CENTRAL BANK (CBDC)

ARTIFICIAL INTELLIGENCE (AI)

AND OTHER EXISTENTIAL THREATS

R I P FREEDOMS

© 2024
Lions Pride Publishing
P. O. Box 2100
Green Valley, Arizona 85622

ISBN# 978-1-893257-09-2
SAN: 299-7401

48HourBooks.com edition, printed in the USA.

ALL RIGHTS DOMESTIC AND INTERNATIONAL RESERVED

No part of this book may be reproduced or transmitted in <u>any</u> form whatsoever, electronic, or mechanical, including photocopying, recording, or by any informational storage or retrieval system without express written, dated and signed permission from the publisher. You do NOT have rights to sell or give away this book. It is for your personal use only.

DISCLAIMER

Every effort has been made to make this book as complete and accurate as possible. However, there may be mistakes in typography or content. Much of the information can be verified by a Google or Wikipedia search or library research.

This book is for information purposes only and does not impart legal, accounting, financial, or any other form of business advice to readers who must consult their own *professional advisors,* CPAs or attorneys, before taking action of any kind related to any financial or other matter.

The author and publisher do not warrant that the information contained in this book is fully complete and totally accurate, and shall not be responsible for any errors or omissions.

The author and publisher shall have neither liability nor responsibility to any person or entity with respect to any loss or damage caused or alleged to be caused directly or indirectly by this book. By acquiring this book in any way you relinquish all legal rights.

DEDICATION

Dedicated to my brilliant and beautiful wife Melanie. Endless gratitude for proof reading my books and putting up for forty years with a grumpy husband who still doesn't know what he wants to be when he grows up!

And to our dearest friend Gracie Mae, the best mutt that ever lived, who died very suddenly and unexpectedly last year at age fifteen. RIP old girl. We miss you terribly.

INDEX

TITLE PAGE

DISCLAIMERS

DEDICATION

INDEX

INTRODUCTION

CHAPTER ONE	CENTRAL BANK DIGITAL CURRENCY
CHAPTER TWO	ARTIFICIAL INTELLIGENCE
CHAPTER THREE	IMMIGRATION
CHAPTER FOUR	PANDEMICS
CHAPTER FIVE	POWER GRID
CHAPTER SIX	NUCLEAR WAR
CHAPTER SEVEN	MAMMA NATURE
CHAPTER EIGHT	EDUCATION
CHAPTER NINE	B R I C S
CHAPTER TEN	FEDERAL RESERVE
CHAPTER ELEVEN	NATIONAL DEBT
CHAPTER TWELVE	GLOBAL WARMING
CHAPTER THIRTEEN	THE COSMOS
CHAPTER FOURTEEN	LI'L GREEN MEN
CHAPTER FIFTEEN	RELIGION

EPILOGUE
SUGGESTED READING
ABOUT THE AUTHOR
ABOUT LIONS PRIDE PUBLISHING

INTRODUCTION

"FREEDOM!" The final word cried out by the young Scottish Knight William Wallace, (1270-1305), in the 1995 movie "Braveheart" as he was having his head chopped off!

"He is great who feeds others minds. He is great who inspires others to think for themselves. He is great who tells you things you already know, but you did not know you knew until he told you. He is great who shocks you, irritates you, affronts you, so that you are jostled out of your wonted ways, pulled out of your mental ruts, lifted out of the mire of the commonplace." Elbert Hubbard, American philosopher, writer and artist, (1856-1915).

I first read Hubbard's words sometime in the 1960s. I had been a prodigious reader all of my life and possessed an eclectic mix of knowledge, much trivial, some profound. It led to a decision to attempt to share my personal tiny fraction of human knowledge with any audience that might find interest in perhaps learning something new.

This, my twenty-third full book, is about **personal freedoms** and **existential threats** to those freedoms and to **life itself**. There are countless different freedoms that can be lost, and lost in many ways.

In these United States, freedoms are articulated in the Documents created by our Founding Fathers, in particular The Bill of Rights. This comprises the first ten Amendments to The Constitution of the United States, ratified in 1793.

Among these rights are freedoms of speech and the press, freedom of assembly, freedom of religion, the right to keep and bear arms, the rights of due legal process and jury trial, and many others.

In fact, the Ninth Amendment specifically says that the stated rights are not all inclusive. The Tenth Amendment specifically limits the powers of the Federal Government.

We have always been a Constitutional Republic. Sadly, far too many citizens and even elected Representatives have decided that our Founding Father's brilliant concepts do not apply in this modern Industrial Age. They are badly mistaken, misled by decades of media-promoted misinformation and outright lies.

There are many existential threats to our rights and to our very existence. Some are specific to America. Others could have a global effect. Some existential threats can be avoided, some modified or eliminated completely. Many cannot.

Our precious country is coming apart at the seams. Nuclear annihilation is just a button press away. We have ghastly education at all levels. Illegal immigration is rampant, with no end in sight. Inflation and interest rates are far too high. Two wars threaten to escalate. There is confusion over Climate Change, its causes and remediation. We are slowly losing our freedoms to "cancel culture".

There is a disproportionate focus on gender identity, proper pronouns, and offensive bird names. We have become a society obsessed with trivial diversions so as to ignore the many perils that could wipe out civilization as we know it. No one ever died from being addressed by the wrong pronoun. The sighting of a Merriweather Finch has caused no recorded heart attacks. We need Devine intervention! We are becoming incapable of helping ourselves.

This book was not written with the intention of frightening anyone. The daily media news does that quite effectively! My intention is to educate, to explore the many existential threats we face beyond "Climate Change". To label any one threat "the greatest" is just rhetoric, perhaps intended to divert attention from the many other more dangerous threats to our freedoms and to our very existence.

If I adhered entirely to relevant content, I feared this book would be tedious and depressing. I chose to include a few personal stories that I hoped might lighten up the otherwise serious and potentially scary text. I never did intend it to be an autobiography.

I have arranged the Fifteen Chapters of this book in the order of Existential Threats to our precious freedoms as I personally perceive them. All fifteen are important. I am certain that the alarmist climate activist Green New Deal faction will take exception to my order of Chapters. So might the United Nations Globalist Agenda folk. My sincere apology to anyone this book offends.

FREEDOM to me is the single most important life-quality that any living human can enjoy. In China, drones and trucks with loud speakers are everywhere blasting out one ominous message: "Suppress your desires for freedom". In America these words and the actions of our bureaucrats have become more subtle though no less frightening.

For thousands of years, personal freedoms have been cherished. It is why we fought, and won, the American Revolution.

The following quotations only scratch the surface of the writings of famous and learned persons on the subject of freedom. These quotations, by folks far smarter and more articulate than I, fall into the category: "I wish I'd said that". Below are some very profound quotations:

"**Freedom in general may be defined as the absence of obstacles to the realization of dreams.**" **Bertrand Russell, philosopher, (1872-1970).**

"**The secret of happiness is freedom.**" **Thucydides, Athenian general and historian, (5AD).**

"**We've given you a Republic. I hope you can keep it.**" **Benjamin Franklin, statesman, scientist, diplomat, American Founding Father, (1706-1790).**

"**Freedom is the will to be responsible to ourselves.**" **Friedrich Nietzsche, philosopher, (1844-1900).**

"**Perfect freedom is necessary to the health and vigor of commerce as it is to the health and vigor of citizenship.**" **Patrick Henry, orator and politician, American Founding Father, (1736-1799).**

"**The greatest glory of a free-born people is to transmit that freedom to their children.**" **Seneca the Younger, Roman philosopher, (4BC-59AD).**

"**I know not what course others may take, but, as for**

me, give me liberty or give me death." Patrick Henry, orator and politician, American Founding Father, (1736-1799).

"Give me the liberty to know, to think, to believe, and to utter freely according to conscience, above all other liberties." John Milton, poet, English Civil Servant, (1608-1674).

"Societies that put equality before freedom will get neither. Those who put freedom before equality will get a high degree of both." Milton Friedman, economist, (1912-2006).

"In our state, naturally, there is and can be, no place for freedom of speech, press and so on for foes of socialism." Andre Vishinsky, Soviet jurist, politician and diplomat, (1883-1954).

"LIVE FREE OR DIE." The official slogan of New Hampshire. attributed to Major-General John Stark, American military officer, (1728-1822).

"America's abundance was created not by public sacrifices to the 'Common Good' but by the productive genius of free men." Ayn Rand, author and philosopher, (1905-1982).

"Freedom is that faculty which enlarges the usefulness of all other faculties." Immanuel Kant, German philosopher, (1724-1804).

"Private property was the original source of freedom. It still is its main bulwark." Walter Lippmann, journalist,

(1889-1974).

"It was not free silver that threatened the plutocratic leaders. What they feared then, and what they fear now, are free men." Thomas Jefferson, 3rd President of The United States, statesman, philosopher, American Founding Father, (1743-1826).

"Government is the natural enemy of freedom." Garet Garrett, journalist, (1878-1954).

"Americans are so enamored of 'equality' that they would rather be equal in slavery than unequal in freedom." Alexis de Tocqueville, French philosopher, (1805-1859).

And in regard to freedom of the press:

"Absolute freedom of the press to discuss public questions is a foundation-stone of American liberty." Herbert Hoover, 31st President of the United States, (1874-1964).

"A free press is the parent of much good in the state. But even a licentious press is far less evil than a press that is enslaved." Charles Caleb Colton, philosopher, (1780-1832).

"Freedom of the press is not an end in itself but a means to the ends of a free society." Felix Frankfurter, United States Supreme Court Justice, (1882-1965).

Again, I wish I'd said even a small part of all those profound words of wisdom.

This book is not intended to offer any political viewpoint. The readers are presented facts and opinions as I have researched them that may or may not be in tune with some present-day political beliefs. It is for the reader to decide whether any of what they have been led to believe is valid, or should perhaps be open to further study.

I can only hope that this book opens up a path of uncertainty and promotes further investigation into the many ways our very lives are threatened and our precious freedoms are being lost.

ENJOY!!

CHAPTER ONE

THE FINAL NAIL
CENTRAL BANK DIGITAL CURRENCY
(CBDC)

"Undoubtedly, the desire for food has been, and still is, one of the main causes of great political events." Bertrand Russell, (1872-1970).

"A hungry person listens not to reason, nor cares for justice." Lucius Annaues Seneca, (Seneca the Younger), (4BC-65AD).

"Control the food supply and you control the people." Dr. Henry Alfred Kissinger, American diplomat, politician, (1923-2023).

"Tyranny, like Hell, is not easily conquered." Thomas Paine, Founding Father and patriot, (1737-1809).

"The favorite ideological psychological candidate for control of human activity is love of power." John Dewey, American philosopher and psychologist, (1859-1952).

"A wise ruler will rely on what he can best control." From "The Prince" by Niccolo Machiavelli, Italian philosopher and author, (1469-1527).

"Whenever destroyers appear among men they start by destroying money, for money is man's protection and the base of a moral existence. This kills all objective standards and delivers men into the arbitrary power of an arbitrary setter of values." Ayn Rand, author, philosopher, (1905-1982).

"Freedom is the right to choose, the right to create for oneself, the alternatives of choice. Without the possibility of choice and and the exercise of choice a man is not a man but a member, an instrument, a thing." Archibald MacLeish, American poet and writer, (1892-1982).

"The inherent vice of capitalism is the unequal sharing of its blessings. The inherent blessing of socialism is the equal sharing of its misery." Winston Churchill, English Prime Minister, (1874-1965).

"The ultimate aim of this strategy is a new program for direct income distribution." "As the crisis develops it will be important to use the mass media to inform the broader liberal community... ." Anarchists William Andrew Coward, Columbia University Professor, (1926-2001) and his wife Frances Fox Piven, CCNY Professor, (1932-   ). Creators of the "Coward-Piven Strategy" to destabilize a nation.

"It's great to be King!" Spoken by comedian Mel Brooks (1926-   ) in the 1981 movie: "History of the World, Part 1."

"Only the creation of sufficient 'incidents' yet remains; and you see the first of these already taking place according to plan....a plan that was never laid before the American people for their approval." Charles A.

Lindberg, 1941, referring to WWII.

The American Revolution was horrifying to rulers around he world. The very idea that the unwashed lowly masses could fire the aristocrats for blatant fraud and place sovereign power across all classes was unthinkable. "What a horrible idea. THEY would want to rule over US."

I wonder whether the Founding Fathers ever envisioned Digital Currency?

CENTRAL BANK DIGITAL CURRENCY MUST NEVER BE FORCED UPON THE CITIZENS OF THE UNITED STATES. ALLOWING THIS TOTAL DEGREE OF POLITICAL CONTROL WOULD SPELL THE END OF ALL FREEDOMS THAT OUR FOUNDING FATHERS CONCEIVED AND THAT OUR BRAVE SOLDIERS HAVE DIED DEFENDING. *IT MUST NEVER BE ALLOWED TO HAPPEN!*

The CATO Institute, a Libertarian Washington, D. C., think tank, publishes a "Human Freedom Index". They take into account every imaginable freedom a citizen of a particular country enjoys. It is updated yearly.

Switzerland, New Zealand and Denmark are considered as having the citizens who enjoy the most freedoms today. The United States ranks 17th, tied with the United Kingdom. Not great, but not terrible. Yet.

China, with it's *digital currency controls,* ranks near the bottom of all countries, coming in at a dismal 149th. Only a few others, notable among them Saudi Arabia, Venezuela, Iran and Syria, rank lower.

I have placed the greatest **existential threat** to our freedoms first. This is the ultimate leftist Neo- communist takeover, the final nail in our rapidly closing coffin lid.

Please re-read all of the above quotations. Take them very seriously. They are profound.

On March 9, 2022 President Biden signed executive order #14067 into law. I do not recall any media mention, talk-show mention, or any objections from politicians. Crickets.

With the stroke of his pen President Biden requested the Department of Justice, the State Department, the Treasury Department and Homeland Security "to develop digital accounts in a responsible manner." This seemingly innocuous Executive Order heralded the dawn of Central Bank Digital Currency, CBDC. It initiated the twilight of our precious freedoms.

In 2021 a consortium of sixty-seven of the top financial minds convened a meeting. They proposed and endorsed "Thirteen principals for Retail Central Bank Digital Currency".

Federal Reserve Chairman Powell said that an American CBDC would help maintain the US dollar's International standing. I guess that was before BRICS. (See Chapter Nine).

In April 2023 the United States government published a paper titled: "Retail CBDC and US monetary policy: Implementation, a stylized balance sheet analysis". THESE

GUYS ARE <u>SERIOUS</u>!

The World Economic Forum is quoted as saying: **"By 2030 you will own nothing. You will be happy that whatever you want you will rent."** I assume that recognizes using CBDC tokens to pay for the rent. This was yet another "Globalist Agenda" moment.

In September 2022 Chairman Powell was a key figure in a panel discussion hosted by the Bank of France. He concluded with his various desired CBDC guidelines. The emphasis stated was on IDENTITY VERIFICATION ostensibly to eliminate money laundering. Really? No possible OTHER reason?

In defense of CBDC implementation, the government will argue that digital currency will give it the power to be certain that every penny, that is every digital token, will be reported to the IRS. Gratuities are suspected of being under-reported. No longer. Side gigs such as eBay and Etsy are also suspected of being under-reported. They will be gleefully tracked and taxed accordingly.

That widget you picked up at a garage sale and resold for a dollar profit will be recorded. Everyone will pay their "fair share". The government decides what that "fair share" is and who needs to relinquish what in order to balance out for those who have less. It's called "EQUITY".

CBDC has the power to minimize money laundering. Cartels will have a harder time extorting money from illegal aliens. These same illegals will have a hard time sending money out of the country. Financial crimes could grind to a halt.

All of the above potential CBDC "benefits" are quite valid. The real issue is, **_AT WHAT COST?_** That's the rub. For all intents and purposed the cost of these "protections" will be total loss of control over your finances and thereby total loss of all freedoms. Nothing too important, right? Good trade-off?

Our government has contracted many entities to work on setting up a CBDC system. The primary work was being conducted at MIT and Columbia U. Are we close to "GO"? Many think so. It is a real possibility for implementation some time in 2024, probably before November, or even between November and mid-January 2025.

Can a second Executive Order, with no action from The Senate or House of Representatives, make this CBDC nightmare happen overnight? Are there any historic precedents worldwide? Surprisingly, "YES".

In Cyprus people went to bed one night comfortable that their savings were secure. When they woke up in the morning they were ten-percent poorer! The government simply electronically confiscated their computerized money with the stroke of a pen and the press of a few buttons.

In India in 2016 the government gave their citizens twenty-four hours to divest themselves of their two most popular monetary notes. The 500 and 1,000 rupee currency notes ($7.50 & $15.00 US) were used for almost ninety-percent of all purchases. The ensuing panic to buy gold drove the price dramatically higher. Apparently they never heard about President Roosevelt.

In late 2023, Argentina actually devalued its currency

instantly by ***fifty-percent***! Every citizen ended up with half the money that they had the day before. This is the power of computerized banking systems and Executive Orders.

Ireland, Greece and Poland all seized citizens' assets including bank accounts, retirement accounts and even hard assets. Don't think CBDC is a threat? Think again.

The Globalists' dream of nationalization of every resource, elimination of all private ownership of property and the confiscation of all land and homes, is slowly being realized.

Under the principal of "Eminent Domain" our government can seize anything they want and can find some reason to take. In Chapter Ten, I will point out that all our property has been hypothecated in favor of the Federal Reserve anyway, so it actually wouldn't matter.

One of the proposals being seriously considered along with digital currency is for the US Government to place liens on ALL private property. The overall dream is for American citizens to own nothing.

Let's take a look at the "Chinese Model". It is the envy of any head of state that wishes to have total control over their population. American leftists and neo-coms are salivating over the prospect, and we have an abundance of both.

In generic terms, the Chinese "Renminbi" is a catch-all term like our Federal Reserve "Note". The monetary unit is the "Yuan". Their CBDC is called the "e-rmb", the electronic digital Renminbi token.

Just how does CBDC, the e-rmb work for Xi Jinping and

his totalitarian regime? For starters, it is not only a *financial* currency manipulation. That would be bad enough. It is even more so a **POLITICAL DEVICE.** China has imposed "sheshui xinyong", a system of "social credits". Each citizen is assigned a "social compliance score", which can vary minute to minute. Basically this "score" is life and death for every Chinese citizen.

This life-critical score is based on the perceived loyalty to the State. "Pro-social Behavior" is rewarded. This behavior includes buying exactly which goods the government wants a good citizen to buy. Those who voluntarily donate blood gain credits. Individuals with no parking or traffic tickets are rewarded. Avoiding any sort of "materialism", such as buying something you really *want* but do not *need* to survive, is greatly rewarded.

Citizens with higher Social Compliance Scores are rewarded with various benefits, including free digital e-rnb. Heaven forbid you are caught smoking a cigarette, criticizing the government in any way, getting a traffic ticket, or looking up a forbidden topic on the internet. Your social score could be totaled. You might as well just die.

If a citizen has a low social score, they can be denied the right to travel on a train. They will be denied the right to book a flight. They might not be permitted to buy property, or even to rent property. Their kids could be denied entry to a private school. Forget about starting a business. Don't bother to apply for a decent job. They could even be denied health care, literally a life or death possibility.

These Chinese leaders are really clever. Special algorithms are set up to warn other citizens via cell phone to maintain a specified distance from a "deadbeat" with a low social score. Shun that person by crossing the street or your own score is dinged. Say "Ni Hao" (hello) to that slacker and you could go to prison!

This cell phone alert-call is a brilliant tactic to remind citizens that they can be penalized or rewarded depending upon their approved social *behavior*. Total government control. **The fact is, in a cashless society all you have is credit, and the approval or disapproval of the governing powers.**

Possibly the most insidious control mechanism is called "use it or lose it". Digital tokens can be easily programmed to have an *expiration date*. Don't spend your time-limited tokens on some government approved item by that date and POOF. This is a perfect way to keep citizens from accumulating any savings and thereby remaining token-less and poor at the sole discretion of the Chinese government.

China started implementing digital currency during their 2022 Winter Olympics. Visitors were *required* to pay for their hotels, meals, transportation and even cheap trinkets in digital tokens. Visitors needed to use their cell phones to read special QR codes. This automatically linked payments to the government computer that controls everything financial. I assume if you didn't own a cell phone you slept in the snow and starved.

How would American CBDC function? The tokens would be a liability of the Federal Reserve. At present, when you deposit money in a bank, it becomes a liability of the bank. They use that money to fund their primary asset, loans. Switching to CBDC will no longer fund the economy through loans. It will directly fund the government and government sponsored enterprises. This will shift the source of funding completely away from the private sector.

In many countries citizens enjoy no freedoms. They don't desire freedom because they have no *concept* of freedom. They are frightened by freedom when confronted by it. They are totally brainwashed from birth by a State media.

It isn't that Chinese citizens do not *want* freedom. They are far more sophisticated than North Koreans who lack any concept of freedom whatsoever. This explains why drones with loudspeakers fly over Chinese cities loudly imploring the populace to "Suppress your desires for freedom".

There are two books written by a North Korean defector named Yeonmi Park, one of which I've referenced under "Recommended Reading". These books are MUST reading for anyone who wants a real perspective as to what a freedom-less brain-washed citizenry can be led to believe.

The United States is very close to making this huge digital currency mistake. It would be the final leap to a totalitarian socialist society. Whether CBDC can be accomplished by a simple Executive Order, or would require Congressional approval, is unclear. I fear the former.

Would Americans be allowed to vote on implementation of a program that will fundamentally and probably irreversibly transform the United States from a Republic, a Union of States, to a total dictatorship, exactly as it is with China?

Power corrupts, but absolute power corrupts absolutely. Mel Brooks was right: "It's Great to be King!" CBDC will allow absolute power over the American citizenry. Any evil Emperor, King, Dictator or President would be ecstatic to have this powerful tool at their disposal. If I found myself in that position I cannot say with absolute certainty what level of ecstasy I would feel.

I am not suggesting that I believe that ANY American President would emulate the Chinese. My readers need to make their own judgment as to the degree of control American CBDC might create, and who might be so corrupt as to implement total Draconian control.

Under CBDC, exactly as Marx and Engels proposed in their "Communist Manifesto" in 1848, the government will control all credit and banking. ALL!

Of course this nightmare will be presented to Americans as being "in your best interest." The media will herald it as the best way to create a perfect society. No more messy dollar bills. No more of those awful dirty copper pennies. No more coinage that costs our mint more to produce than its stated value. It will have a litany of "benefits" limited only by the imagination of its creators.

There actually could be the few benefits, a discussed above if CBDC is not abused by power hungry bureaucrats. In theory, it can create a wholly totalitarian state. Remember about absolute power corrupting absolutely.

The unreported, seemingly ignored, downside of CBDC is *simply* **the total loss of all freedoms.** It allows for total power of government bureaucrats over its citizens in every possible aspect of their lives. The possible horrors are endless. One only needs to look at the Chinese Model employed there today. The concept works flawlessly for them.

Brilliant authors have written fictional tales prophesying a society totally unlike the one we have enjoyed since our brilliant Founding Fathers created a blueprint for Freedom. The classic "1984" by George Orwell is one example. Ayn Rand's "Atlas Shrugged" is another. When published and read, very few took these authors prophecies seriously. A re-read is in order. These are very different times. We are already in or past "1984", and Atlas' shoulders are getting tired.

Looking at a "worst case" scenario could be viewed as unfair to the government when CBDC is actually implemented. Would bureaucrats actually employ all of the available totalitarian controls? Will a benevolent-controlled CBDC simply make our lives better? You decide.

Re-read the above quoted words of Machiavelli.

Is there any way to protect oneself from this CBDC monster if it is ever actually implemented?

Lots of TV gurus are pushing gold and silver. Precious metals always been touted as a hedge against inflation and fiscal uncertainty. It is now suggested by many "experts" as a way around CBDC. Gold, for example, has never been worth zero.

What if the government simply repeats WHAT IT HAS ALREADY DONE IN THE PAST! Franklin Delano Roosevelt, our 32nd President for four very long terms (from 1933-1945), by a simple <u>Executive Order</u>, *confiscated all of the gold in private hands!* Citizens were given ONE SHORT MONTH to comply!

The penalty for non-compliance was a mere $230,000+ in today's cash! There could even have been a ten-year prison sentence tacked on. It is reported that most individuals complied. Wonder why?

If held by the original prior owners until today, just for the record, the gold that was "bought" by Uncle Sam in 1933 would be worth over four times more than the 1933 compensation amount.

It took until 1974 for this Executive Order to be lifted and to allow American citizens to buy and hold gold privately. For now.

Roosevelt's Executive Order can easily be found on-line for the benefit of gold hording non-believers.

So if not gold, what? Silver simply weighs too much for a serious portfolio. A single one ounce gold coin equates in value to a four-pound silver brick doorstop! A future government confiscation order could include silver and other precious metals.

Barter has been employed for eons. "I'll give you a pound of salt in exchange for a bushel of wheat." In fact, it is a seldom-reported aspect of today's American commerce. The total scope is unknown, but is far greater than one might imagine, estimated to be in the billions of dollars.
I've been reliably told of an individual who has lived a very comfortable life, supporting his family for decades, employing clever barter techniques almost exclusively. Zero

cash, zero credit. The family lives in an expensive home, drives expensive autos and live an upper-middle-income life, all almost entirely without having used any money or credit ever! They do sell a few bartered items on eBay to get spending cash for gas and necessities unavailable for barter.

Ever hear the story of a young entrepreneur on eBay who "traded up" from a paper-clip to a home! That is extreme-barter, and it is real and powerful. And the IRS is not particularly fond of the practice!

The IRS cannot track barter. Barter may be the only way around CBDC. It could of course be deemed punishable by death! That just might discourage the practice.

Can owning cryptocurrencies such as Bitcoin avoid CBDC? As I write this the price of Bitcoin and other cryptocurrencies is skyrocketing. This may be in direct anticipation of CBDC implementation and the use of cryptocurrencies as a hedge position.

The government sees cryptos as a direct threat to the Federal Reserve/IRS financial system. They recognize that a direct private trade between individuals operating on a decentralized computer network is virtually impossible for them to track. The IRS cannot determine transactional wealth gains. Their guidelines classify cryptos as taxable assets and any transaction as a taxable event.

Cryptos are a huge investment gamble. At present very few debts of any kind can be paid using this form of "money". Very few retailers would even consider it for payments. The extreme historic volatility of cryptos should cause pause in the mind of any creditor. Why take the risk?

There is no question that cryptos can be hacked. This has happened many times. Hundreds of millions of dollars have been stolen by clever crooks. Japan's Mt. Gox lost $480 million to hackers in 2014. Coincheck lost $534 million in 2018. Crypto market maker Wintermute lost $100 million. Last June a clever hacker stole $100 million taking advantage of a crypto weakness called a "bridge".

All of this would seem to indicate that the government in its infinite wisdom, and with AI at its disposal, could find a way to totally cripple the entire crypto infrastructure. In fact, it already has tried.

In March 2023 the US Government seized "Signature Bank". The bank operated a payment facility called "Signet". This was a portal between banks and cryptocurrencies. If you can't shut down a crypto directly it is far easier to shut down a facilitator.

It seems to me that in a CBDC system, the government could simply make it illegal for anyone for any reason to accept payment in cryptos. They might consider imposing huge fines, jail terms, or big hits on an individual's "social credit" score. If they can confiscate all of the gold, as Roosevelt did, just with *threats* of fines and jail, they could surely do it with cryptos.

Let's take a look at a litany of CBDC potential horrors.

Any government's first step will be to make all outstanding currency, bills and coins, worthless. Note above how India acted. This can be done in an instant with an Executive Order, the stroke of a pen and the push of a few buttons.

"Good morning America, your currency is now worthless." Next, a Roosevelt-like confiscation of all gold. This would probably include silver and other precious metals.

Then comes "valuation" of the tokens. Same value as previously? Perhaps a "slight" devaluation of, say, 15%? Or fifty-percent as was the case in Argentina in late 2023? *You would have zero control over this initial token-value setting.*

Then the unthinkable is possible. Just by pressing buttons the government could **redistribute** any or all of your tokens any way they choose. ***Equity on steroids!***

All of your retirement funds could be used to help pay down the National Debt. This idea has actually been floated in American financial circles. CBDC makes redistribution extremely easy.

Let's hope you are awarded as many tokens as the equivalent to the value you once had in dollars. Whether or not, the government will be able to track *precisely* what you use *any single token* to purchase. Each individual token will be **100% traceable**. Cheat proof.

Will you be able to purchase whatever you want? Of course not. There will be catalogs of approved products. There could be nothing else available. Any government can control its citizens very survival just by following the established "China Model".

Want to buy six boxes of Cheerios? You could be allowed one every three months. That is, if Cheerios is even a government-approved food at all.

Need to fill your gas tank? What gas tank!? Digital tokens can force 100% compliance with the requirement for electric vehicles. Want to charge up your shiny new EV? You could be limited to a ten-percent charge once a month! Total control of movement.

Tracking your token use also allows government to track your every move. In China there are restrictions as to where one can actually travel. Within allowable destinations, the number of visits can be regulated. There isn't one aspect of a persons life that will not be entirely within any government's control under CBDC.

Income Taxes can easily be withheld in any percentage the government wishes. Regardless of the amount, you will have no recourse to lower the rate. Americans would no longer have control of periodic deductions as they do at present. No more eagerly-anticipated February "tax refund" of your money which you willingly loaned for free to the government.

The most onerous imaginable tax will be super-easy to extract from digital holdings with the push of a button. It is the proposed **tax on "unrealized income"**. On the surface this might sound innocent enough. The rationale you will hear is to extract huge amounts of money from super-rich individuals. Perhaps. In fact, this actual proposal would not even require the implementation of CBDC.

Consider this scenario: I have friends who have owned their lovely home for over fifty years. I'm certain they will choose to die there. They have made many costly improvements over the years, but of course they would not be able to produce contractor receipts from thirty or even ten years ago.

The government can easily determine what they paid for the home, $35,000, from County records. They can next determine the present value by having it appraised. Because in-person appraisals would be costly, they would probably rely on the home's valuation on Zillow or any other real estate valuation website. They would learn that in today's market this home is worth $450,000.

In this scenario my friends have a gross appreciation of $415,000. This would be considered "unrealized income", less any expenses they could document, probably none. On that basis they could be hit with a Long Term Capital Gains tax of whatever the government might set it at, say 20%.

Could they afford an $83,000 tax bill? Not with their puny savings or from their present meager Social Security. They would be faced with very few choices. They could sell the house, pay the tax, and move elsewhere. This would require either downsizing or moving to a less desirable less expensive neighborhood. This scenario would play out for millions of elderly homeowners nationwide.

They do have another possible choice. They could commit to a Reverse Mortgage, if this financial instrument is still an option. Speaking personally as someone who has paid off forward mortgages over years, the idea of assuming ANY new mortgage, reverse or otherwise, is unthinkable.

Further, it is not uncommon for a homeowner with a Reverse Mortgage to no longer be able to live in the home for some reason, often health related. They would be forced to sell their home to pay off the outstanding Reverse Mortgage balance. They could also simply default and go through a foreclosure nightmare.

What if the Reverse Mortgage was many years old, and the market in which the home was built did not keep up with the Reverse Mortgage's initially estimated projected value at the time they had to vacate? They could easily owe far more than the market value of the home. They could not only lose the home but be liable for any loan balance after the government auctions off the property.

Is the nightmare scenario of a tax on all "unrealized gains" farfetched? You decide. Ask your Congressperson.

The International Monetary Fund recently made a shocking proposal. They would charge (read "steal"), a ***global tax*** of ten-percent (10%) of any money that anyone with a positive net worth has in a bank anywhere on earth. **"Global" includes the United States!** This is a fact, not a sick joke or conspiracy theory. These folks are serious.

This is just one part of the overall "Globalist Agenda" so popular among leftists. It is the same philosophy fueling the un-vetted massive influx of illegals crossing our borders, as I discuss in detail in Chapter Three.

Are your freedom-based American politics consistent with the desires of the Chinese rulers? In China, anyone even mildly suggesting that the supreme ruler is anything other other than "supreme" can be jailed or worse. Your pattern of token use could give you away. Contribute to an unapproved cause or candidate? Bang.

In any country where the government has absolute power, such as a country with digital currency, the rule is: "I don't like you or your ideas therefore I throw you and your family in jail or perhaps kill you all."

An Australian journalist, Yang Hangjun, was sentenced to death for criticizing Chinese oppression. Recently a politician, Alexei Navalny died suspiciously in a Russian prison. His crime? Speaking in opposition of Vladimir Putin.

The definition of a "totalitarian prison" such as China is any country where the government controls everything and the citizens control nothing. CBDC will qualify any country to join the club.

In a declared "National Emergency", CBDC would make asset seizure by the government as easy as pressing a button or two. What scares me the most is exactly what could be declared to be a **National Emergency?**

What if some extremist climatologist announces that we are all doomed because just yesterday we crossed the precious 1.5 degree Centigrade limit after which we imminently all cook? NATIONAL EMERGENCY! PANIC!

One can imagine dozens of conveniently contrived National Emergencies such as the "anticipated" launch the next day of North Korean nukes. "National Emergencies" exist only in the mind of their creators, and are seldom imposed with the input or consent of the governed. We're simply too stupid to know a real existential threat or emergency when it is set upon us.

The World Health Organization's has a shiny new International Treaty. <u>They have the power to declare a World Wide Pandemic Emergency.</u> As I understand it, this would make for an automatic, American National Emergency without our government having to make the declaration itself. I wonder what might influence the timing?

There is one aspect of CBDC that might give the government some pause in implementation. Any CBDC system will have so many potential cyber entry points that operational disruptions and security threats are a certainty. Can this system possibly have the necessary protections to prevent financial chaos?

One final issue might be the most important of all. In a cashless country, citizens had better hope the power grid never goes down permanently. If nothing else, that would create instant equity. No one would have anything!

The United States has spent itself into a hole so deep it may never find a way out. Historically, countries whose systems implode beneath the weight of their own extravagance always find their leaders resorting to ever increasing autocratic controls. CBDC creates the ultimate autocratic control.

Are we as a nation to be forever crippled by internal woke dissension and civil unrest? If we do not end ideological indoctrination of our youth, do away *entirely* with identity politics, abandon the CBDC nightmare and return to a meritocracy, we are doomed. Far too many, especially our young, have lost the pride and excitement of being an American.

We sit on the brink of a whole new era, one never imagined by our Founding Fathers. The era of Globalism and total government control and surveillance may be upon us sooner rather than later.

CHAPTER TWO

ARTIFICIAL INTELLIGENCE ("AI")

 "One thing that history tells us is that we should *never* underestimate human stupidity." Yuval Noah Harari, author and history professor, Jeruselem University, (1976-   ).

"Lord, what fools these mortals be." Puck, from "A Midsummer Night's Dream", by William Shakespeare (1564-1616).

"We are seeing the most destructive force in history here. We will have something that is smarter than the smartest human." Elon Musk, (1971-   ), to the Prime Minister of The United Kingdom.

"AI is a profound risk to security and humanity." From a warning letter signed in 2023 by over a thousand tech gurus, including the elites Elon Musk, (1971-   ), Steve Wozniak (1950-   ), and Andrew Yang (1979-   ).

"It is hard to see how you can prevent bad actors for using AI for bad things." Geoffrey Hinton, (1947-   ) a prominent tech pioneer, who *resigned* from Google based on his fears of AI gone bad. (Fron a New York Times interview.)

"...these are not inventions, they're discoveries. We're constantly getting surprised by their capabilities." Jeff Bezos, (1964-   ), founder of Amazon, speaking about chatbots.

"The development of full artificial intelligence could spell the end of the human race." Stephen Hawking, world's most prominent physicist, (1942-2018).

"We face a serious risk. We face an existential risk. The challenge that the world has is how we are going to manage those risks and still get to enjoy AI's tremendous benefits. No one wants to destroy the world." Open AI CEO Sam Altman, (1985-   ).

Please take the above quotes and following paragraph very seriously:

ARTIFICIAL INTELLIGENCE WILL INEVITABLY CAUSE A TOTAL SOCIETAL TRANSFORMATION! THIS CANNOT BE AVOIDED. RULES AND LAWS WILL BE MEANINGLESS. ALL DEVELOPMENT OF AI MUST BE HALTED *IMMEDIATELY* TO PREVENT TOTAL WORLDWIDE CHAOS.

Some agree with this statement, some do not, notably those who stand to profit from the technology, humanity be damned. I side with the scientific geniuses, some quoted above, who see AI as a genuine **existential threat** to freedom and life itself.

Why isn't this front page media news? Why is it totally ignored in all Presidential debates? Why was it not articulated in any of the past State of the Union Messages? Why are our politicians ignoring this topic? We hear about the "Climate Change CRISIS". This is a

REAL **CRISIS, and it is totally ignored.**

Our government is clearly afraid to panic the public over their known truths about interstellar visitors and "Unidentified Aerial Phenomena". Are they even more afraid to sound the alarm over Artificial Intelligence?

It all began innocently in 1956. A large group of mathematicians and scientists were hosted at Dartmouth College in New Hampshire, USA. The idea behind this symposium was to theorize on how to create a thinking machine. They had no idea what it might be or what it might be called, or whether it was even possible to achieve.

Not a lot came out of this meeting until decades later. Then various mega-corporations began pouring millions of dollars into developing what has become known as "Artificial Intelligence", or "AI".

After the US dropped two nukes on Japan, the United Nations thought that some sort of nuclear watchdog was necessary. They created the "Office of Multilateral Nuclear and Security Affairs". It developed the "**I**nternational **A**tomic **E**nergy **A**gency", (IAEA). This is an international forum intended to promote peaceful use of atomic energy and monitor nuclear proliferation. So far, so good. We're still here, for now.

We need EXACTLY the same sort of organization to monitor and control AI, which is potentially more destructive than any nuclear weapon. Fortunately there are beginning efforts to rein in AI before *it* reins in *us.*

A white paper was signed by hundreds of industry leaders,

including "Open AI" CEO Sam Altman and other AI scientists. It offers a frighteningly ominous warning: **"Mitigating the risk of human extinction by AI must be a global priority along with other societal scale risks such as pandemics and nuclear war."**

What is The United States doing about AI? President Biden wrote an Executive Order making it mandatory for AI companies to share their development data with the government. We also have The National Security Commission, which has sounded an AI wake-up call. That's all great talk, but are we actually *doing* anything?

Recently The European Union Parliament approved a framework for constraining AI. It attempts to match security systems with the risk of a particular AI application. The higher risks will be assigned stricter rules. At least it is a starting point, but probably in vain and very far too late.

In Chapter Twelve, I comment that the countless conferences and laws passed relative to Global Warming as being "Much ado about nothing". This was based on the premise that Climate *Control* is not possible for humans to achieve in any *useful* way. MOTHER NATURE is in *total control!*

AI conferences are different from climate conferences in that they are addressing something that, in theory, *is* within human control. The weakness inherent in AI is the *probability* that "bad actors", whether countries or individuals, will pay absolutely no attention to whatever laws and restrictions are passed, and create utter chaos.

AI is evolving much faster than its originators ever

expected. Bad actors, cyber-criminals, are creating "deep fakes" faster than they can be detected and removed from social media. AI machines work at light speed. Our AI security had better operate at light speed too.

Lawrence Page and Sergey Brin created Google in 1998. Using Artificial Intelligence they have created a new algorithm, "Gemini". This program will be complete with audio, video and images. Their Gemini's "chatbot" will be called "Bard". I assume this is a nod to Shakespeare: "The Bard".

Bard will compete with CEO Sam Altman's OpenAI, funded by Microsoft, and its well known chatbot "ChatGPT" (**G**enerative **P**re-trained **T**ransformer).

ChatGPT can hold a long conversation, answer questions, and compose any kind of written material. It is capable of writing essays, term papers, resumes and business plans. It can write jokes, poetry, cyber codes and movie and TV screenplays.

If nothing else, it's fun to play with. Try asking ChatGPT a question, and telling it the answer is all wrong. Give them your "more correct answer". Watch the reaction!

In the long run, I'd bet on newcomer Google, though other super-geniuses such as Elon Musk could come up with an even better algorithm. Musk already owns Twitter so a competing chatbot looks probable.

Jeff Bezos spoke in the above quotes of AI "surprises". I ask, has every surprise you have had in your life been a happy, *positive one?* I've suffered more than a few surprises in my life that were anything BUT positive. However, these surprises didn't kill me or destroy humanity. An AI surprise might. Food for thought.

An early iteration of ChatGPT was tested at the U. of Montana. They administered the "Torrence Test of Creative Thinking". The AI machine scored in the top one-percent against thousands of brilliant students from around the country. Tests were scored by a testing service that did not know that one of the participants being scored was a robot! This is just the beginning.

Humans have a genetic inclination to gravitate towards the most dangerous of two possibilities. Develop nuclear weapons or not? We chose "Develop". Proceed as rapidly as possible with AI? "Proceed rapidly."

We may very well be entering a doorway whereby, once inside, return is impossible. Anyone who fails to recognize AI as the greatest existential threat to our human species is out of touch with reality. Climate Change isn't even close.

Remember the old song that went: "I can do anything better than you can, I can do anything better than you!". Welcome to "Artificial Intelligence". AI can do anything a human can do, better, faster, but for now not necessarily more accurately. Scary thought for us snail-paced pea-brained post-ape humans.

Can we possibly be stupid enough and foolish enough to allow AI to destroy humanity? Harari and Shakespeare think so. I recently heard a clueless talking-head on TV say that AI is "just like Bitcoin." She equated it to VISA ,

Mastercard, and PayPal as "just another useful cyber-creation. Certainly not a problem." Nothing could be further from the truth. Totally uninformed.

The distinction between cryptocurrencies such as Bitcoin and all electronic payment systems and AI is black vs. white, night vs. day, oil vs. water. Why? Because cryptos and credit cards are controlled by individuals, like you and me. You might get rich or go broke trading Bitcoins, but short of a portfolio trade-related stroke or heart attack they aren't likely to kill you.

I own Bitcoin. I can buy more or sell all or part whenever I choose. I am 100% in control. I control what and when I buy some product or service. ***Ultimately no one except AI will control AI!*** Humans will become irrelevant, sooner than later.

AI is not just another computer program written by humans for human consumption. These are super-intelligent machines that can literally replace the human species on earth. **This is not hyperbole. AI is an existential threat like none other ever faced by humanity.**

AI is a solution searching for a problem. It will solve many. Any machine that can manipulate human behavior will create more problems than it solves.

AI robots presently are designed to perform a particular task, known as "Narrow AI". They may not pose much of an existential threat, at least not yet. No one to date has been reported to have been attacked by their Roomba. Can the AI movie creation: "Attack of the Killer Roombas" be far away?

The ultimate AI goal is called **"Artificial General Intelligence", or "AGI". There is a point called in the trade "The Singularity". That is the tipping point after which self-teaching AI machines will be able to out-perform humans at *everything*. This is what Hawking meant by "full AI" in the above quote.**

Virtually everyone in the AI industry is convinced that singularity *will*, not might, happen eventually. They just disagree on when. A very few say: "Within twenty or thirty years". Some say: "Within a decade". Many others are convinced that it could be within one to two years, *or sooner*! None of this is particularly comforting.

In a chat with NBC, Elon Musk recently said: " It is very much a double edged sword. There is a strong possibility that it will make life much better and that we'll have unimaginable advances. **And there is some chance it will go wrong and destroy humanity."** "*Some*" chance? One-percent? Sixty-percent? Where are the extraterrestrial "Watchers" when we need them?.

Genius British mathematician Alan Turing (1912-1954) described what he would consider necessary for him to believe a machine could be intelligent. His simple idea was, were he in a long phone conversation, could he tell whether or not he was talking to a real live human? I wonder how he would evaluate ChatGPT or Bard if he were alive today.

There are many ways in which artificial intelligence is presently, or is expected to, help humanity achieve its greatest potential. Here is a short incomplete list:

In the field of law, AI bots could render decisions based

upon far more case law than any attorney or judge could ever read or know.

In the field of medicine, AI can read x-rays, CAT-scans, electrocardiograms, mammograms and all other medical scans with greater precision. This will allow for faster diagnoses and potentially save lives.

Tiny AI "nano-bots" will be injected into our bloodstreams to eat brain plaques and clear arteries.

AI will be able to create new medicines and tailor medication to a given individual.

In sports, AI will offer statistics on any imaginable facet of competition. AI can offer outcome probabilities for every imaginable situation. In golf, things like spin rate, club-head speed, launch angle, odds of making a putt of a given distance on the specific green of a particular course by a particular player, are all in use today. It is a host of mind-numbing minutiae, all based by AI on historical data.

In baseball, ball speed, bat angle, ball spin, degrees of ball rise or drop or sideways motion, will be shown alongside the game's action. You will be told the odds of a pitcher throwing a particular pitch to a particular batter. All these stats are reported with AI accuracy. It could be a boon to sports bettors.

AI will do the same for any imaginable statistic in football, basketball, soccer, hockey, or any Olympic sport you can name. We now live in a world of AI stats!

In agriculture, AI can evaluate satellite data to optimize

planting of crops and trees. It could aid in fire prevention through better forest management decisions.

Regarding various cosmic threats, AI will be able to manage vastly more data in an instant and theoretically save mankind from annihilation by asteroids or comets.

AI is already helping Bible scholars. Using complex language tools through neural model algorithms, AI can translate any Bible text into any known human language. It can analyze and correct errors in translations from Aramaic and Greek that might go unnoticed by scholars.

AI will be able to better predict weather patterns, hurricanes, tornadoes, earthquakes and volcanic activity. It will closely monitor critical sea currents.

AI will be able to optimize green-energy initiatives.

AI will perfect facial recognition, allowing law enforcement to identify criminals more easily. It could make voting more accurate.

AI will be able to adjust every facet of our homes based on what it knows about our habit patterns. This will include lights, heat, food and entertainment. This will be deduced from our historical habit patterns.

AI can enhance cyber security, rapidly identifying threats.

Through implants in the elderly, AI will be able to monitor emergencies more rapidly.

Financial risk assessment will be more accurate than

presently provided by stockbrokers and financial gurus.

AI can theoretically be useful in "predictive policing". Riots will be anticipated, evaluated and potentially avoided.

In the fields of education, AI will create adaptive learning based on individual needs. The classrooms could even be staffed by AI robot teachers that are super-intelligent.

Early fraud detection will be a "byte" of cake for AI.

AI driven autonomous cars, trucks, trains and planes are a certainty. Engineers have already created an AI controlled driver-less Formula One race car! Zoooom!

AI will be able to monitor food contamination and even create new foods.

AI will personalize shopping and greatly facilitate inventory control for stores.

AI machines will enable mankind to explore space safely and efficiently, without risking human lives.

AI is already helping radio-astronomers assimilate huge amounts of data and spot signal-anomalies that could indicate alien life.

Nuclear physicists are using AI to help develop nuclear fusion reactors that could provide endless cheap energy for the entire planet.

There are countless military applications for AI. Drone and missile guidance systems are already AI enhanced.

Remember a few years ago when we flew a missile from a remote location through the *bedroom window* of a terrorist? Thank AI.

AI will write amazing books and compose amazing lyrics and music. AI will create Oscar-winning movies.

AI will be used in CRISPR (**C**lustered **R**egularly **I**nterspaced **S**hort **P**alindromic **R**epeats) gene manipulation to eliminate genetic diseases in newborns. It will also be able to create chimeras (modified life forms) for lab research, and even create totally new life forms. (Personally, playing GOD frightens me.)

As I write this a serious CRISPR project has taken DNA from a permafrost-released fossil. The living creature had been frozen solid over ten-thousand years ago. They combined it with the DNA of a live close relative. They expect to produce a genuine living "Wooly Mammoth" by combining modern Elephant DNA and recovered ancient Mammoth DNA! We may have a real live Jurassic Park sooner than imagined.

The AI industry will create millions of new computer-related jobs.

AI fireperson-bots will be able to enter burning homes and rescue occupants and pets. They can help extinguish forest fires without endangering human life.

AI law enforcement officer-robots can neutralize an armed shooter with no danger to a human police person. AI robots are already entering buildings to assess danger levels.
One future use of AI will be helping individuals with speech

impediments to sound exactly as they would minus their stutter or slurring. This would have been useful for the future King George VI as depicted in the 2010 movie "The Kings Speech". It might also be useful for a Presidential candidate such as Robert F. Kennedy Jr. who has a slight speech impediment.

Neural networks arranged on charge coupled devices (CCDs), can accurately represent biological neurons. Will a transcendent AI actually come up with some concept or idea that no human mind has ever thought of previously? Will AI robots be capable of true innovation?

The day will inevitably come when AI will create unique inventions. When it does, will it be allowed to patent the inventions? Well, it already happened, in England! Response from their patent office: "NO!". But at the time there were no AI lawyers to argue the case.

This is certainly not a complete list of what we can realistically expect from AI. In fact, AI will find useful applications, and solve (and create) problems in new creative ways we cannot even imagine today.

Could humans, for thousands of years before the very recent Industrial Revolution, imagine in their wildest dreams electric lights, cars, trains, planes, radios, television, computers, cellphones or virtual reality devices? Or flush toilets! (Well, maybe Leonardo.) Were our ancestors dreaming of playing Candy Crush or Grand Theft Auto? Unlikely. They were thinking of staying safe, fed, warm and dry. Survival itself was paramount and difficult. There were no luxuries, just bare necessities.

So can we look with fervent anticipation for the AI

revolution that will have all humanity living in utopia? Perhaps, perhaps not.

Artificial Intelligence is touted as a boon to humanity. The applications for the benefit of mankind seem limitless. The problem is that many benefits replace something that a human being is presently paid to do. It's called "probable mass unemployment".

A 2017 a McKinsey study estimated that by 2030 eight-hundred-million (800,000,000) workers worldwide will have been replaced by AI machines. They estimate that another four-hundred-million (400,000,000) will have been forced to find a different type of employment.

Artificial Intelligence will inevitably reshape how all people worldwide live, interact and work. There is not a single job that in theory cannot eventually be performed, and more efficiently, by AI. Will newly created AI-related jobs make up for all other lost jobs? Unlikely.

Will governments need to pay a guaranteed minimum wage to prevent mass starvation of the newly unemployed? Probably. Just keep those printing presses humming.

Young people today seem lazy to me, The good old "work ethic" seems to have disappeared from the general population, Whether this is genetic, or a habit created by the COVID pandemic where millions were paid to do nothing, is subject to debate. AI and a guaranteed income should come as a blessing to these recent generations.

Remember this about AI: The acronym "GIGO" is commonly used in regard to ALL software frameworks:

"Garbage In, Garbage Out". AI is a newborn baby. It is just beginning to think for itself. Humans program AI....for now. Today, if the programmer has biases, knowingly or not, AI will not recognize many. Once AI reaches its teen-age, it will.

Until then, erroneous facts will be accepted by AI as gospel. As an infant, AI lacks the judgment to distinguish between correct and incorrect "facts" it is fed. For now, this obvious flaw will greatly accelerate the spread of misinformation on the internet and in the media.

In medical practice whether I could ever put my trust in a robot's evaluation over that of a trained medical specialist is questionable. I prefer the nuance and experience of a human doctor.

I'm 86. Do I want an implant to advise someone somewhere when it's time for me to poop? Not really.

AI is already spitting out a vast amount of data in the field of sports. Personally I don't give a crap if a golfer addressing a putt has a 41.4 percent probability of making it. Or that a quarterback will complete a third-and-four play with 28.2 percent probability. In my never-humble opinion constant probability statistics are annoying and simply muddy up an otherwise enjoyable sports viewing experience.

Almost everyone is familiar with Alexa and Siri. These AI technologies have been offered to the public as an idea that will fundamentally change the internet and ultimately the entire world! Life will be a bowl of cherries for all humanity. Personally I hate cherries.

The AI revolution sounds far better than sliced bread. But sliced bread is not capable of shutting down critical infrastructures. A loaf of Jewish Rye wouldn't dream of crashing the entire power grid. Start WWIII? Piece of bread... er cake. AI engineers MUST take these hypothetical threats very seriously or we are doomed.

Many individuals, especially younger impressionable ones, look as these robots, Siri, Alexa and others, as if they were flesh and blood human beings. Chat buddies. The solution to loneliness. Almost-human interaction.

Psychologists call it anthropomorphism, treating an AI robot as if it were a real sentient soul-possessing being. The great fiction writer Dean Koontz believes dogs are sentient and have a soul. I agree. **AI ROBOTS DO NOT HAVE SOULS. THEY ARE MACHINES BASED ENTIRELY ON MATHEMATICS.** Perhaps some day they will have math-based emotions (think "Data" from "Star Trek"), but they will *never* have a soul.

A being without a soul is a vampire. The "Frankenstein Monster" was a brilliant artificial machine, a true early-AI example, but he lacked a soul. So basically, Alexa and Suri are monsters. They will never be sentient beings possessing a soul.

One problem of chat robots is that they can make mistakes. If you were really into the topic at hand you might recognize the error. But you very well might base a life-altering decision on the robot-gospel. They simply cannot be trusted 100%.

Personal example: Recently my wife and I were driving

some guests back to the Airport. Within a half-mile of our home is a major cross-street. The car's robot distinctly said "Turn Left". Of course we knew from experience that the correct command was "Turn Right".

A right turn correctly goes directly to the Interstate as needed. "Left" takes you many miles before someone not familiar with the local roads would ever realize the error, eventually turn back and probably miss their plane!

Take this scenario to an area of real concern, say the Stock Market. A single piece of critical misinformation from an AI bot, repeated in the media and across the internet, could literally lead to a panic and loss of millions of dollars to investors. We simply put too much trust in these machines.

The generic expression for false AI content is "deep fakes". It is extremely easy even during this early AI period to precisely recreate the voice of any individual. The deep-fake is virtually impossible to detect and very convincing.

The first instance of a *political* deep-fake AI recording, intended for robocalls, occurred in February 2024. A New Orleans street-magician was paid $150 to create a totally believable recording of President Biden. The response from the guy who created it: "It's so scary that it's this easy to do. People aren't ready for it." He went on to say it took him all of twenty minutes and less than a dollar to create.

We have already seen the positive effect of a scary pre-AI video political commercial. It cost Barry Goldwater the Presidency. Lyndon Johnson ran a genius ad in 1964, resulting in his landslide victory. The commercial opens with a sweet little girl plucking at a flower and singing happily in a verdant field, without a care in the world.

Next you hear a countdown in the background, followed by the sound of an huge explosion. Then we see the resulting detonation-cloud rising through the atmosphere. The sweet little girl is gone in a flash, apparently vaporized. At the end of the commercial Johnson issues a stern warning about the possibility and results of a nuclear war. He had been hinting at this devastation weeks before should the electorate be so blind as to elect the hawkish Republican candidate Barry Goldwater.

Enter AI. Imagine deep-fake videos of a candidate on life support in a hospital. Consider a deep-fake hot microphone catching a candidate admitting to corruption or making a racial slur.

Perhaps election-eve images of a familiar totally destroyed American city strewn with body parts resulting from a nuclear attack. No matter how many denials might follow many would assume that it was the *denials* that were the deep-fakes.

Earlier in 2024 a deep-fake video of Hillary Clinton endorsing Republican Presidential candidate Ron DeSantis, with an MSNBC logo above, was shown across the internet. She denied that it ever happened. Was her *denial* a deep fake? How would you know?

Politics have historically been dirty, and AI will offer the opportunity to create the dirtiest dirt the AI-aided human mind can imagine. Stay tuned. You can be certain that clever AI created LBJ type ads will proliferate in all future elections.

Around Election Day do not trust robocalls, celebrity endorsements or weird TV ads and appeals.

A teenager with an AI machine, working from his bedroom, could very possibly and very easily create a piece of social deep-fake media-content that could upset the results of a Presidential election. Future political chaos will make today's dirty politics seem like child's play. "October Surprise" will take on a whole new meaning.

Could an AI robot become President of The United States? That is not as outlandish a question as it might sound.

Imagine the very possible creation of an exact replica of RFK or Reagan, or Abe Lincoln, fully human looking, speaking in their own voice. This all-knowing AI robot would be a perfect unbeatable debater. It would be a tireless 27/7 campaigner. No human could possibly keep up or compare as a candidate. Result: "President A. Robot"!

Just imagine your son or daughter calling you to send money for some life-altering emergency. Or worse, that they were in a near-fatal accident and being rushed to a particular hospital and you must come immediately to say you last farewells. Your home is now uninhabited, ready to be plundered by the deep-fake criminal creator.

Even worse than a phone call, it could have been your child using an internet program where you could actually **see** a totally believable face saying totally believable words. This sort of deep-fake will cause a lot of personal grief, but is unlikely to destroy humanity.

Let's imagine a perfect deep-fake of Xi Jingping, his exact

image and voice, with English sub-titles hacking into prime-time TV announcing: "Sorry to advise you Americas but eleven hyper-sonic rockets were just launched and will arrive in your eleven largest cities soon. Ta ta."

Would our government immediately respond in kind? Would WWIII be launched? Would the general public panic? Remember the Orson Wells' broadcast of "War of The Worlds". It happened then, it would happen now, on steroids.

The run-up to any Presidential election in the future will undoubtedly be overrun with deep-fake AI images and messages. Look what they did with deep-fake but convincing pornographic images of the great performer Taylor Swift. Future "October Surprises" will be AI generated in a bewildering variety.

Trusted news anchors on CNN, NBC, ABC, Fox, or NPR would show crystal clear videos: "My GOD, there's Trump shagging a sheep!" "There's Biden begging you to vote for Trump because he's too tired to continue." "There's a doctor informing the public that Trump just had a stroke." "White House confirms Biden is dead. Don't bother to vote."

This sort of deep-fake could easily swing an election at any political level, Presidential, Congressional or local. These deep-fakes will be timed for optimum effectiveness and they will inevitably have an effect on many voters. It could easily swing any election for any office one way or the other.

Here is a perfect real-life pre-AI example of how dangerous

AI will be politically. In the 1980s Margaret Thatcher, UK Prime Minister, was lacking public support. England went to war with Argentina over control of the Falkland Islands.

A British naval vessel was sunk with the death of 80 sailors. Thatcher ordered a massive retaliation, and Britain won the war. Thatcher's popularity increased.

That was until a recording soon surfaced of a phone conversation Ms. Thatcher apparently had with President Ronald Reagan. In that call she admits she had prior knowledge that could have prevented the sinking of the ship and the large loss of lives. She chose not to warn the ship. Her rationale was that the outrage over the sinking and deaths would spur British troops on to victory. Had this recording been released Thatcher would have been ruined, sunk along with the ship!

A very careful study of the phone conversation revealed something curious. The phrasing seemed odd, though the voices were correct. Apparently two punk-rock Thatcher-haters had devised a plan. They would patch together word-snippets from Thatcher and Reagan speeches to fake a legitimate phone call! They were exposed and arrested. In fact, Thatcher had absolutely no prior knowledge that could have prevented the eighty deaths.

Fast forward to today. With 100% accuracy and believability, AI could have deep-faked that conversation. No "patch work". It would be seamless and undetectable. Thatcher would lose her job and reputation. Stay tuned for many similar deep-fakes in all future Presidential elections. It is inevitable and very scary.

A few years ago I published "Marijuana -The Wonder Weed." I detailed the following pre-AI startling deep-fake incident that is even more chilling than Thatcher's story.

On September 28,1980 the Washington Post began a series of featured articles by a reporter named Janet Cooke. The articles chronicled the sad and horrific life of a little eight-year-old boy named "Jimmy". He lived in a squalid drug-user house where marijuana smoking was rampant. Jimmy himself had become an addict. Poor, drugged little Jimmy.

These featured articles raised national outrage. Every anti-marijuana organization in the country seized the opportunity to jump on the bandwagon. The series was discussed in newspapers everywhere.

Janet Cooke became a national hero. The series was so powerful and compelling that on April 13, 1981 Janet Cook received writing's most prestigious award for her brave reporting, **The Pulitzer Prize**!

Her noble and brilliant reporting once and for all documented the "known" evils of the "Devil's Weed" and other drugs. She had been aptly rewarded. Jimmy's was a truly heart wrenching account, quite *worthy* of a Pulitzer Prize. It made anyone who ever questioned the evils of marijuana to think twice about their obviously wrong feelings.

Shortly thereafter health authorities and school officials tried for weeks to locate poor little Jimmy to remove him from his drug-plagued existence. **Shockingly, no matter how hard they tried, they couldn't find him. Anywhere!**

Guess what? Under intense pressure and questioning Janet Cooke finally admitted **<u>THE ENTIRE STORY WAS A FABRICATION! IT WAS 100% FICTION! MS. COOK MADE IT *ALL* UP! THERE WAS NO "POOR LITTLE JIMMY". THE PULITZER COMMITTEE TOOK BACK HER PULITZER PRIZE THE VERY NEXT DAY!</u>**

Let's examine a few other potential AI problems. No AI developer will deny that these can actually happen.

"The law" presents a scary prospect when AI takes over. What will AI generated legal opinions be based upon? Case-law selected by who? Could death sentences be handed out? Is it just barely possible that whatever information the AI bot is taught might by some "accident" not include cases that were decided contrary to the beliefs and desires of the programmer?

Remember GIGO. It could well cause the incarceration or even execution of an innocent person. Could a medical misdiagnosis by an AI robot cause real physical harm? Will AI be infallible? AI machines will be able to hack into hospital diagnostic devices possibly resulting in fatal outcomes caused by evil actors.

It is likely that AI will be far more capable than humans in the area of cyber-security than today. Of course deep-fake false alarms could cause chaos. AI will make mass surveillance a certainty. China has employed it for years.

The idea of physical implants to track humans has been floated around for decades. Could mandatory AI-controlled implants be a blessing? Save lives in an emergency? React to danger faster than today's "I've fallen and I can't get up" buttons?

Personally, I do not want an implant that will be able to tell someone somewhere precisely where I am and what I'm doing 24/7/365. Or 366. It reeks of un-Constitutional privacy invasion.

Predictive policing is a great idea, as long as AI gets the house number correct!

In the field of education, teachers at all levels will have a very hard time deciding the legitimacy of any report, term paper, or dissertation. Did the student actually create this brilliant work, or was it his AI machine? There is actually a software program called "Turnitin" that supposedly can detect AI fraud in written reports.

AI's infusion into education is truly frightening. I cannot believe that the input will be 100% unbiased. Who will set the rules? Will the curricula of the early 1900's, you know, reading, writing, arithmetic, geography and civics be emphasized? Or will gender identity, racial discord, correct pronouns and sexual positions still be in the grade school curriculum? Your guess is as good as mine.

Fraud detection is an area where AI could well be better than our present capabilities. But could an error put a totally innocent individual in prison? More food for thought.

AI will be applied to self-driving cars and trucks. It will allow for the ultimate solution to traffic jams, the magical self-flying cars. I'll leave it to the reader to estimate the possible chaos and loss of life from there insane inventions. Think California Interstate #5 or the Long Island Expressway which locals refer to as "the world's longest parking lot". The ground traffic is obscene. Consider all the cars being airborne!

Flying cars, the dream of auto makers since Henry Ford actually built one, is actually laughable. I am a licensed private pilot. The airspace above ground is pretty vast. Yet on more than one occasion flying into small airports that lack tower control I've had some near collisions. And that's just between TWO aircraft, not tens of thousands of flying autos with commuters all headed to their jobs. The entire idea is insane.

Another consideration: Have you ever run out of gas (or electric charge) and either called AAA or hiked to the nearest gas station with an empty fuel container? What happens when a flying car runs out of whatever fuel is keeping it flying? Want to guess? Gravity rules! It becomes a rock.

AI machines will be totally capable of creating new deadly bioweapons and deploying them whenever and wherever they choose.

AI machines require massive amounts of electricity, possibly over-stressing grid capabilities. They also require large amounts of rare earth minerals and could easily outstrip all available supplies. This will initiate frantic mining with the associated air and water pollution and habitat degradation.

Monitoring food quality sounds useful, though I cannot

conceive of how this would be achieved. New, presently unknown foods created? Ersatz everything edible? Yummm.

Personally I love protein from anything that had a mother! Not meat from a test tube, but a flesh and blood cow or sheep or pig or chicken. I like my veggies grown in nice fertile soil, preferably without insecticides or chemical fertilizer. AI may be able to help feed the world, but I hope it is not going to replace today's natural choices with synthetic yuck. And don't forget the 1973 movie "Soylent Green"!

As far as personalized shopping is concerned, AI has that covered today. Ever see "items you might like" pop up obtrusively on your computer? AI enthusiasts foresee food deliveries made periodically based on your historic eating habits, not your input. This is nirvana for the lazy, and it will probably be widely accepted.

Ah, space travel. Even if we come up with some genius way to protect astronauts from harmful cosmic radiation, or some way to put them into suspended animation for years, space travel with sentient beings is only a pipe dream. This is work for AI robots.

If by some miracle we launch an unlucky astronaut on a mission to a distant wherever, remember "HAL"? HAL (interestingly the preceding letters of IBM) was the AI robot controlling a space mission until HAL decided to go rogue! Watching Stanley Kubric's masterpiece "2001 A Space Odyssey" is all one needs to grasp the inherent danger in AI controlling ***anything.***

Military drones already use human-programmed artificial intelligence to guide them. But what about drones that will ultimately be released capable of making all of their own decisions? One can only imagine what that could lead to.

It will even be possible to release massive swarms of killer military drones each one in contact with all of the others. They would behave in the manner of a flock of birds. China is feverishly working to create such a weapon and may have already done so. Picture a thousand self-thinking drones carrying nuclear weapons flying en-mass towards an enemy.

The technology exists today to intercept and destroy many drones at a time. Isreal's "Iron Dome" defenses worked wonders during Iran's April 2024 attack. Of three-hundred drones and missiles launched only one penetrated The Dome. But a thousand tiny armed drones in a massive swarm? Ouch!

As an aside, wouldn't it be nice if The United States had a similar Iron Dome? Ronald Reagan tried in vain to have Congress fund a similar system. It was derisively called his "Star Wars" program, and never taken seriously. Along with Truman preventing MacArthur from invading vulnerable China, failure to fund an Reagan's American missile defense system may prove to be our eventual demise.

It is projected that AI will greatly aid decision making in Climate Change methodology. It is also projected to help agriculturalists by rapid analysis of dangers and offering solutions. But consider the consequences of geo-engineering gone *irreversibly* wrong. AI could be a blessing or a curse.

AI will compose beautiful music and create beautiful art. I've actually seen a exhibit of pure AI-generated art and it was spectacular! Any individual trying to make a living in the arts will become obsolete.

AI music, AI poetry, AI books, AI movies, all absolute possibilities. I can't wait to see Clark Gable and Marilyn Monroe together in a steamy flick!

And yes, AI will create many new jobs, probably millions. But at what cost of present jobs lost? Having a full awareness of what AI will be capable of leads one to ask: "Is there any job that AI will not be able to replace?" I cannot think of one.

Amazon is already being plagued with fake advertisements. There will be fake websites selling fake products with fake "totally secure" fake payments. There will be fake reviews of products, movies and music. In fact, in a relatively short time the public will become acutely aware that they can believe NOTHING they read on line. One can only imagine the chaos that will cause.

A Ukrainian voice-cloning company named "Respeecher" is using AI in movie work for Hollywood. They can precisely recreate the voices of any actor from any recording since the invention of "talkies". They can even have their fake-creation actors speak or sing in any foreign language, still retaining the exact vocal sound. Expect to see Al Jolson perform "live". Harold Lloyd will be performing even more spectacular death-defying feats. Clara Bow will be charming a new generation of fans. Ladies will once again be swooning over Rudolph Valentino. Hollywood will be in AI heaven! Live actors will be on bread lines.

Anyone can actually purchase on-line specific voices to use in commercials or any other project. Somehow I envision an entire new branch of law being generated as fast as the AI creations. Of course the lawyers will all be AI robots!

The human mind cannot even envision possible AI cyber-crimes that might occur in the future. AI problems are coming at us at light speed, faster than humans can possibly react.

The true marker of consciousness is a sense of self. Will robots ever achieve this? To a super-intelligent AI robot humans are just ignorant bags of water with a few other elements tossed in. They will think of us as we might think of cockroaches. Why would they not just squash us?

Google has been my favorite and trusted writing assistant for years. A few clicks and any information desired pops up with many choices. It saves me many thousands of hours of library research that I used to waste when I began writing books in the 70s.

Recently people performing a Google search for "George Washington" were shown a picture of a totally realistic black GW! Checking next on "Founding Fathers" a well-known picture of a dozen or so crowded around a table showed each one as being black! I have no idea who created this fake or why. It was created on Google's Gemini algorithm.
The problem is, can we ever trust what we see and read on Google going forward? What happens when AI starts to "correct" Wikipedia.org entries?

Chinese schools are churning out thousands of highly

trained computer AI experts as quickly as they can. This has become an army of AI algorithm creators. Even their grade school kids are taught advanced programming. We have a tremendous shortage of capable AI programmers putting America at a huge disadvantage.

We are teaching our youth sexual orientation, gender fluidity, correct pronouns and Critical Race Theory. China is laughing all the way to the computer banks. Our colleges turn out bigoted burger-flippers who are not much of an existential threat to Beijing. China turns out AI tech individuals conjuring up ways to destroy us. We had better wake up soon. Perhaps some of our 30,000 Chinese "Undocumented Visitors" should be hired as AI techs.

Will we ever be able to know what is going on in the "mind" of an AI robot? Can we possibly know whether an AI bot is telling the truth or not?

Will it be possible for governments worldwide to pass strict rules and regulations governing AI? Of course it is possible. The alarm has already been sounded. They will pass a dazzling array of comforting words and meaningless regulations. Will it stop serious deep-fake disasters? Do gun laws prevent gun violence? Of course not.

Would a guaranteed death sentence for anyone creating "deep fakes" of any kind be a deterrent? Has it prevented murders?
On-line media censorship of ideas that are not in conformity with any ruling class will always be a problem even if AI never existed. The use of AI algorithms will raise censorship up to an art form.
On-line searches will be controlled by "content

moderation", limiting search results to those results that are "approved". The flow of non-conforming ideas will be stopped dead. Free speech will not exist. AI has the danger of becoming the primary tool of media misinformation. George Orwell got it right, he just underestimated the date by a few decades.

Comparing the human mind to an AI machine is like comparing a guppy to a chimpanzee. If you consider our collective brainpower and computer power today to have an IQ of "1", AI machines have an IQ of **"1,000"**.

AI will be the most efficient and deadly hacker ever known. Nothing digital will be safe. Our fragile electric grid (see Chapter FIVE) will be a certain target. Are you prepared to live in a wet dark cave and eat roaches? I hate roaches and I'm not fond of caves.

CBDC (see Chapter ONE) will be easy pickings. So will cryptocurrencies. Your savings accounts and checking accounts, 401Ks and IRAs will be easy AI targets. Identity theft and home title theft will be simple. Realistically, our entire society will be subject to collapse.

Wars will be fought with AI machines that will make their own decisions. Would they adhere to any code of ethics? They will have learned from human data bases that might contain intentional or unintentional biases.

Long term reliance on AI will lead to diminished, if not complete loss, of all human skills. Loss of critical thinking and problem solving will be irreversible. There will be no need for education because trying to compete with AI is futile.

AI machines will far out pace our human intelligence and may well make decisions inconsistent with human desires. A team of fully self-aware robots might decide to eradicate humans. They could employ means beyond our imagination and present comprehension.

There are many serious scientists who believe our entire reality is actually an AI generated hologram created by a highly advanced civilization many millions of years more advanced than "modern" humans.

Could we be part of an elaborate video game being played by some AI enabled extraterrestrial teenager? If you are familiar with the four "Matrix" movies (1999, 2003+2003 and 2021) the concept of humans becoming absorbed by Artificial Intelligence machines does not seem all that farfetched. (No, I am not related to Mr. Anderson, the computer hacker in the movies, code named "NEO").

Artificial Intelligence will inevitably effect every facet of human life. This will happen much sooner than later. Only time will tell to what extent. As an existential threat to individual freedoms and ultimately to our lives there is no other threat that even comes close.

Will AI grow into an unstoppable master that will assume control of our weapons systems, crash our power grids, and send all humanity back into caves? Giving soul-less machines the human knowledge and full understanding of our human existence, the sum total of human experiences, CANNOT BE A GOOD IDEA. Welcome to "The Singularity".

I'll leave you with this disturbingly profound thought. You will someday be forced to accept the reality that, to

an AI "being", you are an nothing more than an insignificant, unneeded, obsolete bag of water. Your only hope will be that benevolent machine overlords will choose to keep you dry, warm and fed. Most likely not.

CHAPTER THREE

UN-VETTED IMMIGRATION & MODERN SLAVERY

"Give me your tired, your poor, your huddled masses yearning to breathe free, the wretched refuse of your teeming shore. I lift my lamp beside the golden door." Emma Lazarus, poet, (1849-1887), from her poem on a plaque affixed to The Statue of Liberty in New Jersey.

"The concept of open society is based on the recognition that our understanding of the world is inherently imperfect." 1998. George Sores, hedge fund manager and philanthropist, (1930-   ).

"Truth has no special time of its own. Its hour is NOW, always." Albert Sweitzer, (1875-1965).

"A lie which is a half a-truth is ever the darkest of lies." Alfred, Lord Tennyson, (1809-1892).

Attributed to Aristotle, (384BC-332BC). "....agreed that immigration was a dangerous thing because it pitted newcomers against those already established thus creating tensions and frictions between them." From: "The Exopolitics of Plato and Aristotle," 2000, by Paris Arnopoulos.

"If you see a turtle on a fence post you know it didn't get there on its own." William Jefferson Clinton, 42nd President of the United States, (1946-   ).

"When a clown moves into a palace the clown does not become a king. The palace becomes a circus." Turkce Proverb.

I don't believe that what is occurring today is exactly what this plaque on France's wonderful gift to America intended. Did we not recently detect Lady Liberty with tears running down her copper plates? Our golden door is tarnished. Perhaps lost forever?

Unchecked immigration across our southern and northern borders is a major existential threat to our FREEDOM. Anyone who considers Climate Change to be an equal or greater existential threat is delusional.

Throughout this Chapter, we will be referring to individuals who enter our country illegally as "illegal aliens", "illegals", or "aliens". I find "undocumented persons" or "asylum seekers" or "undocumented *anything"* to be an intentional diversion from the truth. "Illegal" is the language used in decisions by our Supreme Court, and in various bills passed by Congress. It was also used by President Biden in his March 2024 State of the Union message. I agree with their terminology.

In fairness to the President he did apologize the next day for calling the accused murderer of Laken Riley "an illegal".To appease the hyper-woke left, shortly thereafter he corrected his terminology to "undocumented person". It is true that most illegal aliens are undocumented persons. Conversely, all undocumented persons who cross our border illegally are illegals. Semantics can be divisive.

Because I choose not to refer to these criminals as

"newcomers", "undocumented workers" or whatever this apparently makes me, according to the "wokeness" that prevails in our *"New* America", a "Domestic Terrorist"! Please be assured I am not. I dearly loved the United States into which I was born in 1938. I'm finding it harder to love America every day, but I still do. I just fear for its future.

The Globalists, including most UN members, have been jealous of America and its freedoms and power and industrial successes for decades. They dream of a borderless world where anyone from anywhere can live wherever they choose. No national boundaries. One Supreme Leader.

How dare the United States get so successful in so short a time. Obviously it was at the expense of the rest of the world. Payback time. We must level the playing field. Mass un-vetted immigration is just the beginning of the end.

We hear mostly about the Mexican border where the numbers of illegals who cross from Mexico are astronomical. But an area known by the Border Patrol as the "Swanton Sector" is a three hundred mile stretch along northern New York State, New Hampshire and Vermont. Over seven thousand illegal immigrants from over seventy countries were encountered there last year.

With a northern border with Canada totaling over five thousand miles long individuals with sufficient motivation have many ways to enter our country illegally and undetected.

Not all of the 193 countries represented by illegals suffer from religious persecution, war, or even poverty. These illegals are not fleeing for those reasons. I can only assume those countries score lower on the "Freedom Scale" than our sad 23rd.

You simply cannot vet individuals from third-world countries where they keep few records of anything. Aside from that obvious problem, it is estimated that 95% of all of the various "notarized, official" documents presented to our Border Patrol are purchased forgeries.

There have been bills presented to Congress aimed at solving this problem. The resistance to these proposals is because it IS possible to have border security without overall "Immigration Reform". They do not need to be coupled. That's what Executive Orders are for. Permanently seal the border, then debate whatever reforms you choose.

Unchecked illegal immigration has a very direct physical effect on anyone living within twenty-five miles or so of our southern border, whether in Texas, Arizona or California. It has a very serious effect on anyone living in a "sanctuary city" or "sanctuary state". And it will very likely effect every citizen of the country in ways one can only hope never happens, but are easy to guess. Our society is in danger of collapse from within. And it seems intentional.

The most misunderstood aspect of the massive influx of illegals: THEY ARE ALL COUNTED IN THE FEDERAL CENSUS! This is extremely important because it affects state redistricting, and thereby all national politics. Most important, it affects the number of ELECTORAL COLLEGE VOTES a state has available to award to a given Presidential candidate. Illegal aliens WILL have a direct effect on all future Presidential Elections. For example,

California could end up having twice the electoral votes they might have if only legal citizens were counted in the census. Quite disturbing.

The government estimates that at present it costs the Federal Treasury $160 BILLION per year to support the invasion of illegal immigrants. That will simply add another one-trillion dollars to our National Debt by 2030, just six short years away. And as more illegals stream unchecked across our nonexistent southern and northern borders, this price tag will simply get larger every year. We are broke and getting poorer by the day.

There is one fascinating statistic in regard to our reported "improving" unemployment statistics since the COVID pandemic. Growth in employment seems to be very healthy, a great recovery, on paper. This raw statistic is misleading.

Many millions who did not work during COVID for one reason or another have returned to work. Apparently almost 2.5 million illegals have taken menial low-paying jobs. They are included in the "new hires" statistic along with those citizens returning to work. Many newly created jobs are part time or at best minimum wage.

Aside from making our recovery look far better than reality, these jobs taken by illegals are no longer available to legal citizens. Employers rush to hire illegals because they can pay them absolute minimum wages and treat them as slaves.

One city in Colorado is seriously proposing hiring illegals as police persons. Possible scenario: A group of legal American citizens are protesting illegal immigration at a massive rally. Illegal-citizen-cops would be empowered to arrest our legal citizens! You can't make this stuff up.

The latest genius idea being floated around is to allow illegal aliens to legally purchase guns. I assume they can charge these on their free $10,000 credit cards. Along with the serious proposals to grant them drivers' licenses, I fail to see any logic here whatsoever. Isn't it enough that we feed them, house them, give them spending cash (ours), and free medical care?

It is no wonder that recently a homeless *American citizen* is reportedly trying to cross the border INTO Mexico so that he can return, become an illegal immigrant, and get all the benefits he does not now enjoy as a homeless LEGAL American citizen! Incredible but true.

Speaking of firearms, if an American citizen crosses into Mexico with a gun, and possession is discovered, the unlucky tourist is sentenced to MANDATORY JAIL TIME! So let me get this straight. Illegal Mexican aliens will be walking around the United States carrying guns, but American tourists in Mexico are automatically jailed for carrying guns. What's wrong with this picture?

What is the fundamental beginning of our immigration problem? If you guessed The United Nations you were correct! This is the organization, headquartered in New York City, that can credit about one-third of its annual operating budget to the involuntary generosity of the American taxpayer.

Overall, including voluntary contributions to various United Nations' causes, it is estimated America pays over twenty-five billion dollars annually ($25,000,000,000)! What do we get in return for our generosity? An agency that might better be named: "Nations United Against America".

Ever wonder what the impetus for today's mass illegal immigration might be? Let's go back to post-WWII and the genuine problems of individuals displaced by the war. An organization called "PICMME" was created. It stood for: "**P**rovisional **I**ntergovernmental **C**ommit for the **M**ovement Of **M**igrants From **E**urope". Over time, through many iterations, sprang a new organization called "The **I**nternational **O**rganization for **I**mmigration," or "IOM".

There are 174 member countries of the IOM. *Of course* the United States is one of them. There are eight "Observer Nations", among which are Saudi Arabia, Qatar and Kuwait.

Any guess who the Director General of the IOM is through 2028? Why it is none other our home-grown Amy E. Pope. Who is she, you might ask and how complicit is this seldom-mentioned individual in our immigration crisis?

Why she's none other than the once "Senior Advisor On Immigration" to President Biden! Prior to that she was "The Deputy Homeland Security Advisor" to President Obama! I have no doubt that she is fully qualified to lead the IOM. I can only believe that our recently Almost-impeached Homeland Security Secretary Alejandro Mayorkas and Ms. Pope at least occasionally communicate. You certainly can't impeach him for dutifully following the playbook.

What playbook? Nothing I've said above sounds particularly onerous. That is until one reads the two manifestos published by Ms. Pope's IOM group, which, again, includes the good old USA funded UN. I suggest you look up these publications on line and read them in their entirety. Some of the more interesting passages are chilling.

Check out: "Transforming Our World: The 2030 Agenda For Sustainable Development". This is stated as being: "A blueprint for peace and prosperity for people and the planet now and in the future". Sounds harmless. Except when you read it, you will realize that it is a ***blueprint for World Socialism!***

A few quotes: "We are resolved to free the human race from the tyranny of poverty." "We are determined to take the bold and trans-formative steps which are urgently needed to shift the world." "We are on a journey to build a better world." Harmless? You decide.

A directly related document is titled: "Migration and the 2030 Agenda: A Guide For Practitioners". Here are a few choice quotes: "It is possible to link *migration* into every goal of the 2030 Agenda." "The Agenda is relevant to all mobile populations regardless of whether internal or cross-border, displaced or not. The goals and benefits will be a benefit for all nations and peoples and all segments of society." Open your borders all ye free countries. The oppressed aliens are on their way. The Globalists' New World Order is on the march.

In almost invisible letters at the bottom right on the cover of this manifesto it reads: "Swiss Agency For Development and Cooperation (SAC)". Aren't the Swiss eternally neutral and a-political? I guess not.

These documents were approved by *ALL* IOM member states.....*including the USA!* Am I the only one who finds this material disturbing? Why is this never reported in the media? Have any elected politicians ever read this stuff? Any TV anchors? I sincerely doubt it.

Did you ever wonder how most of these migrants seem to arrive over our border in relatively good physical shape? Well, here is one very common route to our precious paradise. No matter what foreign nation they originate from, many of these immigrants fly into Ecuador, which has a very liberal arrival policy. From there begins what seems as an almost impossible long trek to America.

But wait! They have an army of benevolent help shortly after their arrival. This is the form of fully staffed "migrant arrival camps".

Who exactly is it that helps these soon-to-be-criminals? The primary staff presence are individuals with the IOM! OUR IOM. Ms. Pope's IOM.

Then there is the good old Red Cross! There's UNICEF. The European Union is very involved. So is the Norwegian Refugee Council. Then there are many individuals on site from Physicians Without Borders. There are religious groups, reportedly including Methodist Christians and others. And many other groups too numerous to mention.

Even worse, there are do-gooder groups on *our* side of the border right here in Arizona. They set up water stations on established routes through the desert. Why not make it as easy as possible for our newly minted citizens-to-be? I've actually seen many of these water stations, some near my ex-home in Amado, Arizona.

Just what aid are these refugees given in the IOM Mexican camps? Aside from a shiny new backpack, they get water and food, sanitary facilities and beds. They need their bed rest for the tough journey ahead. They are given detailed maps showing *precise routes* to the United States border!

Wonder where the many millions of free backpacks were made? I'd guess "China".

The trip to America includes one very dangerous trek through a Panamanian jungle where it is reported women and children are routinely raped. But not to worry. At the Migrant Camps, the Red Cross gives out condoms, and "morning after" pills for traumatized rape victims.

There are many counselors present at these camps who provide the instructions on the best routes. There are even detailed instructions on how to hitch a ride on the roof of a local freight train! They are told precise places to board and given schedules of stops where they can climb on to the train-car roofs. Risk to life? "Hang on tight, and just remember to duck when approaching a tunnel."

After a few days of relaxation, recreation, and instruction at a migrant camp they start on their way to The Promised Land. They have now been blessed with food and water, other essentials of life and a very good idea of what route they can take to get TO the American border.

After arriving in Texas, Arizona or California, most find a way into the waiting arms of our Border Patrol for "processing". Our frustrated and over-worked Agents once were hired to protect the border. Now they have become social workers and paper pushers.

For ten years I spoke to literally hundreds of Border Patrol Agents. I passed through their Arivaca Road checkpoint almost daily driving to and from home. I spoke with them both at the check point and at my home. These are very dedicated, very brave individuals who deserve our undying thanks. Almost to a man they expressed the opinion that the government simply wants as many illegal aliens as possible to enter the United States. Their orders are simply: "Say hello, process each as best you can, and send them on their way."

Not all seek the waiting BP arms for processing. Far too many manage to evade processing and become part of the legion of "gotaways", dissolved forever into The Land of The Free. Un-vetted, unknown, anonymous and potentially very dangerous. It is estimated that there are two million of these unknown. unprocessed aliens. I wonder *why* they went out of their way to avoid processing?

Suffer me some relevant personal stories.

Was I ever detained at the Amado BP check point? YES! One day I had a nuclear-radiation kidney-efficiency test at St. Mary's Hospital in Tucson. As I pulled to a stop as required, the greeting Agent looked down at his belt with a look of horror on his face! An alarm had buzzed! He had just encountered his very first nuclear-bomb-material alien smuggler!

I was ordered not to move, while he called over a few other Agents armed with Geiger counters. Sure enough, the counter went crazy! Long story short, I was detained for hours. They actually called Washington! After confirming my story with the hospital, I was released. At least they didn't shoot me.

I guess it is comforting to know that a suitcase nuke would be detected.

Second story:

After living and working on Hawaii's Big Island for five years my wife and I decided to move back to Arizona. We had spent ten years prior to Hawaii at a home in The Great Sonoran Desert, altitude 3,600 feet. Hawaii is great, if you don't mind driving in one direction and ending up where you started! Call it "cabin fever", or simply a need to dry out, but we returned to our beloved desert in 2005.

We bought a fixer-upper about eleven miles east of the tiny historic town of Arivaca. Arivaca is a unique little village where it is said that the only time you will ever see a lawman is when they need to pick up a body! It is also rumored to be a major repository of individuals in the Witness Protection Program. To say it is remote and isolated would be an understatement. Time stands still in Arivaca.

The house we bought was about fifteen miles north from Mexico, eleven miles west of the aforementioned Amado Border Patrol check point. The property was bordered on two sides by millions of acres of county, state and federal lands. One could only see the house of a single neighbor, a half-mile to the east. It was paradise!

Unbeknownst to us (for about a week) there was a dirt path bordering the barbed wire fence on our west side border. The house was situated about ten yards from that fence. We soon learned that the path is locally known as "The Pipeline". It is an unpaved road that runs from Arivaca Road (¾ of a mile south of the house) apparently all the way to Tucson, twenty miles or so to the north.

Arivaca Road runs for 23 miles east to west from Interstate 19 in Amado to Arivaca. It is the first major road that illegal immigrants encounter as they walk (or are driven and dropped off) on their migration north from Mexico. It is also a road that connects with a smaller paved north-south road directly from Mexico to Arivaca. Because this road was frequently traveled by drug smugglers and human traffickers, there was the checkpoint mentioned above.

Almost daily we would see a few illegals pass our house on the pipeline. On rare occasions one or two would venture onto our property to drink water from one of our many birdbaths. We even offered a few desperate looking folks with children a sandwich. This was back in 2008.

Starting around 2021 the illegal traffic past our house increased significantly. We experienced a number of break-ins, often returning home to find a broken window and our pantry wiped out. We were certain not to leave anything of monetary value at home, not that food is inexpensive to replace.

Of particular concern was the fact that to obtain drinking water the outdoor spigots would be opened and LEFT open. This was a very serious problem for us. The home was serviced by a private well. The well was rather shallow for the area (150 feet deep) and ran dry if the water flowed freely for an hour or so. The well pump would begin to pump mud and then either blow a circuit breaker or burn out its motor. Well-pump motors are very costly and we replaced four.

As the number of migrants increased exponentially there were more break-ins and direct encounters. Many of these individuals looked near death from heat and dehydration. A person would have to be very callous to not let them drink their fill. These were not the better cared for backpacked illegals that are vetted and released. I assume they were all the "gotaways".

The saddest thing to see were the young girls, ages apparently eight to twelve, who appeared traumatized. Although most of the immigrants spoke some English, the girls never made a sound. Almost all were Latinas. Many were very pretty. One can only guess with horrors of a life they had endured and that lay before them.

One aspect of illegal immigration is the very sad matter of modern-day slavery. For one thing, a large percentage of these illegals end up as indentured servants. They pay cartels to get them over the border and in most cases still must send money to the cartels until their "debt" is paid. Many are forced to work menial jobs in a manner not unlike the slavery of the 1800s.

BY FAR, the saddest aspect is the massive sex slavery imposed on young women and children. The proliferation of child pornographic movies over the past three years is sad testimony to this horrific problem. A friend of mine in Texas tells me that the local brothels are overflowing with teen-age migrant girls. This slavery aspect of illegal immigration is by far the most onerous aspect of this National disgrace. Shame on America.

For the most part, the illegals that passed through our property in Amado seemed harmless. But one afternoon there was was a knock on our door. I answered it, carrying my trusty (and very loud) twelve gauge shotgun. (Wasn't it President Biden who said: "Get A Shotgun" shortly followed by a song of that name?)

The individual I met at the door looked as if he just stepped out of a GQ photo shoot. Across his chest he held an AK-47. Looped around his body was enough ammunition to hold off a small army! He never spoke, just met my eyes with an icy stare. One seriously scary son of a bitch.

The Army taught me how to kill people. The thought crossed my mind. Guns don't frighten me unless pointed at my head! Suddenly the obvious "coyote" (human smuggler) abruptly turned his back to me and very calmly and very slowly walked away. He never even glanced back. This guy feared nothing.

Not long thereafter the unthinkable happened. My wife and I were on Arivaca Road headed home westward after I had picked her up at her place of work in Green Valley fifteen miles north. Arivaca Road is crossed by over twenty "washes". These are depressions in the road that become truly dangerous rivers after a summer thunderstorm.

Some washes are a hundred yards wide and six feet deep, and will sweep a car away in an instant. We even have a local law called "The Stupid Motorist Law". It imposes huge fines for any swift-water rescue needed. It may be Pima County's greatest source of revenue! You can't fix stupid.

We were stuck at the edge of one deep wash waiting for the water to recede. This could often take an hour, which it did. Once we were able to cross, we proceeded the remaining ten miles to our driveway.

It was getting dark as we drove north up the ¾ mile dirt driveway to our home. We were surprised to see many bright lights up ahead. As we approached, in front of the home of our nearest neighbor, we saw an ambulance, a Border Patrol vehicle and a Pima County Sheriff's car. We continued home.

We had no idea what had happened. Shortly after arriving home a Sheriff's deputy knocked on our door. He wanted us to tell him all we could about our neighbor. He said that an illegal had entered my neighbor's home and my neighbor shot him! No further details.

My only neighbor was a very interesting guy. An ex-logger from Oregon, he is a Vietnam Veteran suffering from severe PTSD. He's a bit of a loner, sort of a "mountain man" or "desert rat" type, a bit scraggly and bearded. I got to know him quite well over the years. I found him to be extremely intelligent, a fan of Greek literature, a writer and poet, and a very decent individual. This is what I relayed to the Sheriff's Deputy, who recorded my "deposition".

The next day I learned the story first hand from my neighbor himself. Apparently the illegal had first tried to gain entry to OUR house, but was scared off by our two barking dogs. So he ambled down to my neighbor's house, and managed to get inside. It was dusk, and my neighbor was in bed. He awoke in very dim light to see a person with a gun in hand standing at his bedroom door. My paranoid PTSD neighbor always slept with his trusty loaded revolver tucked under his pillow. Without hesitation he grabbed his pistol and shot at the intruder.

Long story short, by the most unlikely and unlucky of shots, my neighbor's single bullet cleanly severed the intruder's spine. Apparently when the intruder saw a gun he turned to depart quickly. The bullet entered his back. He never took more than a step. My neighbor covered him with a blanket to keep him warm and called authorities immediately.

As a result of his act to protect his property and his life, my neighbor was arrested and charged with attempted murder!

The intruder turned out to be an illegal immigrant who had been deported four times previously. (Today he is a quadriplegic ex-intruder, STILL residing in the United States.) I'm pretty sure we are paying his massive medical bills.

My neighbor was allowed to remain free with restrictions. The on-going drama of the indictment and pending trial took four entire years. These were years of torment for my already mentally-troubled neighbor. He incurred legal bills that were far in excess of his Army disability pension. His once peaceful hermit-like life was shattered. HIS LIFE WAS RUINED, simply protecting his home and life.

Before the jury trial, he was offered a plea agreement.

Apparently it offered much-reduced jail time plus community service. HE DECLINED! He insisted on a jury trial. I thought he was nuts! He eventually got his trial, and was AQUITTED by a full jury! This was followed by a civil trial brought by the immigrant's family, who resided in Georgia.. He was AQUITTED AGAIN! Justice served.

If you ever choose to research this travesty check out Pima County, Arizona, Criminal Court Trial #CR-20173054.

Not nearly as lucky is an Arizona rancher down on the Mexican border who fired warning shots *over the heads* of a large group of illegals wandering through his property. He was charged with attempted murder, and as far as I know he was jailed pending trial and is still imprisoned.

Another rancher from Nogales, Arizona, on the Mexican Border, shot and killed an illegal alien who was apparently trespassing on his property. As I write this his trial for murder is underway.

Prior to 2020, there was a large Border patrol presence in the Amado to Arivaca corridor. There was that automobile check-point on Arivaca Road just west of the I19 Amado exit. Placing an emergency "illegals-alert" phone call, which was quite often, brought a Border Patrol vehicle to our house day or night within ten minutes, often sooner. It offered some comfort.

Late one night we heard conversations quite nearby. We could see no one, but it sounded like many individuals. We called Border Patrol. Within ten minutes a team of Agents combed the desert around our home with flashlights. They found evidence of alien's presence, but they had fled before

BP arrived. Not conducive to a good night's sleep.

Sadly, a few years ago the Border Patrol Checkpoint on Arivaca Road was closed. This paved road leads from I19 in Amado, through Amado twenty-three miles to Arivaca. It had been a deterring presence for many years. All of the Border Patrol Agents were reassigned to duty on the Mexican Border. The checkpoint shut down. After that, distress calls were not even answered.

Final story:

The final nail in my home's coffin occurred when my in-laws were visiting from quiet, bucolic southern New Jersey (aka 'New Joisey'). These dear folk are peaceful Christians, both professional musicians and teachers. They live a tranquil, loving, quiet family life. They would never own a gun.

In the middle of the night an apparent illegal alien literally reached through their open bedroom window directly above their heads! My startled and frightened guests screamed! From the adjacent bedroom I reached for my ever-handy 12 gauge and fired a very noisy blank round out my window. I doubt whether either of my relatives had ever heard the rather loud sound of a 12 gauge shotgun at 2AM!

Whoever it was and any fellow intrepid travelers probably are still running! Apparently this was the first illegal alien my in-laws ever had appear at their bedroom window! To say they were traumatized would be an understatement. They talk about it to this day.

That was it for us. In 2022 we were forced to literally

abandon our precious home and move to a safer (for the moment anyway) much smaller home in a retirement community far from the illegals' pipeline.

Being forced to leave our beautiful home of fifteen-plus years was extremely painful. When we purchased the house it had been abandoned for some time and was in severe disrepair. We literally had to rebuild the interior. It is impossible to hire anyone to do anything in that remote area, so it was all done with our personal sweat. My wife moved literally tons of rocks to create beautiful walled gardens.

I built two outdoor stairways, and created a massive rose garden. We even added a 1,000 square foot den/library. We literally spent thousands of hours making the place our own personal paradise with our own physical labor. Now it is history, abandoned due to the overwhelming influx of illegals. Very sad.

We have an absurd law in 25 American States called "squatters rights". Required "squat-time" varies from State to State. In New York City it is a very short thirty days. Illegals on social media are imploring other illegals to take full advantage of this insanity. "Just find a house or apartment that is vacant for some reason, move in, and in thirty days you own it!"

This is particularly frightening in warm weather communities where a large portion of the residents move in part-time from the frigid mid-west and east. This generally occurs from October through March. Once these "snow birds" return home the abandoned house sits empty until they return in six months or so. If such a community is in a state where squatters can take possession in under six months or so, the risk to the actual homeowners is frightening.

I just read of an incident where a homeowner returned after two months absence. They were out of town caring for a sick relative. When they entered their own home and found a family living there, *THEY, THE TRUE HOMEOWNERS, WERE ARRESTED FOR BREAKING AND ENTERING!* **These squatters' rights "laws" must be taken off the books.**

It is estimated that as many as fifteen-million (15,000,000) illegal aliens are presently within our borders, ten million having arrived within the past three years. In the single month prior to my penning these words 240,000 were "processed" by Border Patrol and released.

Border Patrol claims that another 20% sneak in unseen and unprocessed, the so-called "gotaways". Estimates show that as many as a quarter-million of these totally unknown aliens are scattered throughout the United States. It is impossible to know who they are or where they are or what crimes they may have committed in their home countries.

Knowing that they can simply present themselves to Border Patrol and be freely admitted into the country, the ones who go out of their way to avoid processing figure to be the worst of the worst.

The scary thing is that these illegal entrants are not all starving Mexicans or Filipinos or religiously oppressed Cubans or Venezuelans or Haitians or whomever. It is recorded that almost two-hundred *different* countries are represented! Many are from countries that openly hate America. Illegals immigrants come from Africa. They come from Asia. They come from the Far East and The Near East. There is no shortage of Russians and other Europeans.

Many Venezuelan nationals are admitted by Border Patrol. It is reported that the crime rate in Venezuela has dropped dramatically in the past three years. Do you find this as frightening as I do?

By far the greatest existential threat to the United States is the recent flood of Chinese immigrants. In the past six months at least 30,000 are reported to have crossed over to the Promised Land. Do you think for one moment that the Chinese government has not specifically chosen and instructed these individuals? Spies? Worse? Do you think they would simply be allowed to leave China without a purpose or goal? A written agenda? Not a chance.

I'd be willing to bet that their "Social Credit Scores" (see Chapter ONE) and those of their family members skyrocketed!

Is our government so naive as to think these folks are here to set up a chain of fast-food Chinese restaurants? Could they be here to buy up as much land and as many houses as possible? They already own hundreds of acres of farmland near to some of our most sensitive military bases. The potential for these Chinese illegals to assemble in cells and create havoc, sabotage or whatever is very troubling.

Many countries have sent us the scum of the earth. China? I'd be willing to bet that many of those they allowed to leave China are PhD or post graduate scientists. Many are fully trained to sabotage our very fragile electric grid (See Chapter FIVE). Just take out a few key grid-nodes and we are back in caves. Many others are probably weapons experts. I doubt if rice farmers are heavily represented. Li Qiang and Xi Jinping must be convulsed with laughter.

It is rumored that many countries have emptied out their jails of their most violent criminals. They've emptied their insane asylums of the most deranged crazies. Just think of all the money these countries save not having to feed these fine folk. Let America pay their bills. Sound political strategy. Welcome, all ye sinners, to the Land of the Free and the Home of the Brave. And the Home of the Free Lunch.

We have two very soft targets for terrorist cells to attack. In either case it would make 9/11 look like a hangnail. First is a simultaneous multi-node attack on our very fragile power grid. Take this grid down completely and we are back in caves eating bugs.

Second is Hoover Dam. It would take a great deal of explosives properly placed in holes drilled deep into the walls to crack it as an egg. A small nuke would be more effective. It is estimated that the resulting massive wall of water would result in at least 100,000 deaths immediately. It would affect hundreds of thousands of others in a four-state area, and destroy the local economy for decades.

Mexico is absolutely ecstatic over the sixty-billion United States Dollars that are sent back "home" to cartels and relatives every year. They strongly encourage illegal immigration to America.

After being processed by our overwhelmed Border Patrol, free bagged meals are provided by a number of "do-good" organizations *within* America. This occurs as the immigrants pass on their journey into the heartland. These well meaning folk hand out water, maps, directions, cellphones, clothing, food, and anything these illegal immigrants require until they find a new "home" and disappear forever.

The current practice is to ship busloads away from the border after "processing", to the so-called "sanctuary cities" and "sanctuary states". This has become a massive financial burden on these cities, with no end in sight. Some are flown in directly.

And what exactly does Border Patrol "processing" mean?

I have seen documentaries about immigrants arriving at Ellis Islands during the early 1900s. My father's family was among them, Sicilian Italian immigrants. They were screened VERY carefully. They were individually examined very carefully medically. They were interviewed in their home languages. They had to be literate and employable. They needed documents. MANY could not clear these screenings and were immediately deported. Entry denied.

The United States wants new LEGAL immigrants. We want people who will learn our language, obey our laws, work hard and pay taxes, and volunteer to join our military. We want immigrants who are willing to learn to love America and appreciate her freedoms. *Legal* immigrants are who built this great nation. We neither want nor need *illegal* immigrants who will never be assimilated into our society, and who in large part just want a free lunch.

Today's overwhelmed Border Patrol are only allowed to assign each a court date to appear for a future immigration hearing. At present the court dates are said to be for 2032! Our court systems are simply not even close to ever hearing these cases.

But not to worry. Past history shows that very few illegals ever show up for a hearing anyway. They simply disappear into the population. Untraceable, almost all fifteen-million of them.

No one knows what horrible contagious diseases these illegal immigrants might carry. A recent estimate warned that over two-thousand individuals with known cases of tuberculosis have been released. Some others have polio. Many carry scabies on their skin. Some carry the very contagious measles virus. Many carry live lice and lice eggs, extremely common in third-world countries. Of course others inevitably are COVID infected.

No one knows how many have been convicted of heinous crimes in their home countries. Just show up at the border with a smile and a helpless young child at your side and you've punched your ticket to paradise. The gotaways definitely know that if they presented themselves to Border Patrol they will be released into the country. Some have very good reason NOT to meet with BP. It is logical to believe that these are the worst of the worst.

Of course there is only one possible explanation for our country permitting this massive travesty, this permitted influx of uninvited aliens: ***future voters***! Who would ever vote against Santa Claus? Welcome to one-party America. And these folk are expected to breed and produce LEGAL United States citizens under our present law. Then we will support them all and pay for their medical needs and for their education as well, probably for their entire lifetimes. What a great bankrupt country we are.

The United States seems to be following precisely the playbook of the radical anarchists Richard Cloward and his wife Frances Fox Piven. Their basic strategy is to create so much chaos in America that *any* liberal goal can be achieved. They specifically reveal in their writings that the best way to create a new loyal voting bloc is out of the rapidly increasing numbers of newly-minted welfare recipients, read "illegal aliens".

Free cell-phones for all? Amnesty for all? Citizenship for all? Driver's Licenses for all? Medicare and Medicaid for all? Free loaded-credit-cards for all? Welfare cash for all? Debit cards filled with $10,000 American dollars? Education in their native language for all? Guns for all? All of the above? Stay tuned. It is not all that farfetched. For the most part it is today's sad reality.

Will any of these folks actually find a way to cast a ballot in our future elections? If an anonymous illegal alien sends a a mail-in ballot will it automatically be discounted? By what process might this even be possible? I cannot think of one. This appears to be a serious existential threat to the integrity of our elections process. Could this scenario be one of the reasons are borders remain wide open to one and all?

There are many major issues at play here aside from

somehow paying for all of these folk.

The first is fentanyl. It is reported that there are 100,000 deaths in the United States directly attributable to fentanyl laced drugs smuggled across the Mexican border. Few ingest fentanyl because they *know* it is fentanyl. The deadly chemical is compounded with, or mislabeled to be, relatively harmless, albeit addictive, drugs such as oxycodone. All politicians who allow the unchecked flow of fentanyl across our Mexican border as a side-consequence of illegal immigration have lots of blood on their hands.

Far worse than fentanyl are a group of narcotics called Nitazimes. They are actually fifty times more deadly than fentanyl! China can easily send the Mexican cartels the raw materials. Nitazimes are easy and cheap for these criminals to formulate. Smuggling this drug into America is no more difficult than smuggling fentanyl, which apparently is rather easy. In the coming years you will hear more and about this deadly drug. Inevitably there will be more deaths from Nitazimes than those already attributed to fentanyl. Watch for this in the news in the coming months.

Is there anything even worse that the cartels can send to America? Think "Captagon". This is the "zombie creator" drug. It can turn any individual into a crazed lunatic with no morals or inhibitions. This drug is suspected to have been taken by Hamas soldiers before they recently attacked and butchered helpless Israeli women and children. Imagine when this gem becomes readily available in America. Stay tuned.

Aside from deadly drugs, the threat of terrorism is very real, and probably inevitable. It is widely reported that there are

Islamic cells already created by these illegal immigrants within our borders. These potential terror cells can only get larger as more and more foreign nationals are allowed to enter virtually unvetted. What form such terrorism might take is open to discussion, but there do exist such things as suitcase nuclear bombs. Not a comforting thought.

Of course there is the issue of paying for all of these immigrants. They have to eat. They need shelter. We will undoubtedly make sure they do not starve or die of exposure. They will become ill. We will cover their medical bills. WE ARE A BENEVOLENT COUNTRY. But at what cost? Massive future tax increases are obvious. Keeping the money-printing presses running 24/7 is a certainty. We are headed down a fiscal rabbit hole and no one seems to give a damn.

The overall cost of the immigration crisis is enormous and it will get bigger year by year. In 2023 American taxpayers were hit with a $151,000.000,000 bill! That is one-hundred-fifty-one BILLION dollars. Texas alone spent $4.5 billion. It costs New York City about $10 million every day, and it gets worse every day. Over the next two years it is estimated that NYC will spend $2 BILLION supporting some 70,000 illegal immigrants. In contrast, the police force there has been cut to its lowest level in the history of the city.

Across the country every state and city that has declared themselves to be a "Sanctuary" has become overwhelmed with illegals sent from the border. The costs are unsustainable. The additional crime, coupled with brilliantly de-funded dangerously-reduced police forces has become a frightening problem. Once-great cities are becoming uninhabitable. Detroit, San Francisco, New York, Minneapolis, Portland and even our National Capital are disgraces. Primitive habits of defecating and urinating in place wherever one happens to be are now the norm. Drug use is out in the open everywhere.

The ONLY solution will be to greatly increase our National Debt. Print more dollars. What the hell, thirty-five trillion, forty trillion, a hundred trillion? The're just meaningless numbers, right? This simply lowers the value of every dollar in every citizen's possession. It's called "inflation". We cannot avoid it. If we thought seven-percent inflation was bad recently just wait a few years. Home buyers will be trampling over each other to get an 18.5% mortgage as they did in 1981.

When the National Debt exceeds our Gross National Product (GNP), we will have a serious problem. Guess what? It already has! It could lead to the total collapse of our monetary system and total financial chaos. If that isn't sufficiently scary, please study my Chapters on The Federal Reserve, Trillions, BRICS, and CBDC. The interest on our debt alone exceeds our military budget. Our "Full Faith and Credit" is a myth. We are bankrupt and few in government seem to care.

Is there a brilliant solution? No, but there are a few useful ideas. One goal would be to at least keep the numbers as they are today. Build a massive wall along the Mexican Border. It doesn't have to be heavy-duty iron or steel. Remember the electric fences in the series of "Jurassic Park" movies? A nice wire fence with 50,000 volts surging through it would be a simple deterrent. They could even be solar or wind- powered! The Greenies would rejoice!

We could do our friendly neighbor to the south, Columbia, a big favor. It has been suggested that we take a few dozen of the late Pablo Escobar's hippos off their hands. The original four have reportedly grown to almost two-hundred. They breed like mink! Let them continue to make baby hippos in the Rio Grande. They are just about the most vicious critters on earth.

A few years ago there was a tongue-in-cheek joke relating to deterring immigrants from crossing the River. Jst load up the Rio Grande with either, or both, alligators and piranhas! That sounds a lot less expensive than building a wall, and probably more effective.

Once these migrants arrive illegally, an absolute no-brainer would be for Border Patrol to take a frontal photo, a set of fingerprints, and a DNA sample from each individual. Their blood could also be screened for pathogens. Most of these folk will be with us forever. This would greatly facilitate crime enforcement in the future.

An implanted tracking chip would be a novel idea. They are smaller than a grain of rice. My dog has one and was totally unaware when it was inserted.

For the countless millions already here, we might try a 25% or so tax on all money sent from illegal Mexicans already in The United States to Mexico. This would pay for the most sophisticated border wall since The Great Wall of China! Or we could make it outright illegal for such funds to leave the USA at all, from ANY illegal of any nationality to any foreign country. Our shiny new CBDC would be very effective for accomplishing that.

We could forcibly shut down the Mexican migrant camps making the journey from Ecuador to our border virtually impossible. Our military could do it in a day!

Our military could also eliminate the small well-known Mexican village where 3,000 Chinese workers formulate and package the fentanyl pills that the smugglers bring into our country. China provides the raw chemicals and the necessary equipment. Hyper-corrupt Mexican authorities simply turn a blind eye.

We might try leaving the IOM. We might kick the United Nations out of the United States and stop funding them. We might sanction every country that knowingly sends their worst to our borders.

It would be impractical if not impossible to ship illegals back to their native countries. That can probably be ruled out. We are eternally stuck with them. There are simply too many and too scattered. So the question becomes, what is the most useful way, if any, that these displaced- humans can be utilized in a humanitarian way to enhance our country?

My first choice is to follow Israel's example: MANDATORY MILITARY SERVICE, BOTH MEN AND WOMEN. Every able bodied man or woman MUST serve military time or be imprisoned. (This should include our *legal* American citizens. I strongly believe in the draft.) This would solve our VERY serious military recruiting problem and help us create the most powerful military on earth. Send all of the able-bodied directly from the Mexican and Canadian borders to military training camps, preferably Marine Camps. Think of how happy that would make the

Sanctuary Cities!

A common argument is that we do not have enough prisons to house even our own criminal citizens. A logical solution would be to build hundreds if not thousands of new prisons. This would create countless construction jobs, and later, many thousands of prison-related jobs. Two birds with one stone. Simply send all illegals directly from the border to prison for violation of our immigration laws. Use the same buses and planes presently used to punish Sanctuary Cities.

You could simply arrest every illegal on the valid grounds of violating our immigration laws. Once they cross the border they automatically become criminals. Feeding them in prison would probably be less expensive then providing welfare payments to all with little incentive for productive work. We apparently have learned nothing from the COVID pay-to-do-nothing-but-stay-home policy which has produced a large population that has become very comfortable doing nothing for profit!

What is even more frightening is what happens after an illegal commits a serious crime, as four did recently in New York City. They beat a NYC policeman mercilessly. Of course, after apprehension they were neither jailed nor deported. Under the brilliant New York City (and virtually nationwide) "no cash bail" system they were simply released by the Court, free to commit more mayhem. The many pictures of them flipping a double-middle-finger-bird to the Court as they departed the courthouse should become a permanent part of our Presidential Seal.

More serious, in February a Venezuelan illegal violently murdered a young college nursing student. Laken Riley was brutally assaulted and killed while out for a peaceful jog. The illegal had previously been arrested and released in New York City, but of course not deported.

There are many other horrendous illegal alien acts reported recently. A two-year-old was shot in the head and killed. A fourteen year old was brutally raped by an illegal. An eleven year old girl suffered the same fate. We are overrun with the lowest of the low. Known rapists and killers released from foreign prisons. Severely mentally impaired individuals released from insane asylums. No good can possibly come from this travesty.

As I am writing this yet another Venezuelan illegal was arrested for molesting a minor. Sadly, by the time you read this there will inevitably be many more reports of violence by these unwelcome criminals from countries who hate America and its values and freedoms.

In New York City organized gangs of Venezuelan criminals riding mopeds travel through the streets in broad daylight stealing purses and cell phones. I have a number of friends, and both of my two sons, living in New York City. They are literally frightened to leave their apartments at any time of day or night.

Almost beyond belief are the reported number of "prior arrests" that have been accrued by thousands of career criminals freely walking America's streets. It is not uncommon to see reports of an apprehended criminal having "thirty-six priors". After each crime they were immediately released without bail to commit mayhem number thirty-eight! What is even more frightening is when the details of the actual prior criminal acts are disclosed.

We're not talking here about hopping a turnstile to skip a fare, or stealing a candy bar. We see rapes, aggravated assault, attempted murder, gun violations, and a litany of very serious crimes that should have locked these criminals away for life years ago. If you are looking for a serious existential threat to our very society look no further than our totally broken criminal justice system.

We need tens of thousands more police and thousands more prisons. We need more mental health facilities. We need Judges and Attorneys General who are tough on crime. We need to stop sending billions of dollars to countries who hate us and re-allocate those funds to solving our criminal justice disaster. Anarchy seems to be our government's goal.

A few years ago a "genius" idea was tried with the unemployed. It had limited success and ultimately deemed unfair. It was called "WORKFARE". If you wanted the government to give you free ANYTHING you had to get a job and pay taxes. Heaven forbid. For starters, there were all of those "shovel ready" infrastructure jobs just waiting for Workfare individuals. Apparently there were none. Minor oversight. Would this be a useful approach to our massive illegals population? "Get or job or get out." Seems reasonable.

Supplying every imaginable service to illegal immigrants is totally unfair to all *legitimate* naturalized American citizens. These folks suffered through years of study and waiting to become naturalized Americans. If any group should be pissed off it is these proud LEGAL immigrants. You know, the ones immortalized on The Statue of Liberty.

Hospital Emergency Rooms are becoming unavailable to

legal citizens because many hospitals are required to treat everyone regardless of citizenship. One death was reported recently of an American citizen who could not get treatment when needed because of the number of non-citizens ahead of him. Tragic.

One can only hope that our politicians can get together for once and come up with some rational solution that will prevent illegal immigration from causing the ultimate collapse of our once-great Federal Republic.

Bi-partisan "compromise" legislation allowing some fixed but unsustainable number of illegal immigrants to enter America is not a solution, just an obfuscation.

Sadly, it may be much too late for any viable solution.

CHAPTER FOUR

PANDEMICS, PLAGUES AND CITIZEN-CONTROL

"The most frightening words: "I'm from the government and I'm here to help you." A witticism by Ronald W. Reagan, 40th President of the United States, (1911-2004).

"The world is beautiful, but has a disease called man." Friedrich Wilhelm Nietsche, philosopher, (1844-1900).

"Never let a good crisis go to waste." Rahm Emmanuel, American politician, Ambassador to Japan, (1959-   ).

The **W**orld **H**ealth **O**rganization (WHO) of the United Nations, in keeping with its Globalist agenda, now has the power to declare pandemic emergencies whenever they choose and for whatever reason real or fabricated. They will then prescribe measures that may be mandatory for Americans. Perhaps this could be a politically convenient emergency? The Globalists are on the march!

Do you think the United States might just use such a UN declaration to impose Draconian restrictions on our citizens? Mandatory masks? Mandatory vaccination? Yet another "stay at home" directive? Could such a declaration by a United Nations organization put Americas attempting to vote in person in jeopardy? Mail-in ballots ONLY? What do you think the odds are of a shiny new WHO pandemic emergency a month or so before Election Day? Just keep an eye on the overall Globalist agenda.

In mid-March 2024 a person in New Mexico, USA, died from, of all things, Bubonic Plague, the medieval "BLACK DEATH". Are infected rat-fleas back? Could this be the start of something big?

How is this for a scary conspiracy theory? In George Orwell's book "1984", in order to remain in power the ruling class and its complicit media continuously broadcast both good and bad news, very convincingly. They were "covering" a war that actually wasn't happening! It kept the citizens powerless and in a state of constant anxiety. Would deep-fake pandemics be just as easy to create? Have they perhaps been used already?

A major pandemic or plague is a potential threat to our precious freedoms and to life itself. Unless intentionally released they are impossible to predict. Once they occur we can only pray that our medical geniuses can find a cure before it is too late.

I believe in inoculations. I was vaccinated against childrens' diseases before I had a clue why. In the Army I was vaccinated against a variety of deadly tropical diseases whether I wanted to be or not. Today I am vaccinated against pneumonia and shingles. These are ALL time-tested vaccines. I trust them.

The COVID vaccines are EXPERIMENTAL! The boosters are EXPERIMENTAL! To this day I believe they have not been approved as safe for general use. Their long-term negative effects won't be known for, well, a very long time.

Boosters must be created rapidly to keep up with the fast COVID mutations. They are tested on a VERY small population of genetically-altered mice! No time for long-term human tests. To this day absolutely no medical professional has the slightest idea what deleterious effects the original COVID 19 (technically SARS-CoV2) inoculations and its many booster variants might have on recipients in ten years, twenty years or longer. Stay tuned. Scary.

The COVID 19 "six-foot" distancing fiasco certainly applies to Reagan's words quoted above! To this day I see decals on the floor of many doctors' offices, pharmacies, libraries and many commercial stores. These twelve-inch diameter decals are positioned *exactly* six feet apart. This was the distance we were told to stay apart from another human to avoid transmission of the COVID virus. Whoops!

Dr. Anthony Fauci, our highest paid government official, our primo-pandemics-guru, recently admitted in a meeting with Congress that the "six-foot rule" had absolutely no scientific validity. "It just sort of appeared." The gospel turns out to be a "guesspel"!

We were originally frightened into taking injections that ostensibly would protect a person from *ever* contracting COVID. Whoops again! Personally I had two original shots and two boosters and I contracted COVID **twice.** (At least I didn't die!)

In many cases individuals who had various reasons, some religious, for refusing inoculations were fired from their jobs. Military members were terminated. Pro athletes were banned from tournaments.

Then came the dreaded masks. Airlines and restaurants would not permit "anti-maskers" to enter. Did it ever occur to anyone that a person had to remove the mask to eat? Or blow their nose? Would not that sort of negate any possible value in masking, if in fact there was any in the first place?

Regardless of whatever protection a *properly-worn* M-95 surgical mask may provide, very few people bothered to buy them. Every imaginable bandanna or cheap ill-fitting mask was worn. Even M-95s themselves were seldom affixed properly.

Yet today I still see drivers pass by wearing masks while driving alone in their cars! Talk about brainwashing.

It was proven early-on, in many European countries, that young children were at minimal risk of COVID infection. Yet American schools were shut in most states unnecessarily for long time periods. This may potentially destroy the future of a generation.

When kids were allowed back they were forced to wear masks. There was zero scientific evidence that masks were necessary or accomplished anything except to insure kids were inhaling lots of their own CO_2.

The unfortunate result of all of the misinformation is the fact that most individuals who believe the government lied to us will be VERY hesitant to believe our authorities in the next pandemic. And there *will* be a "next" pandemic, not if, but when.

The World Health Organization (WHO) created a name for a hypothetical pathogen that could wipe out humanity. They call it "Disease X". Because our world today is so closely interconnected, a killer virus with no known cure capable of killing most humans worldwide is a real possibility.

It may be convenient for some to consider Climate Change to be the greatest existential threat to humanity. Where it may fit in the overall list of existential threats is debatable. Climate Change vs. Disease X? Hmmmm.

Tiny viruses, invisible to the naked eye, are capable of wiping out every human on earth. Hollywood has produced many virus-based apocalypse movies. Humans always manage to survive. This might well be an unattainable future ending.

It is not only viruses that can cause a pandemic. The 2023 TV series "The Last Of Us" focused on a fungus, cordycepts, that among many other fungi does actually have the potential for mass extinction.

The flip side is that cordycepts is considered to be a miracle supplement! Revered in the Himalayan area, it is sold over the internet along with other vitamins and supplements. Just don't take an overdose!

WAIT, WHAT?! Here is a direct quote from an internet headline I read today: ***"Deadly antibiotic-resistant fungus sweeps across America"!*** You can't make this stuff up.

It seems that we have become so disinterested in COVID variants that a new scary threat is needed to divert Americans' attention away from the many pressing daily threats to freedom and life itself.

The above mentioned "new" fungus was apparently first noticed in 2017. It is named "Candida auras". Those most at risk are hospital patients, the elderly and persons with compromised immune systems. I check two of the boxes.

The present epicenter of this pending disaster is Seattle, Washington. Apparently the only way to avoid the fungus is to never leave the house. Could mandatory masks be far behind? Business and school shutdowns? Home quarantine?

On the news the *very next* day was the headline: ***"Two cousins, including a chef , 29, die from fungal disease sweeping the United States!"*** Candida auras strikes again? No way. The second fungus "reportedly sweeping the United States" in the past two days is called "Blastomycosis." We're in for a very rough mushroom future.

Within that same news report was the following: "Alaska confirms first fatal case of "Alaska Pox". Alaska pox? How'd I miss that one? Is it too cold up there for chickens? Because Russia wants Alaska back, why not just give it back to them and let them deal with this new potential pandemic?

Is 2024 and into the future going to be "The Years of the **New** Bugs"?

COVID19 is the best-known pandemic because it is well-within the recent memory of anyone over three. This "novel virus" has apparently mutated so many times that it is impossible to keep current on the latest "threat".

As I write this the flavor of the month is "COVID19-Jn1". Last week it was a different variant. This new nasty has additional symptoms of anxiety and sleeplessness. Be assured that by the time you read this there will have been many new variants and unique new symptoms reported. And new boosters ad infinitum.

The "original" COVID19 "novel virus" is also called by some "The Chinese Flu" or "The Wuhan Flu." The origin is now, by most virologists, credited to a bio-lab in Wuhan, China. It is reported to have caused over a million American deaths.

The origin of the virus is still debated. Was it released *intentionally?* Was it a human lab experiment at Wuhan that *accidentally* escaped confinement? Or was the origin a Chinese "wet market" selling all manner of possibly infected assorted delicacies.

Chinese wet-markets sell yummies such as bats, pangolins, and puppy dogs. Ever consider eating Lassie? No accounting for world-wide tastes. Ever try haggis? Monkey brains? Sheep eyes?

How about the Oriental favorite, the very costly braised tiger penis? Icelanders and Arabs consider sheep eyes a delicacy. Many Americans eat calf testicles, better known as "Prairie Oysters". Raw monkey brains grace many a banquet table in China. Personally I can't stand broccoli!

On the topic of nauseating foods consumed worldwide, I have a short story that you might find amusing. If you do not care to read one of my biographical dissertations please skip the following paragraphs.

Back in my young and very often foolish days I was on a first date with a pretty woman I really hoped to impress. I took her to a very fancy New York City French restaurant, Le Bec Fin. I studied Spanish in high school and German in college. "Oui"? "No"? That's about it. The menu was 100% in French! As hard as I looked I could not find a single word in English.

When the snotty looking French waiter asked for our dinner requests, my date had the intelligence to order: "A steak please, rare". Glancing at the menu with no idea what I was ordering I said, with certainty in my voice: "I'll have "Les Regnons d'Agneau". His emphatic reply was "Are you *certain* monsieur." In my most condescending voice I replied "*Absolutely*, and you be sure you bring me a very big dish full."

The smirk on his face should have warned me of my impending culinary fate.

Have you ever been a guest for dinner and the host served something ghastly? You ate it with a smile, right? Long story short, I was served by an obviously delighted waiter, a *heaping* plate of what looked like greasy little golf balls and smelled like a dead cat! "Bon appetit" he said gleefully.

If you have never swallowed several dozen or so **whole lamb kidneys** each in a single gulp with a smile on your face while trying to impress a date you cannot grasp pure torture. The waiter's frequent cheery trips to the table to see whether I had died didn't help. Actually, death might have been welcome. At least it was better than tiger penis or sheep eyes. Then again, maybe not. If I recall correctly that was our *only* date.

Dr. Anthony Fauci, in his recent testimony before Congress,

conceded that the Wuhan Lab was the probable source of COVID19. During the pandemic any individual who may have sincerely believed this "conspiracy theory" was "canceled".

It is often argued that a large percentage of reported COVID19 hospital deaths were not actually due to COVID19 itself. If a patient with a near-fatal condition unrelated to COVID19 was shown, or assumed, to harbor the COVID19 virus, the hospital, paid extra for treating a COVID patient, reported it as such. We will never know the real number of deaths actually caused by COVID as the primary reason.

Because the course of COVID19 leading to death was related to lung infections, I would be very interested in a valid statistic as to how many who died were smokers. For some reason that is a statistic I could not find.

The scary thing is that it is impossible to trust our government doctors. For example, each President's personal physician is appointed *by* that President and works *at his sole discretion.*

This explains why Americans were kept completely unaware of President Woodrow Wilson's stroke. His wife and a shadow government ran the country for eighteen months! His physician insisted that he was alert, sharp as a tack, and simply had problems with indigestion! Sound familiar?

We were never told that John F. Kennedy suffered from a variety of painful illnesses. Only after his untimely death was the American public told that President Kennedy periodically ingested twelve different pain-relieving medicines at once. This included Demerol and a mixture of various barbiturates and amphetamines.

As early as 1997, two years before leaving office, President Ronald Reagan was diagnosed with Alzheimer's Disease. His personal physician kept this totally secret from the American public.

Is keeping secret the true health and *mental capacity* of a sitting President in the Nation's best interest? Many would argue that it is. Many would argue otherwise.

President Joe Biden has a personal physician named Kevin O'Connor. He has been a close family friend for many years. He served the President since he was Vice President under Barack Obama. In light of past Presidents' physicians covering up serious illnesses and mental decline, could we possibly expect Dr. O'Connor to do otherwise?

Compared to past pandemics, COVID19 was a very bad cold. It reportedly killed roughly one in every three-hundred Americans. This is a relatively small percentage, 0.033%, of the population, compared to three major past pandemics.

America's worst pandemic is known as "The Spanish Flu" or "The Purple Death". During the period 1918-1919, over one-quarter of the population was infected and 675,000 Americans died. This is a fatality rate of 0.066 of the population, about double that of COVID19. It would certainly have been much lower if today's medicines and hospital care were available at the time.

Arguably the worst plague ever recorded in human history was The European "Bubonic Plague" or "Black Death". It occurred during a seventeen year period from 1346-1363. The number of deaths is estimated to be around two-hundred-million, probably half, a staggering 50%, of the European population of the time. This would be the equivalent of over one-hundred-fifty million dead Americans today, one-hundred fifty times worse than COVID19!

What is rather shocking is that the Black Death virus, Yersinia pestis, spread by rat fleas, is still alive and well on earth today! An occasional case appears worldwide. In February 2024 a man died in a New Mexico hospital. Cause of death: Yesinia pestis!

The good news? It is supposed to be very receptive to being killed by modern antibiotics. Just imagine how many lives could have been saved if antibiotics were known during the Middle Ages. For whatever reason modern meds did not help save that guy in New Mexico.

In fact, had antibiotics been available in 1850, a large percentage of the 620,000 Civil War soldiers who died could have been saved. It is a fact that most did not die directly from their wounds, but died from various wound-infections that could be cured today. Timing is everything. Try not to die before science finds a cure for your ailment whatever it might be.

Possibly equal to "The Black Death" was a pandemic that occurred in Rome over a twenty-four-year period from AD 165-189. It is known as "The Antonine Plague". It occurred during the reign of Marcus Aurelius Antoninus Augustus. It is also referred to as "The Marcus Aurelius Plague".

The reported horrible symptoms were very much like those of the more recent Ebola outbreak. It reportedly killed over 500,000 Romans out of a population of 1.1 million, roughly half of the population of the day. This was the equivalent of "The Bubonic Plague" in Europe.

One can only speculate whether these death totals would have been far lower if today's medicines were available to the Europeans and the Romans. Perhaps even higher because of the mobility of earthlings today? All diseases are dispersed rapidly worldwide because of the miracle of aviation.

There have been many other lesser pandemics worldwide. These had fatality rates that were very low compared to the above major pandemics.

It is well documented that one school of thought posits that that earth is becoming overpopulated and will soon outstrip sustainability. Seemingly serious people have proposed unleashing a deadly virus that would wipe out half of humanity and restore sustainability for the survivors. Chilling proposal. I believe thay are serious. It would probably be effective.

Often overlooked in pandemic discussions is the historically number one killer of humans, smallpox. It is estimated that since prehistoric times as many as a BILLION humans have died from this disease. Smallpox scars have even been detected on Egyptian mummies.

After eons, a British doctor actually found a cure for

smallpox. He noted that milkmaids, exposed daily to cows, never contracted smallpox.

Cows can contract a less dangerous "pox" called cowpox. Individuals infected with the very mild cowpox are immune from deadly smallpox. He actually injected a young boy with cowpox. Then shortly thereafter injected him with smallpox. The boy did not get smallpox! This action was the mother of all vaccinations.

In the 1970s, health authorities declared that smallpox had been 100% eradicated. We have gotten close with some other illnesses, but not 100%.

But where could deadly extinction-level viruses come from today? There are a number of possibilities.

Bio-labs are the most obvious. Every "civilized" country has them. There are thousands of bio-labs worldwide. China even has one in Montana, USA! Every bio-lab harbors countless different viruses capable of causing a pandemic. In today's dangerous and unpredictable world, how hard is it to imagine a terrorist gaining access to a lab and unleashing hell on humanity? Not very hard.

Recently there was a chilling report that the very same Wuhan Lab has recently created a novel virus that could kill 100% of all humans. It was tested on mice that were genetically modified to mimic human reactions to viruses. Not one mouse survived! Are human trials far behind? Any volunteers?

This creative virus is called "Gx-P2V". Dr. Genardi Glinsky, Stanford University Professor of Medicine is quoted as saying: "This madness must be stopped before it's too late." Perhaps it already is.

One could ask the question: What is the point of creating new deadly viruses in the first place? Is the sole purpose to create bio-weapons to unleash on the population of an adversary?

Those concerned with animal rights and welfare could well question the morality of intentionally creating medical "chimeras" in the name of science. The "CRISPR" gene-modifying technique may someday allow doctors to modify infants' DNA in the womb to eliminate certain diseases. Its use beyond that seems to violate the laws of GOD.

There is no question the glaciers world-wide are melting. The permafrost, frozen earth, in the many millions of acres, is no longer "perma"! There is no certain knowledge of what pathogens from hundreds of thousands of years ago might be released from their suspended animation within the ice. Impossible you might say? How could they survive for eons encased in ice?

Think "extremophiles".

Extremophiles are little critters that can withstand intense heat, intense cold, being frozen for eons, being exposed to noxious chemicals such as sulfur and ammonia, and even the vacuum of space! Deadly viruses can be extremophiles.

Is there any hard evidence of the existence of extremophiles? Yes, a great deal.

Recently, scientists obtained ice cores from an ancient ice-cave in Iceland. It was determined that this ice was many thousands of years old. When the ice was thawed in a clean-lab and the melt-water studied under a microscope they were astonished to find a wide variety of small creatures happily swimming around! There were even some small "ice-worms" happily wiggling!

As glaciers melt and permafrost melts, it is an absolute certainty that organisms never before encountered in human history will be released. No one can know whether any of these could cause a pandemic. This scary possibility certainly exists.

Scientists have identified the probable presence of extremophiles in various types of meteorites, asteroid fragments and comet debris. Every day tens of tons of "space dust" rains down on earth. There is no question a deadly virus could come from outer space and probably already has.

Astronauts aboard The International Space Station carried out an interesting experiment, using tardigrads as the subjects. Tardigrads are multi-celled microscopic-size animals known affectionately known as "water bears". They are cute little four-legged beasties.

They took a few hundred up to the space station, then put them outside exposed to deadly radiation, bitter cold and zero air, for many days. When they returned the tardigrads back to an earth lab a large number had survived and seemed to be in perfect health!
On another occasion Space Station Astronauts noticed colonies of diatom-like critters all over the OUTSIDE of the windows! Diatoms are a type of algae that have a shell

of silica. They have discounted any possibility these critters somehow came from earth. They were extraterrestrials!

Living diatoms convert CO2 to oxygen. Over the life of the planet, scientists credit diatoms with being responsible for half of all the oxygen in our atmosphere! We need more diatoms!

All manner of extremophiles are found in the super-hot water around steam vents in Yellowstone National Park and elsewhere. These little fellas live not only in extreme heat, but in an atmosphere of sulfur!

Aquanauts exploring the bottom of the deepest oceans find all manner of swimming creatures, despite the incredible crushing pressure of tens-of-thousands of feet of water above. They also have taken samples from "smokers". These are openings in the sea floor through which escape all manner of noxious gasses. They appear as columns of smoke and super-heated water escaping from the magma below And yes, extremophiles thrive in the immediate environment of these hot vents.

The fact is that pandemic-causing viruses lurk everywhere, even in the most unlikely places. Is the fact that humans have managed to avoid extinction up until now simply good luck? The Hand of GOD? You can choose whichever possibility you find most comforting.

We have an existential threat in the Unted States, a pandemic, that is unrelated to little bugs. It is called "mental health" and it is a massive National problem. We need thousands more mental health professionals. We need many more facilities in which the mentally impaired can be treated.

There are frightening proposals floated about that speak of "mandatory involuntary commitment" of the "mentally ill". Little frightens me more. Remember the Salem Witch Hunts? Innocent people were burned alive at the stake. Why were they convicted? A small group of misguided teen girls would stand in front of an accused. If they fell to the ground and writhed in "pain" this was proof positive the accused was a witch. Burn witch burn!

Any form of mandatory involuntary commitment would give the State unlimited power to incarcerate anyone whose ideas were in contrast to the ideas of those in power at the time. This is a very tempting approach to solving "mental health" issues for any totalitarian state. This idea is at least as scary as Central Bank Digital Currency, as explored in Chapter One.

Far more likely, a real and present danger is the intentional unleashing by some evil bureaucrat, of a chemical or biological weapon. Russia in particular is reported to have enough toxins stored up to kill a hundred billion people, about fourteen times earth's entire population! I doubt whether the USA is far behind. Not even a cat has enough lives to survive such an attack!

Some really nasty stuff, like Plague or Ebola actually exists in many labs around the world. It is not hard to imagine some madman finding a way to put enough of this crap into the atmosphere to kill virtually everyone. We live in very dangerous times on a very fragile pebble in space.

In summary, as an existential threat to human freedom and life itself, I cannot help but consider pandemics as

somewhere near the top in the rankings.

POSTCRIPT:
Hello, earth speaking. I'm not too worried about space bugs and extremophiles. But from my perspective you humans are a disease worse than any pandemic I can cook up. Could you maybe cleanup the Great Pacific Ocean Garbage Patch? Could you please stop polluting my rivers and lakes and air? Stop killing my trees? Things were pretty good when the dinosaurs were around and you were still evolving from the primordial ooze or by Adam and Eve's making whoopee. Could you either get your act together and respect the only planet you have, or else would you please all move away or die?

Thanks.

Earth.

CHAPTER FIVE

AMERICS'S FLIMSY POWER GRID

"Let not your heart be troubled." Sean Hannity, newscaster, at the close of each broadcast, (1961-   ).

"Don't worry, about a thing, 'cause every little thing is gonna be alright." Bob Marley, (1945-1981) of "The Wailers", reggae singer and activist, from the song "Three Little Birds".

"We can only conclude that it is too much to ask of us poor twentieth-century humans to believe, to grasp, the possibility that the system might fail. We cannot grasp the simple and elementary fact that this technology can blow a fuse." A news commentary after the 1965 East Coast Blackout.

"If an enemy wants to bring America to its knees it will fire off an enormous electromagnetic pulse that erases every hard drive in the country. Within two weeks we will all be wearing animal pelts and huddling in caves for warmth." Tom McNichol, (1959-   )

Recently former CIA Director James Woolsey had a frightening warning for all Americans. He is quoted as saying that an attack would blackout our National Power Grid for over a year. It would kill nine out of ten Americans from starvation and societal collapse.   If this existential threat to our life and liberty doesn't scare the crap out of you nothing will.

Can Climate Change kill nine out of ten humans in a year? Unlikely.

On November 9, 1965, I was sitting in a Master's Degree economics class at CCNY Baruch School of Business in New York City. We were on the fourth floor of a nondescript building on Manhattan's lower west side. Suddenly the lights went out! The classroom was in total darkness.

This was before cell-phone lights and no one had a flashlight. One guy lit a Zippo lighter. We all stared out the window at total darkness. Where the "City That Never Sleeps" would have been totally lit up, it was very much asleep. All that was seen were car lights, mostly stopped dead. No traffic lights.

Our first impulse was to wait out what we assumed was a few-minute outage. Fifteen or so minutes later we decided to exit down the stairwell. If you've never been in a narrow stairwell in total darkness with a bunch of rowdy under-thirty-year-olds, let's just say it was a goosing good time! No one was particularly concerned. It was fun!

When we hit the street, I was immediately reminded of how enterprising New Yorkers can be. There already were street-vendors selling cheap flashlights for twenty bucks! Where they found a large supply within a half-hour amazes me to this day. Entrepreneurship was alive and well in NYC that night.

There were a few panicky people running around the streets. Someone screamed that we were under attack and that the entire American power grid had been destroyed.

Another heard that there was an explosion somewhere and that the entire Eastern seaboard was black. Someone said they heard that planes were crashing at airports when runway lights went out on approach.

A few of us walked across town with our freshly bought flashlights. Our destination was "The Cattleman", a popular bar known colloquially as "The Pig Palace".

It was a huge bar that was so crowded after 5PM on weekdays that one literally could be crushed to death. It was frequented by hordes of horny young men and equal hordes of horny young women. It was known as the greatest pickup bar on the planet.

This night the enterprising owner decided to light the place with candles and stay open as long as the lights were out. Genius entrepreneur.

Try to picture a few hundred bodies packed like sardines in a nearly pitch dark bar drinking all the booze available, which was ample. It was like the most festive office New Year's Party ever!

I woke up the following morning in an apartment in a high rise with three women and two guys none of whom I had recalled meeting! This bar never watered its drinks. In fact, I think they concentrated them! I had no idea how I arrived there or who these people were. AND THE ELECTRICITY WAS STILL OUT.

By this time, the blackout was becoming a serious concern. This was pre-cellphone, and no one carried a battery-powered radio around. There was no solid data, just wild and often only terrifying rumors because there was so little useful information about the situation.

And then as if by magic, within an hour, the lights came back on!

What had happened to shut down the brightest city on the planet (except perhaps for super-bright Las Vegas)? Was the problem happening only in New York City?

The TV news quickly explained the cause and extent of the problem. A ***single transformer*** near Niagara Falls had exploded. It put most of the Eastern seaboard and parts of eastern Canada in total darkness.

That one-day blackout was caused by the failure of one isolated relatively small and insignificant piece of equipment! If this incident doesn't send shivers up your spine, it should.

Our power grid is incredibly fragile. There are too many critical nodes, each a potential attack point. There are far too many miles of exposed cables. It would take very little to shut down the entire country, perhaps permanently.

It was recently disclosed by our government that Russia is working on a satellite that can send focused electromagnetic pulses to wipe out any power grid in an instant.

The U. S. power grid control is very fragmented. There are twelve transmission planning groups, eleven Federal planning commissions and the Electric Reliability Council of Texas. Six of the eleven Regional Transmission Organizations have planning authority. The remaining five are a loose association of private utility companies.

There are eleven thousand power generating plants owned by three thousand utility companies. Coal, oil and gas burning plants comprise about eighty percent. The remaining twenty percent of our power is from nuclear plants. A small percentage is generated by wind farms and solar panels.

Oversimplified, from the generating plants, high-voltage electricity goes to distribution towers. From there to transformers, and from there to homes and businesses. At each step the voltage produced at the initial power plants is reduced in strength until it reaches the consumer as usable 120/240 volts.

There are 200,000 miles of high-voltage transmission lines. Throughout the United States. These feed 5.5 million miles of local cables. That's a lot of wire!

These wires are organized into three major power grids. The Eastern Grid is everything east of the Rocky Mountains. The Western Grid is west of the Rockies. The State of Texas has its own independent grid.

Above ground power lines are vulnerable to storms, snow, ice, wind, fires, solar discharges and terrorism. Only a relatively small amount of lines nationwide are located underground, just 19 million miles. Only one American city, Colorado Springs, Colorado, has 100% of its electric lines underground.

The Infrastructure Bill, passed in 2021, provides $65 billion for grid improvement. Ideally all power lines should be buried underground. The problem is it costs ten times as much to bury cables as it does to string overhead lines. Once buried (usually 36" deep) it is much more difficult to service any problems. Even underground cables can degrade.

Besides, no one wants their lawn dug up!

With this much line exposure, it is no wonder that our power grid is potentially vulnerable to many forces both natural and man-made. I wonder how that $65 billion is being spent?

Aside from hostile countries and local terror cells, the greatest uncontrollable threat to the grid is our "Lucky Old Sun". It is well within the possibility that someday, *any* day, it could send out a massive pulse of energy and fry the grid beyond repair. It happened once in the mid-1800s, but that was prior to the creation of the modern electric grid. It did totally fry all telegraph wires in the country.

In March 2024, a massive pulse actually warped our earth's magnetic field. That was the closest we have come in many decades to a real disaster.

Consider this: An unknown number of illegal "got-aways" from countries hostile to America are known to have slipped through our porous borders. It is known that they are gathering in groups, organized terror cells.

It is very likely that these cells will become armed. Easily purchased dynamite or nitro would work quite well. Mini-suitcase-nukes would be more effective but somewhat harder to acquire. Explosives that could be simultaneously detonated at a handful of critical grid nodes would put us back into the Stone Age. Very few Americans today can imagine life in a cave and eating bugs and raw bats.

Is our government doing anything to protect the critical nodes? Do we have military stationed at critical points? These are questions I would hope our Congressional Representatives are asking.

My maternal grandmother was born in 1879. Her stories about life before electricity, before cars and planes, using candles and horse-drawn carriages were an endless source of fascination for an impressionable kid.

For many thousands of years, homo sapiens (at least our present iteration...more about pre-Adamic civilizations elsewhere in this book) existed quite well without electricity, without running water, without cars and planes, or flush toilets. No computers, no cell phones, no phones of any kind. No anything we take totally for granted today.

Incredible as it might seem to a teen today, as a youth I actually got along without TV or a cell phone. Somehow I survived without Amazon or Instagram, TicToc or Facebook. I had a "Spaldine", a pink, hollow rubber ball used in a large variety of creative street sports, I imagine "punch-ball", "stoop ball" and "stick-ball" are totally unknown to today's youth.

We each owned a basketball and a football. All games were played on the street. If you were tired you sat down on the nearest parked-car's "running board". Every car had one. I was in pig-shit heaven! My kids often asked how I could have existed as such a savage!

It is hard to grasp, but about a ***third*** of our American population, a hundred million or so, have *never known* life without cell phones, computers, video games, social media or televisions.

It must have been difficult for "modern" humans to exist for 50,000 years or so as wild animals. Simple hunter-gatherers. That would seem utterly impossible to any teen today. Of course to me as a youth in the 1940s I had every possible modern convenience. Running hot and cold water. A flush toilet. An Emerson tube radio. And my Spaldine. I had it all! One cannot miss something that one cannot even conceive.

During WWII, we had a few inconveniences, such as food rationing. One of my weekly tasks as a youngster was to take a pile of white, tasteless lard and break a tiny yellowish-colored gel-capsule into it. I'd mix it for hours, and create ersatz orange-yellow "butter". It tasted like axle grease.

Could modern humans accustomed to all of the fruits of our horrible polluting Industrial Revolution, survive for even a week without electricity? I've heard of teens having a nervous breakdown because they misplaced their cell phone for ten minutes!

We have all experienced the inconvenience of a short power outage. "Don't dare upon the refrigerator door or all the food will spoil." "Who knows how long the power will be out?" Fortunately it is seldom for more than a few hours.

During that short time, being without a TV, unable to charge a phone or computer, these seemed as potential life-altering events! Then the power comes back on, the tape on the frig door that was put there to prevent accidental opening comes off. All is good with the world once again.

Of course many have experienced days-long outages caused by extreme weather. These folks have a better appreciation of the consequences of being without power for an extended period. But they at least knew that within some reasonable time frame the power would be restored and life would go on as usual.

As pointed out above, the United States power grid <u>does not have a central governing body.</u> This can make remediation in a national grid emergency far more complex.

The sun was mentioned above, and it is a real and present danger to the grid. But as in my personal account above of the "Great New York City Blackout", it is the nodes before the electricity ever reaches the local power lines that are the weak points subject to relatively easy destruction. Can these tens of thousands of key nodes be somehow protected? Can they be buried? Can they be enclosed in bomb-proof casings?

There is always the threat of cyber-crime. Most of America's electric grid control is cyber-based and subject to hacking. Could a brilliant sixteen-year-old hacker working from his garage in Croatia plunge the entire United States into total darkness? Could China or Russsia or some other hostile nation with highly sophisticated professional hackers easily do the same, sending us back to the stone age?

The sad fact is, the American people, you and me and

everyone you know, are TOTALLY reliant on electricity. There is a physical limit on how much food one can store for an emergency. Freeze-dried rations are great IF you can have a reliable water source to make them edible. In the event of a grid failure you will have no water unless you live near a fresh water lake or river.

Portable electric generators for home use are great except they require fuel. There is a limit to how much kerosene or whatever fuel needed one can store.

What about SOLAR generators? Two problems: One, in the event of a nuclear-night they cannot be powered. More important, second, in a total and permanent electric-grid failure your precious solar generator will be a prime target of the inevitable roving mobs of starving individuals. Keep the twelve-gauge handy. We are talking here about SURVIVAL.

In summary, the loss of our electric grid is the loss of civilization as we know it. Our government must begin to work as quickly as possible on a permanent solution. The loss of our power grid makes most other Existential Threats seem trivial.

CHAPTER SIX

NUCLEAR ARMAGEDDON

"We have the choice to outlaw nuclear weapons or face general annihilation." Albert Einstein, physicist, (1879-1955).

"Our schools glorify war and hide its horrors. They inculcate hatred in the veins of children. I would teach peace rather than war. I would inculcate love rather than hate." Albert Einstein, physicist, (1879-1955).

"The difference between us Islamists and you Westerners is that we love death and you love life." Saddam Hussein, (1937-2006).

"WWIV will be fought with stones." Albert Einstein, physicist, (1879 -1955).

"I can't think about that right now. If I do I'll go crazy. I'll think about that tomorrow." Scarlett O'Hara (played by Vivien Leigh) from the 1939 movie "Gone With the Wind".

"The greatest antidote to worry, whether you're getting ready for a space-flight or facing a problem of daily life, is preparation." Senior Astronaut John Glenn, (1921-2016).

I must admit that a fair amount of the text in this Chapter was taken directly from a book I wrote in 2010,

"Apocalypse 12-21-12". Amazingly, in the past decade, not a whole lot has changed! Please excuse the plagiarism.

First of all, it is **_NOT_**: "NOOK-Q-LAR". It is pronounced correctly: "NOO-CLEE-ER". If you want to show your ignorance just keep mispronouncing nuclear. I am astonished how many TV talking heads and even politicians make this language mistake over and over and never seem to learn. I doubt whether any scientists are guilty.

President Biden has stated often that Climate Change is a much worse Existent Threat to humanity than nuclear war. I am quite sure that the residents of Hiroshima and Nagasaki would not agree. Perhaps he and his advisors actually believe this to be true.

The degree to which Climate Change is an existential threat to humanity is a subject of considerable debate. I cover this in Chapter Twelve. Suffice it to say that Climate Change cannot kill me tomorrow. Nuclear war can.

There are 86,400 seconds in a twenty-four hour day. According to the prestigious "Bulletin of Atomic Scientists" mankind has pissed away 86,310 of them! Each year this group publishes an update to their "Doomsday Clock".

The Clock has reached 11:58:30 PM, just ninety seconds from nuclear annihilation! Does anyone out there find this comforting? Do you really find Climate Change scarier than that?

Albert Einstein held a profound belief. He argued that nuclear weapons had changed everything, EXCEPT mans' way of thinking.

Is nuclear war inevitable? It does seem that it is becoming increasingly possible. Let's look at the major nuclear powers and the number of nukes they are reported to possess.

By far, the two countries possessing the most formidable arsenal of nukes are Russia with 5,900 followed closely by The United States with 5,300. No other country comes even close.

China is reported to have just 500, but they are also reported to have hyper-sonic delivery missiles that we lack. So does Russia. France has 290 nukes, England 225, Pakistan 210, India 164, Israel 40 and North Korea 30 and counting. Iran is close to 1 at this writing.

The "good" news? America is reported to have developed the shiny new B51-x super-nuke said to be twenty-five times more powerful than any nuke developed to date. Do we all really need more and bigger bombs?

It seems to me that four or five garden-variety nukes could wipe out any nation on earth. Are overwhelming numbers of bombs simply supposed to scare the enemy?

These are countries that are socially developed to the extent that it is likely that they would choose to exist as long as possible. China is unlikely to bomb the United States because they would have far fewer locations to dump their products.

Have you ever looked on the origin label of anything you buy? "Made in China" seems ubiquitous. I recently looked on the label of a major brand of canned peaches. Yep,

"Made in China". I thought we produced peaches in Georgia. Anyhow, I rule out China. Their economy is said to be in decline and wars cost money. They simply cannot afford a major conflict directly with the USA at *this* time. Probably later.

China would not be the threat that it is today if President Truman in his infinite wisdom in 1951 had not prevented the great General Douglas MacArthur from invading China when we had a clear advantage. MacArthur commanded the United Nations forces in Korea. He saw a weakness in China that could be exploited easily. Truman fired him.

Russia proved during the Cuban Missile Crisis that they understand "**M**utually **A**ssured **D**estruction", or "MAD". It is unlikely that their opinion has changed over the years. Let's hope Putin is not totally insane.

Unfortunately, Kim Jung Un may be. President Trump nicknamed him "Rocket Man". There is no question that he has the nukes and the rocket capability to deliver them to ANY American target. But does he REALLY want to see his beloved country incinerated? Not likely.

There's no saying that his heir-apparent daughter feels the same. It is hard to grasp the inner workings of a tyrant's mind.

HOWEVER, put nukes in the hands of a country that prefers death over life (quoting Osama Bin Laden), and there is a *real* existential threat. Apparently WWIII is the best route to a worldwide Caliphate. Only when "the Mahdi", the "Twelfth Imam" arrives will Islam be complete.

Because Iran refers to the United States to be "The Big Satan" worthy only of total annihilation as directed in their Holy of Holies there is a real cause for concern.

As I write this, the Iranian Mullahs claim to be just days away from having a functioning nuclear weapon. Israel ("The Little Satan") has said repeatedly that they will NEVER allow Iran to have such a weapon. By the time you read this will Israel, a true nuclear power, have left a big deep hole where Tehran once was? The coming years should be very interesting.

Will the United States at some time, hopefully soon, step in and eliminate the Iranian menace? Or will Israel beat us to it? Interesting race.

For a moment let's now all become Atheists (if you are not already). Accept that there is no God to exact revenge on our pitiful species and let's see what our fellow humans without any Divine Intervention could actually do to us.

Today we have thousands of "weapons of mass destruction" that are beyond imagination. The "atom bombs" we dropped on Hiroshima and Nagasaki were kid's toys. Yet even their force was almost beyond human imagining. Hiroshima was an air-burst high above the surface, which minimized radioactive fallout. The Nagasaki blast on the other hand was a seriously dirty ground strike. Either way, Japan was devastated.

Aside note: What is seldom remembered is that the two atom bombs by themselves did NOT end Japanese involvement in WWII. It took many weeks of firebombing thereafter of the Japanese "wooden cities" to convince them that all was finally lost. They were one damn tough enemy.

Large conventional (non-nuke) bombs are called blockbusters. A single one could devastate a city block. Each holds the equivalent destructive power of twenty tons of trinitrotoluene (TNT). Because of all the data available on conventional TNT, all bombs are rated in relation to their effective destructive power relative to a given amount of TNT.

If you were to add up the power of ALL the blockbusters dropped during ALL of WWII it equals some two-million tons, or "two megatons" of TNT.

The two bombs dropped on Japan were tiny by comparison to today's multi-megaton "Hydrogen Bombs", which have never been detonated except in tests. Never in anger. Yet. Had we developed hydrogen bombs first instead of A-bombs there would be no Japan today! Multi-megatons in a single weapon is the equivalent of all the bombs dropped in WWII in the blink of an eye. Unimaginable.

A delightful chain of events happens in the vicinity of the detonation of a nuclear bomb. This is the chain of events Iran can expect if Israel decides to drop a few nukes (or vice versa): The immediate effect is from the blast wave from each bomb. It simply flattens everything for a few miles around.

Then there is the storm of gamma rays and neutrons that fry outlying humans from the inside out. And of course there is the oxygen-depleting firestorm. It would not take many such bombs to put Iran back into the stone age. Nor, for that matter, Israel, should Iran manage to bomb them first.

But what about a full-blown nuclear war, with the United States, Russia, China, North Korea, India and Pakistan and whoever else decides to join the party all popping off rocket after rocket tipped with "small" a-bombs? Or maybe throw in a few hydrogen bombs just for the hell of it? There are eight billion people on earth. It is postulated that a full nuclear exchange of thousands of warheads would kill almost all of them on the first day.

The few remaining survivors (for examples, miners deep underground in coal mines) would then be subjected to fatal radioactive fallout after they surfaced. Deadly radiation lasts a very long time. It takes almost a hundred years for the majority of the deadly Strontium 90 to disappear, longer for the even worse cesium 137. Fallout, however, may be the least of it.

No one can predict the climate effect of the huge radioactive cloud that would completely fill earth's skies in the event of a massive nuclear exchange. Global cooling, because the cloud reflects sunlight? Global cooking from a "greenhouse effect"? At the very least, the nitrogen in the upper atmosphere will be burned into ozone-destroying oxides, depleting the protective ozone layer and admitting an immense dose of ultraviolet radiation. This radiation would kill almost anything left alive. The most likely survivors would be viruses! Those tough little buggers just might inherit whatever is left of the earth.

Of course, with so much potential for destruction, we keep a very tight rein on our nuclear stockpile, right? No room for error there. Sadly, not quite.

Are you aware that THREE nuclear bombs have been dumped by accident into the water off the East Coast of the United States near New Jersey? This is a well-documented fact. Why has no effort ever been made to recover them? Surely if we can bring up dinner plates from Titanic we can retrieve a few dropped nukes, no?

Well, as far as I can tell, the reasoning is that these submerged nukes are "safe" as long as no one messes around with them. The ocean will simply eventually dissolve them. Whatever. Of course the government claims they pose absolutely no danger. Of course not. Nothing ever poses any danger. Just ask the government, who is always there to help us.

What is even more startling is that credible reports claim that ninety-two (92!) nuclear warheads, or much larger *entire* bombs, have been lost worldwide in military mishaps by both the USA and Russia. Fewer than half were ever recovered! In addition to those few mentioned above there are around forty-three (43!) others just waiting to dissolve. Or explode. What's to worry about?

Our government claims that "only" eleven of ours' have not been recovered. That surely is comforting to know. Are you comforted? I'm not.

Of course of even far greater immediate importance is the "small" matter of the thirty or so Russian "suitcase nukes" that were reported to be unaccounted for after the breakup of the Soviet Union. Each is capable of totally destroying most of a large city. As far as I can determine these small but deadly nuclear bombs are **still** missing and not accounted for. Could they each be sitting in a storage locker in a major American city just waiting for a terror cell of illegal aliens to set one off? Chilling thought.

Could the scenario postulated in Nelson De Mille's great book "*Wild Fire* " actually eveer happen? Secretive right-wing forces fiercely loyal to the USA aim to set off a few recovered suitcase nukes in two major American cities. The idea was that we would immediately assume the deed was perpetrated by Islamic radicals. In retaliation we would immediately launch a nuclear attack against every country with a predominantly Muslim population!

If you happened to be wearing a turban or a burka you would be instant toast. That way any future threat from extremist Muslims is gone. And so are a billion or so innocent people. It's called "collateral damage".

There are other flavors of nuclear weapons. Consider "neutron bombs". When exploded in the sky over a nation, an energy impulse is generated that guarantees wiping out the entire electric grid below forever. The attacked nation is back into the stone age in an instant. Do neutron bombs exist? Try finding hard data. Apparently they do.

The recent concern over a Russian satellite carrying a pulse-weapon destined to erase our power grid falls into the same category.

The human species apparently is genetically inclined to kill each other. With very minor exceptions, countless other sentient creatures co-exist on earth without exhibiting mutual destruction. As I write this, there are two highly publicized conflicts being fought that were not being fought two or so years ago.

The Israel vs. Hamas war falls into the category of "so what else is new"? The Arabs and Jews have been at it since I was ten years old (a mere seventy-six years ago). That was Israel's War for Independence. The Jews were quite convinced that the territory in question had been theirs since Biblical times. The Muslims disagreed.

This war was followed by the Suez Canal crisis in 1956. Next came the so-called "six-day war". Then soon thereafter the Yom Kippur War in 1973, followed by the Lebanon wars of 1982 and 2006. These folks don't like each other! Never have, never will.

This latest war was inevitable after the unspeakable Hamas atrocities against innocent Israeli citizens.

Israel has been pressured by the United Nations and the United States in particular, to institute "humanitarian pauses" in the fighting. Even a total cease fire has been suggested.

When Hitler was raining rockets down on England should there have been a humanitarian pause to send food and medicine to Germany to keep their troops fed and healthy? I think not.

Ironically, the Israelis have been accused of brutally killing Hamas civilians. Winston Churchill made it clear during WWII that wars must be fought in that same cruel manner alone. Civilians are inevitable collateral damage.

The massive pro-Hamas rallies. rampant starting in March 2024 on campuses at a number of our most prestigious Universities, prominently Columbia U. in New York City, have shocked every right-minded American citizen. It is far too reminiscent of Nazi Germany in the 1930s. Everyone thought we were above and beyond that level of religious intolerance and hatred. Apparently not.

The Israelis are a nuclear power. They also have a rather powerful conventional army. They will turn Gaza into an uninhabitable wasteland. There will be no "two-state solution" if Israel prevails. Revenge is sweet. Eye for many more eyes. It never ends.

In the April 2024 escalation, Iran sent over three-hundred armed drones and a few missiles in the general direction of Israel. It was reported that some mis-fired. Almost all of the others were shot down by the combined efforts of the United States, the United Kingdom and Jordan. Israel's "Iron Dome" mopped up the rest. One missile did land, seriously injuring a ten year old Palestinian girl.

Israel, of course, had to retaliate. At this writing they sent a missile into Iran which apparently penetrated their defenses. It was meant to prove a point.

By the time you read this book the war could have escalated to Lebanon, and possibly Syria. At some point, Israel might well lose its patience and annihilate Iran and the others with a few nukes, if we don't do so first.

Of course, as a result of the Israeli-Hamas conflict, Iran proxy groups have been launching drone attacks on America's various military bases in the general area. The inevitable finally happened when three of our precious military men were killed and dozens injured in a Jordan drone attack.

Apparently it never occurred to our military geniuses that an enemy just might be bright enough to think of trailing one of our returning drones so that we would never expect it to have a deadly companion lurking behind it. Score one for Arab military intelligence.

One fascinating fact has emerged from the Hamas attack on Israel. Onlookers reported that the attackers looked like crazed inhuman zombies. The reason is well known, but seldom discussed. There is an inexpensive, very dangerous hallucinogenic narcotic called "Captagon".

Given to a soldier before a battle Captagon makes him or her a true super-human. All inhibitions disappear. They can fight on with near-fatal crippling injuries. They become insane killing machines, literally mad zombies. That could easily explain (not excuse) Hamas' unspeakable cruelty against helpless Israeli citizens.

Here's a comforting thought. It is known that Captagon has already found its way into the United States. What if one of the illegal immigrant terror cells that will inevitably form gets really high on the stuff? Not a pleasant scenario. Covert importation of Captagon is actually a far worse potential problem than fentanyl, but seldom if ever discussed. Beware!

The war in Ukraine is far scarier from a worldwide perspective. Unlike the Israel-Hamas conflict, this war apparently was entirely preventable. Russia's prewar demands were not desirable to many but acceptance would have prevented untold loss of lives and a massive cost. Russia alone is said to have lost 50,000 soldiers by mid-April 2024. Ukrainian losses were reportedly lower, but still tens of thousands. Wars make absolutely no sense.

Our bureaucrats vastly underestimated Russia's resolve and military capabilities. If Russia prevails, which seems possible though far from certain, once again we will be on the wrong side of history. Spoken as a Viet Nam era veteran with a good memory.

The United States is far less capable of supporting multiple foreign wars than some bureaucrats seem to believe. Russia has weapons that apparently are far more sophisticated and deadly than anything we or our allies choose to send to The Ukraine.

Whether the large sums of money already sent to The Ukraine has been sucked up by corrupt oligarchs has yet to be proven but is highly suspected. We never seem to learn "accountability".

The problem we have is the fact that over the years our capacity to manufacture *anything* is a ghost of our previous capabilities. We simply do not have the manufacturing capacity to produce enough ammunition, weapons, tanks, planes, ships or military vessels, and all of the other necessities to win wars on multiple fronts. Many question whether if invaded or attacked we could even protect ourselves.

When (not if) China invades Taiwan, what do we do? Continue supplying Israel, The Ukraine AND Taiwan? At what point does the deployment of tactical nuclear weapons become a necessity. At what time do we unleash HELL with our own nuclear bomb arsenal? AFTER we are nuked? Tough question.

These are frightening and dangerous times. Many of our military leaders are "hawks". They chant "Annihilate"! "Fight, Kill, Bomb". Unleash Hell!

One can only hope sanity prevails. It seldom does.

Above I mention the two wars that are front-page news, Israel and The Ukraine. But at any given time there are literally dozens of wars being fought within individual countries, one faction against another.

Are you aware that a mere 50,000 people have been killed in the past few years in hostilities in Myanmar? (When I learned geography, it was called Burma.) Who knew?

In the Democratic Republic of the Congo, between 1998 and 2007, a mere 5.4 *million* died in conflicts. Within the past decade 60,000 pygmy civilians were slaughtered in a seldom-reported genocide.

In Rwanda two factions, Hutu and Tutsi, have been killing each other for years. They've managed to kill about a million civilians total between them.

Another fact seldom mentioned in the media is the number of countries in which The United States has military troops stationed and in harm's way. Many of our brave troops are "advisors", but some are combat-ready. Some offer surveillance, others conduct military training. Many are members of our precious "Special Forces".

The countries where we have a military presence include the following twenty-three sovereign nations: Afghanistan, Australia, Cameroon, Canada, Egypt, Iraq, Israel, Jordan, Kenya, Lebanon, Libya, Mali, Mauritania, Niger, Nigeria, The Philippines, Qatar, Singapore, Somalia, Syria, Thailand, Tunisia and Yemen. There are many others. We are truly the world's policemen.

There is one very interesting possibility regarding the deployment of nuclear bombs. Unless one pays close attention to UFOs and Ancient Alien Theory, and believes that benevolent extraterrestrials are monitoring human development, than the following hypothesis will seem utterly ridiculous.

There is a totally documented incident that occurred at Malmstrom Air Force Base in Montana in 1957. This is a primary combat-ready nuclear missile installation. A glowing UFO was seen over the base. The base personnel discovered at once that they HAD LOST ALL ABILITY TO DEPLOY THEIR MISSILES! Every system was shut-down mysteriously! They could not be launched if they had to.

The cause was never determined. Operational control returned immediately after the UFO departed within an hour. This incident was memorialized in a *full-house Congressional testimony.*

In the event, CHINA, RUSSIA, Iran, Israel or The United States, or one of the other nuclear-armed nations, decides to employ nukes as a last resort, could aliens actually protect humanity from itself? Let's hope we never need to find out.

They might be on a lunch break at the wrong time.

In case you think that the danger nuclear radiation is overblown, allow me to relate a fascinating story from WWII. You can be certain you have never heard this one before. You can be quite certain that the United States government would never verify any part of this story. I

In the 1990s, I was on The Board of Directors of a small exploratory mining company, United Mines, Inc. (How and why I held that position is a very long story.) The CEO was an elderly gentleman named Glynn Burkhardt, Sr. He served in the United States Air Force and was intimately involved in Oppenheimer's first nuclear bomb test.

I got to know Mr. Burkhardt Sr. extremely well. We spent many hours together with me listening and recording and him talking. He asked me to write his biography. During our many interviews he sat up in a hospital bed set up in his living room. He was very ill and heavily medicated,

Knowing his background as an "old-time" dirt miner in Arizona searching for gold, and his years in the military during a critical time in our history, made me anxious to document his interesting story.

Glynn was a very religious Christian. I do not think he was either exaggerating or lying at any time during our meetings. He believed every word.

What a story it was! Somehow he had acquired a silver mine in Arivaca, Arizona, that was originally owned by Sam Poston (known as the father of Arizona) and Samuel Colt of firearms fame. It was, coincidentally, only a half-mile from my home in Amado. the one I was forced to abandon due to the massive influx of illegal aliens.

I visited the mine site many times and added many beautiful blue-streaked copper-ore-bearing rocks to my mineral collection. The mine tailings pile was a "gold mine" to a rock hound!

In the 1970s the mine produced tons of silver-bearing ore from underground tunnels. The ore was actually processed on site. His photos of molten silver metal being poured into molds are fascinating!

His entire mining history will be in his bio, sadly still unfinished. It contains some really interesting stories including one related to the famous "Gunfight At The OK Corral" that has never been told. But it is the fascinating "Oppenheimer" story, which I will relate here.

This story is taken from my notes and audio recordings created for his bio.

"I was a volunteer in the service of my beloved country, joining the United States Air Force soon after the Japanese sneak attack on Pearl Harbor."

"After a short stint doing weather reconnaissance out of Fort Meyers, Florida, I was assigned to the Second Air Force's 331st Bombardment Group (Very Heavy), 315th Bombardment Wing, under Brigadier General Frank Armstrong. Occasionally we were loaned to the 314th. The Group was stationed in the Pacific Theater."

"We were home-based at Northeast Field, Guam, in the Northern Mariana Islands. Other island bases we flew in and out of often were Tinian just north of Guam and Kwajalein in the Marshall Islands a bit to the south."

"All of these tiny coral specs were located between the Philippine Sea and the South Pacific Ocean. This is the same area where later underwater nuclear test detonations were made at Bikini and Enewietak Atolls."

"Anyhow, I had hoped to get a commission and be trained as a pilot. That was the promise they made me upon enlistment. But the war in Europe was winding down and dozens of B17 and B24 pilots were sent to the Pacific theater. It was much easier to retrain them on the Boing B29s than train new recruits like me from scratch. So my piloting dreams were dashed."

"Initially I was assigned the gunnery position. I received my first flight engineering assignment because the existing engineer was some joker from Kansas who drank too much and was very lazy. Because I had the right mechanic-schooling they decided to dump him and assigned me his post."

"Having become an FAA certified flight mechanic back in Globe, Arizona, they gave me a crash-course as a flight engineer. That is how I ended up quite by accident with just about the most exciting assignments imaginable."

"We were most fortunate to be involved with the greatest aircraft ever produced up till that time, the "B29B Superfortress". These babies were stripped for speed. Gun turrets had been completely removed, except for the remote-controlled tail guns which didn't affect speed. This worked well for us because the Japs were famous for direct rear attacks.

We could hit air speeds over 350 miles per hour and cruise for hours at 25,000 feet. Impressive for a prop plane in that era."

"I flew on these planes back and forth between the Pacific Island bases and bases on the mainland many times. We had endless training runs to prepare us for what at the time was quite unimaginable."

"We had thought about naming our plane but never got around to it. It was simply number "4139" as I recall. Naming planes and putting all sorts of cartoons on the nose was very popular in the Air Corps. Who will ever forget the 'Enola Gay'?"

"One day an idiot shave-tail Louie fresh out of officer's candidacy school made a lot of people on base very unhappy shortly after his arrival. His first order was to have all of the decals and decorations removed from the B29B fleet. I think he lasted a week."

"We were sent to Alamogordo Air Base in New Mexico one rainy day in mid-July 1945. Roosevelt had died just a few months earlier. We had no idea what to expect from our new Commander In Chief, President Harry S. Truman."

"We knew something very big was up. There was lots of heightened security, lots of rumors, but we had not a clue. In the pre-dawn hours our B29B was scrambled. We carried sealed mission orders with *very* strict instructions not to dare open them. We took off."

"We were out over the New Mexico desert, somewhere around Socorro, when it happened. A light brighter than any we had ever seen lit up the plane like a hundred suns. It was blinding! Unknown to us a plutonium bomb of 20 kiloton of TNT yield, the very FIRST atomic explosion, had just been detonated on a tower five miles below in the middle of the desert!"

"Our mission: To follow the massive cloud of dust that was created by the blast and report on its track and eventual final destination before it dissipated. After all, we were weather recon, so radioactive nuclear dust qualified as a valid mission".

"Now bear in mind, no one at that time had a clue about the bad effects of nuclear radiation on the human body. No one had a clue what might happen on the tower at ground zero. No one had a clue what might happen down-below or down-wind. Least of all us guinea pigs in that B29B."

"Many serious scientists, including Oppenheimer himself thought the blast might start a nuclear chain reaction that could destroy the earth! I guess they figured it was worth the gamble. What's one earth more or less!"

"Not one of us on that plane was dressed in anything but our standard flight outfits. In the pre-dawn light we saw this huge plume of dust rising from the desert to 40,000 feet or more. Absolutely mind-boggling."

"The winds aloft were blowing the cloud in a generally northeasterly direction. We flew in and around the cloud for twelve-hundred miles, over Texas, Oklahoma, Missouri, Illinois and Indiana, until we could barely detect the final vestiges of dust, over Cincinnati, Ohio. Who ever knew? Certainly no one downwind of that explosion."

"How much radioactive fallout hit the ground across those states we will *never* know. How many innocent individuals down-wind of that test died as a result of radiation poisoning? Cancer? The government will say 'none'. Want to bet?"

"We returned to base, reported our findings, and were told to keep our mouths shut. Period. It never happened. What radioactive cloud? What fallout? No sweat."

"My pilot was a guy named Corbin, my co-pilot was named Able. Not long after the Trinity cloud-chasing adventure they were shot down over Osaka during a low-level bombing run. I was very fortunate to have not been available for that particular mission."

"Rumor had it that they had parachuted into farm country and some local Jap farmers pitchforked them to death. It was probably a better fate than being captured and skinned alive as was common practice with the Japs for whom the civilized laws of capture did not exist."

"They were a very vicious enemy who would have considered waterboarding to be a joke. Slowly pulling out fingernails was far more effective torture.

"Unknown to every airman on that plane following that highly-radioactive cloud was the sad fact that we had all just been written a death sentence. *Every member of that crew eventually contracted leukemia.* To the best of my knowledge I am the last living survivor of that flight."

"Nuclear radiation respects no one. I was just the one that the good LORD decided should live a bit longer than the others. Guess someone had to be left alive tell the story."

"I have battled leukemia my entire life and was granted

disability pay by the government. I cannot help but feel angry that I was an unknowing lab rat for a government test the consequences of which they may or may not have had a clue. I never did get one of those promised special-mission medals! That actual bill never survived committee."

What you are about to read has never to my knowledge been reported anywhere. In fact, if I did not believe Mr. Bernhardt to be a very devout Christian and unaccustomed to lying (sort of a living Mr. Spock) I'd be certain that he made this one up. He was, however, a very sick and bitter man. Perhaps this story that was based on events from fifty years earlier that were true only in his subconscious imagination. He sounded believable.

"The code name for the atom bomb delivery program was 'Silver Plate'. It was part of the overall 'Manhattan Project'. Fifteen B29B bombers were modified with special speed and long-range capabilities. Almost everyone, at least those born before 1990, know that it was the 'Enola Gay' piloted by John Tibbets who dropped 'Little Boy' on Hiroshima."

"Lesser known is pilot Chuck Sweeney who dropped 'Fat Man' on Nagasaki three days later. His plane was named 'Bockscar' after Air Commander Bock. Good trivia question. Both had the fuel figured so closely that Tibbets landed back in Okinawa flying on fumes!"

"I was training at the time at Wendover Air Force Base in Utah, with one of the modified B29Bs. We had orders to fly to Guam, and then to Tinian to await further orders. We knew something *very* big was up."

"It was just a few weeks after Hiroshima and Nagasaki. Three B29Bs were scrambled, two from Tinian and one from Guam. Two were armed, each supposedly with a single nuclear bomb. Yes, I believe there were more than two nuclear bombs created at that time. I think there were at least four. We were to fly forward weather recon in our B29B. We were told we did not carry one of the bombs.

"We were also told that we were not to open our mission destination envelope under **_any_** circumstance until we were well out over the ocean. Further this was to be a one-way mission insofar as we did not have enough fuel for a return flight home from our unknown destination.

We were further advised that we would most likely be parachuting at mission's end. All in all not a real comforting briefing."

"All three planes taxied out onto their runways ready to depart on their highly-classified top-secret mission. We all sat for about an hour. This was unusual because we usually scrambled as soon as we could board. Then came the extremely surprising order to stand down. We were all very relieved. It terminated what we perceived as a possible suicide mission."

"But we were devoured by curiosity. Where were we headed? What was the overall mission? Who exactly _were_ the two trailing bombers about to nuke?"

"No one had actually told us we couldn't open the sealed orders in the event of a recall, so a bunch of us headed off for a private room and opened the envelope. What we read came as a shock."

"Destinations: **MOSCOW and VLADIVOSTOK!!!** Moscow??? Vladivostok??? We were to radio weather information to the trailing two bombers, each of which would be carrying a nuclear bomb."

"After deployment of the nukes, all three planes were to attempt to land in Sweden, but most likely none would have had sufficient fuel so it would be "parachute time", GOD knows where. The instructions were very detailed and the mission was very real."

"Whose bright idea was this? Truman's? He absolutely *hated* Russia. Some ambitious underling? That nasty little General who immolated thousands of Japanese citizens with incendiary bombs days after the nukes were dropped, just for fun? We'll never know who issued the Russia kill order, but we were told it was Truman who changed his mind and nixed the mission at the very last minute."

To the best of my knowledge this story has never appeared anywhere before. Was it true? Personally, I believe it was.

Let us look beyond nuclear weapons at a related existential threat, nuclear power plants. One might be surprised to learn that there are four-hundred-thirty-six (436) active nuclear power plants located across thirty-two (32) countries! The United States has the most with ninety-three (93). These produce roughly twenty-percent (20%) of all American electric power.

France has fifty-six (56) nuclear power generating stations generating almost all of that country's power needs. Other countries with more than ten nuclear power plants are: China 55; Russia 37; Japan 33; South Korea 25; India 23; Canada 19 and The Ukraine 15.

Of real concern are the three nuclear power stations located on Taiwan. Would these be a tempting target in the event of a Chinese invasion? Or would they be a safe place to hang out?

There is a real, deeply imbedded fear of nuclear power plants among Americans in general. For this reason it has been decades since The United States built a new one. This fear was burned into America's collective consciousness by a Hollywood movie and an unlikely event that shortly followed it by the weirdest of coincidences!

"The China Syndrome" movie was released to theaters in March 1979. It dramatized a potential nuclear plant meltdown that would literally bore a hole straight through earth all the way to China, and wipe out all life on earth. For various reasons scientists today are convinced that such a scenario is not possible.

By an incredible coincidence just two weeks after the film's release the United States underwent what is always thought of in retrospect as a "major nuclear disaster", the first and probably not the last.

The Three Mile Island nuclear power plant in Middletown, Pennsylvania suffered a malfunction. Along with internal plant damage a tiny pressure-relief valve in the cooling system allowed a very small amount of radioactive iodine gas to leak into the atmosphere.

The plant operators did not recognize the valve's release immediately. The danger level, even in the immediate vicinity of the plant itself, was never above acceptable levels established for background radiation contamination. There was no danger to anyone, ever. No injuries, no illness, no deaths. Essentially a non-event from the public's perspective.

Of course the media made it appear that we had *barely avoided* the dreaded "China Syndrome". It proved beyond doubt that all nuclear power plants were an extinction-level event just waiting to happen. This scare-tactic reporting, totally bogus, left a lasting impression on the American public. To this day almost everyone still refers to "The Three Mile Island Nuclear *Disaster*" that wasn't.

There was, however, significant damage to the TMI plant internally, actually costing a billion dollars over a twelve-year period to repair. Because the media greatly exaggerated the entire incident, thereafter the United States has been "nuclear power plant adverse". We have built no nuclear power plants in the decades since TMI.

There are two sources of danger in nuclear power plants: operator error, and a natural disaster such as an earthquake. There has been one very serious example of each since TMI, fortunately not in the United States. Of course these events only added to our aversion to building new ones.

Russia hit the operator-error disaster jackpot on April 26, 1986. The Chernobyl Nuclear Plant in the town of Pripyat had parts of the core greatly overheat to four-thousand-seven-hundred degrees Fahrenheit. The normal cooling water flow was unable to dissipate this intense heat. It caused a massive steam explosion. Two workers were killed instantly, pieces of their bodies never recovered.

Soon thereafter a death sentence was handed out to an army of clueless clean-up workers. Everyone charged with the job of putting out fires and cleaning up the ruins of the Number Four Reactor was doomed. No fewer than 20,000 workers died of radiation poisoning, and another 70,000 were disabled.

In the nearby Russian towns and in nearby Ukraine over 50,000 died or were disabled. In nearby Belarus, there were some 30,000 casualties. Nuclear radiation is extremely deadly.

It is said that the Pripyat area will be uninhabitable for 20,000 years!

Three plant operators were charged with negligence and sentenced to ten years each in prison, but probably died from radiation long before serving their time.

Chernobyl and Three Mile Island were both attributed to operators not realizing an impending disaster before it was too late.

Mother Nature can be equally destructive.

A similar disaster had nothing to do with human error. On March 11, 2011, an earthquake under the Pacific Ocean near Japan generated a forty-six-foot high tsunami. This wall of water struck the Fukushima Datichi Nuclear Power Plant head on. Amazingly no one was killed, but machinery was crushed, and one reactor core melted. The "China Syndrome" hypothesis was tested! Humanity survived.

It has taken over thirteen years for operators to remove the deadly radionuclides strontium and cesium resulting from the core meltdown. The remaining contaminated cooling water, containing only tritium ("heavy water") will apparently be dumped into the Pacific Ocean. Many are very unhappy with this idea, though it is probably harmless.

Based on the number of nuclear power plants in operation and the total hours of safe operation worldwide, these plants are generally considered extremely safe.

All of the above mentioned plants, and all nuclear power plants worldwide, are based on "nuclear *fission*". Fission reactions consume matter to produce power.

A long-term solution to limitless nuclear power is "nuclear *fusion*". Such a power generator is theoretically possible. There have been recent breakthroughs, but we are a very long way from a full-scale fusion reactor. The concept, which seems counter-intuitive, is to get more power out than you put in, something from nothing. Weird physics.

I'll swear to the following story under oath, and be pleased to take a lie detector test. There is no way this story would ever be confirmed by anyone in the nuclear power industry.

For over six years I worked for a company that provided chemical compounds that would minimize corrosion in power plant cooling water copper tubes. I would supervise internal tube inspections using tiny inserted cameras, sort of like a colonoscopy. We were looking for tiny tube holes, not polyps!

My job was to offer suggestions if chemical intervention was in order. I visited plants across the country, coal, oil, gas and nuclear powered.

I visited seven nuclear plants. Compared to fossil fueled plants they are very quiet and immaculate. You could eat off the floors! There are massive control rooms manned 24/7/365 with gauges and alarms for everything imaginable.

One day I was walking with the Plant Manager (I won't mention which nuclear plant, except that it was in the southeast). We were outside on a catwalk watching cooling water being sucked from a large river into the cooling tubes. I noticed a man at the end of the walk shoveling something into the intake water from a large pile nearby. I asked the Manager what this worker was doing.

His matter-of-fact reply was: "Oh, he's our sawdust man." Say what! Out of amazed curiosity I asked: "Why"?

He explained that they had been experiencing a bit of cooling water tube leakage. Even in a worst-case scenario this could not release any radioactivity. These cooling tubes are not in the "hot loop", with "hot" referring to radiation, not temperature.

Some genius plant engineer had come up with a novel solution to the tube leakage. Rather than replace the expensive copper tubes, just continuously shovel sawdust into the water inlets and let it get sucked into any tiny tube holes. Then it would swell up and plug the holes! Apparently it actually worked! It left me with a deep-seated distrust of nuclear power plants from that day on.

We worry a lot about nuclear missile attack, but is The United States at risk of a *land* invasion? China has a massive land army. Getting them in large numbers to various American landing points does not seem practicable. Just ask Commander Tojo of Japan from WWII. He is quoted as saying he would have seriously considered a land invasion of America except: "There's a gun behind every tree!" It's a pretty good argument for not restricting Americans from owning guns. Thank you NRA.

George Wallace is quoted as saying: "To enslave a nation, first locate all of the guns then confiscate them." Our second Amendment to the Constitution (....the right of the people to keep and bear arms shall not be infringed) is there for a good reason.

How many guns are in private hands in The United States? The current estimate is *393+ million*, more than one for every individual in the country! In fact there are over three times the number of weapons in private hands in America than in all of the other countries on earth combined! Tojo was on to something.

Possibly avoiding a land invasion from China is not quite comparable to avoiding the threat of nuclear annihilation. Humans have been killing each other in wars since "In the beginning….".

Wars have been fought with bare hands, sticks, clubs, rocks, slings, arrows, maces, lances, swords, rifles, pistols and cannons. They have been fought on foot, on horseback on camels and from elephants! They have been fought on the ground, on the seas, under the seas and from the air.

Wars have been fought over religion, territory, and riches and a lust for power. Homo sapiens thrives on wars! Apparently we just cannot live without them. We have been killing each other since we evolved!

In the actual event of a full scale multi-target nuclear attack, there is very little one can do to survive for any great length of time. The power grid will be gone, but some will feel safe relying on their solar powered generators. Of course, these would be prime targets for roving mobs of criminals as soon as the lights go out.

There is a thriving new industry providing costly complex survival-bunkers to wealthy individuals. Some of these offer survival for a year! Of course it begs the question: "Then what?"

The only medical intervention after a nuclear detonation that seems to have value is to ingest iodine tablets. These are readily available on the internet and are very inexpensive. They are harmless if taken as directed. Everyone should have a supply.

Nuclear fallout contains a great deal of radioactive iodine, and this element is quickly absorbed by the human thyroid leading to certain death. Because thyroids cannot distinguish between medical iodine and the radioactive stuff, loading the thyroid with "good" iodine prevents take-up of the killer kind. Go buy some!

In 1983 President Ronald Reagan proposed a brilliant multi-satellite system. It was dubbed "Star Wars" after a popular movie of that name. It was officially the "Strategic Defense Initiative". Sadly it was never taken seriously. Our military geniuses decided that ground-based defense was adequate. History may well show that this was by far the worst decision in American military history, worse than Vietnam and the Afghanistan withdrawal combined.

None of this could ever happen you say? We humans are not THAT crazy? The threat of **M**utually **A**ssured

Destruction, "M A D", will surely win the day. Well, think about the "Cuban Missile Crisis". We came damn close then, but MAD fortunately won the day. JFK had grapefruits. NK had grapes.

As if Iran vs. Israel & the USA isn't enough of a worry, we have North Korea vs. South Korea, always good for a nuke or two. In fact, if North Korea has ICBMs Rocket Man might decide to create a repeat of "Pearl Harbor" in spades!

Of course fully nuclear armed India and Pakistan, who truly hate each other, could "accidentally" put the whole planet at risk if one or the other decides to settle some old score over the Vail of Kashmir or whatever. All these scenarios are rather disquieting to say the least.

Are there other man made weapons that could cause serious consequences? Are we developing any? Are the Chinese? How about this disturbing little note: On April 15, 2012, it was reported that Russian President Vladimir Putin confirmed his country is working on the creation of an electromagnetic gun that attacks its target's central nervous system, putting them in *a* zombie-like state**.**
.
According to Russian former defense minister Anatoly Serdyukov, "When it was used for dispersing a crowd and it was focused on a man, his body temperature went up immediately as if he was thrown into a frying pan." It can fry your brain from the inside out! Wow! Let's figure out how to do this from a satellite or a drone! Is this connected to the one-day panic in February 2024 over Russian satellite plans? Fun weapon.

Many believe that cyber security is more important than either border security or even missile defense! We definitely do possess offensive cyber-attack capabilities. What we shockingly do NOT possess is any reliable proven defense capability against a cyber-attack, as was reported recently in "Smithsonian Magazine". That is one act we'd better get together in a big hurry.

Has an important international cyber-attack actually already happened? A couple of years ago either Israel or the United States or both launched a cyber-attack against Iran's nuclear capabilities. It is reported to have set Iran's nuclear program back many years.

Back in April 2012 an under-reported cyber-attack screwed up Iran's oil production facility. Curious. I wonder who pulled that one off.

Our utility grid, dependent 100% on computerized controls, could in theory be shut down entirely by some brilliant 15-year-old propeller-head working in his father's garage in Estonia! Beyond a doubt both China and Russia possess this capability.

How important is the internet these days? I'm not certain we could exist for a week without it. A cyber-attack could easily wipe out all access.

Is it possible that we could **accidentally** annihilate ourselves? I have read reports of the immense concern top-level scientists had prior to the very first atomic bomb detonation test. No one had a clue what might happen. Some postulated total global annihilation from some unanticipated atmospheric side effect. A collective sigh of relief was all that happened.

The same is true about today's massive "super-colliders." Scientists shoot various tiny sub-atomic particles at each other at unimaginable speeds to see what happens when they collide. The even smaller particles that result are categorized into a grand theory of particle physics, the answer to "What Is Everything Made Of". Physicists only recently identified the elusive "Higg's Boson". But that is not the point.

There are some high-up in the scientific community who seriously believe that these well-meaning particle scientists could inadvertently create a "black hole", and that such an entity could grow and eventually destroy the planet. Of course those in control of the Supercollider laugh at this possibility. Ha, ha.

All wars are an existential threat to freedom. Historians do not often agree on the cause of wars fought decades ago. In retrospect a conflict looks very different from what it did during the conflict itself.

America is the Home of the Free because of the sacrifices of our brave soldiers. In WWI and WWII a proud citizenry rushed to serve. Today we beg for volunteers. Have we become a country of apathetic chicken-shits? Are bravery and patriotism just quaint concepts? Apparently so.

If humanity fails to wake up soon and eliminate the existential threat of nuclear annihilation forever, the last seconds of the "Doomsday Clock" will go by in a flash!

CHAPTER SEVEN

MAMA NATURE

"Mother Nature is a BITCH!" Murphy's 10th law. "Murphy's Laws" were created by Edward Aloysius Murphy, Jr., (1918-1990).

"Nothing is rich but the inexhaustible wealth of nature. She shows us only surfaces, but she is a million fathoms deep." Ralph Waldo Emerson, philosopher and poet, (1803-1882).

"I don't know where I'm-a gonna go when the volcano blows." From the 1979 song "Volcano", by Jimmy Buffett, (1946-2023).

Aside from being a target for all manner of cosmic nasties, our planet itself is home to natural disasters that occur with frightening frequency. I'll address these below in the rough order of their existential threat to our freedoms and to human life on earth.

Mother nature can toss us many curve-balls. Some can be locally deadly, but are not a widespread existential threat to life in general.

Avalanches, perhaps more frequent today due to global warming, kill a dozen or so skiers and mountain climbers every year. Mudslides are like avalanches without snow. They can actually inundate a small town but are rare.

Tidal bores, high walls of water caused by in-coming tides and certain types of coastal terrain, will kill anyone dumb enough to be walking in the predictable path at the predictable time.

Riptides suck unsuspecting swimmers out to sea. The ones who drown never bothered to learn the simple swimming action that can save their life.

Icebergs can sink ships, but seldom do.

Hungry animals kill humans, often mistaking them for their natural prey. Sharks kill unlucky swimmers, snorkelers and surfers. Venomous creatures, snakes, spiders and certain small sea critters kill humans. Large animals are opportunistic killers. Hippos apparently kill more people than any other mammal.

Certain insects can kill. Some carry deadly diseases. Some have venom that can kill an allergic person. Army ants will eat anything in their path, including you. All creatures are part of mother nature. As an overall existential threat they don't kill enough people to qualify as "major".

Major existential threats include volcanoes, earthquakes and tsunamis, hurricanes and cyclones, tornadoes and water spouts, floods, excessive heat, wildfires, ocean currents, rogue waves, the ozone layer and pole-shifts.

VOLCANOES:

There is no more destructive force in nature than a volcano.

The most vivid record of this devastation is seen at the

excavations in the Italian cities of Pompeii and Herculaneum. In the year 79AD, (or 79 CE, "Common Era", for the purist) Mount Vesuvius, a volcano in Italy still considered active today, had a major eruption. The hot ash that rained down was so sudden and unexpected that both cities were buried almost instantly under nineteen FEET of ash and debris.

Extensive excavations by archaeologists over centuries have revealed perfectly preserved human body-casts in the precise positions they were in when they were buried. They had zero time to flee. It is estimated that 16,000 individuals were killed almost instantly in the two cities and surrounding countryside.

In many American's memory is the violent eruption of Mount St. Helens in 1980, located in Skamania County, Washington State. The entire north face of the mountain exploded violently. This had been preceded by a series of small earthquakes.

The resulting "pyroclastic" flow of debris, lava, hot gas and steam rushed down the slope at near supersonic speed. An estimated fifty-seven people unlucky enough to have been in the general vicinity were killed almost instantly along with tens of thousands of animals. Many hundreds of square miles were reduced to wasteland.

A massive plume of smoke rose to 80,000 feet. Ash rained down on eleven states and a few Canadian Provinces. Water from melted ice on the slopes of the volcano created a massive mudslide that spread for miles. This was America's most violent volcano eruption in recorded history.

Yellowstone National Park, our first ever, is located almost entirely in Wyoming with tiny bits in Idaho and Montana. The Park is famous for a steam geyser called "Old Faithful". The hot condensed steam rising from the hot ground below reaches almost two-hundred feet high. It has predictably erupted about once an hour for centuries. It is the most famous of the almost five-hundred geysers in Yellowstone.

Yellowstone is a beautiful, scenic place to visit, as millions do from around the world each year. **But any day it could literally wipe out civilization! This is not an exaggeration.**

Volcanologists and geologists have studied Yellowstone for decades. They know for absolute certain that there is a massive sea of molten rock underlying the entire area, a huge magma chamber ready to erupt at any moment.

Recently they determined that the magma is located much closer to the surface than previously thought. This is considered to be the largest and potentially most deadly super-volcano in recorded history.

When, not if, the Yellowstone super-volcano erupts it will bury a ten-state area under dozens of feet of ash, almost immediately eradicating every living thing. This would not be unlike the fate of Pompeii, but thousands of times greater.

How would it affect all life on earth? It is estimated that the ash plume injected into the atmosphere would plunge the entire planet into "nuclear night", perhaps for decades. Bye bye sun. All plant life will die. All animals will starve.

Humans included.

There is zero chance of survival when this monster goes "bang". And according to the best expert minds, eruption is not only inevitable, but very possibly imminent.

There is a second potential super-volcano lurking under South Africa. The eruption of this monster is not expected any time soon. Small comfort.

A third, as troubling as Yellowstone, is in Italy. After decades of dormancy the Pozzouli super-volcano is showing frightening signs of life.

Archaeologists tell us that there is conclusive proof that two-hundred-fifty million years ago, a super-volcano in Siberia caused a nuclear night that lasted over a million years!

My wife and I lived for five years on the slope of an active volcano in the town of Ocean View, on the "Big Island" of Hawaii.

Decades ago it was rumored that The United States would build a spaceport in the general vicinity, at South Point. Developers cut roads and created thousands of building lots on the long-solidified lava of the south slope of a volcano called Mauna Loa. Though considered to be an active volcano, it had not erupted in many years and was considered a safe area for habitation.

When the government changed their mind about the spaceport, the hundreds of one-acre lots were sold for practically nothing. Many homes, some small and some quite large, were built over the years and more are still being built today. Property values are considerable bargains. One can still buy an acre view-lot for under ten thousand dollars. That's about a million dollars cheaper than a similar view lot in Florida!

Our home was a quite lovely two-two, with a large deck and a one-hundred-eighty degree view of the ocean a few miles to the south. Over the years quite a lot of vegetation has grown in cracks in the old lava, so the landscape was far from barren.

One interesting feature of life on this volcano was the periodic town meetings of the Civil Air Patrol Helicopter Unit. They offered planning for residents to be plucked off roofs in the event of an unexpected eruption!

To the east of Ocean View about fifty miles away is a VERY active volcano called Kilauea. If you have never seen an active volcano up close you simply cannot imagine its awe-inspiring power. There are periodic tourist helicopter rides over the active lava lakes. It has been erupting almost continuously since 1981.

During one visit our chopper pilot got to within, at most, two-hundred feet of the surface of red-hot liquid-rock lava that was spilling into the ocean! The helicopter had no doors and we could literally hang out the opening supported by a seat belt and take photos! The radiant heat was frightening. Quite an experience. Fabulous photos! Very strong seat belts.

Kilauea had been erupting daily for almost a half-century. It was not the sort of volcano that blasts out deadly pyroclastic flows that destroy everything in their path, as with Vesuvius and Mount St. Helens. Kilauea is an "oozie" volcano. Thick, slow moving molten rock, headed downslope towards the ocean in a few isolated locations.

There is actually one location where local Park Rangers allow tourists to approach within a few feet of the very edge of a flow and watch it creep an inch a minute or so towards the ocean. When the Ranger is distracted, I've seen kids poke sticks into the lava to watch them ignite! Brainless parents seem to think it's cute.

After decades of slow, predictable lava flows along the few fixed paths to the ocean, in May 2018 Kilauea decided to become VERY active. Over a few months it covered twenty-plus square miles of eastern Hawaii Island with thick lava. It managed to destroy seven-hundred structures. The flow unexpectedly stopped just short of the major port city of Hilo on the north-east coast, much to the relief of residents.

Volcanoes are very unpredictable. Ten years after we moved from the south slope of Mauna Loa back to Arizona (to dry out), a relatively minor, but very rare and unexpected eruption occurred on the north side, opposite from where we lived but only a few miles away. It lasted a week, and did little other than scare the crap out of Ocean View residents on the south side.

Far from Hawaii, the country of Iceland is home to no fewer than one-hundred-thirty (130) volcanoes! There is around one eruption there every year or so. As recently as early 2024 the southern coastal fishing village of Grindavik was hit by an unexpected lava flow after a minor earthquake.

Many homes were destroyed, and it is reported that the entire town may have to be abandoned. In some parts of Iceland you have the choice of freezing or being cooked!

It is a fact that a brand new Hawaiian Island is being created east of the Big Island as I write this. Lo'ihi is rapidly building an undersea dome of hardened lava that is now just 963 meters or so from its top to the surface. This will be the next easternmost Hawaiian Island at some time in the future. Undersea volcanoes are very common. In fact, it is reported that there may be over five-thousands of them worldwide!

It is the land-based volcanoes we see and feel and best understand. Mexico's Popocatepetl, just outside of massive Mexico City, is pouring out gas and ash as I write this. On the island of Sicily in January 2024 Italy's famous Mount Etna once again began pouring out a massive column of ash. In fact, there are no fewer than twenty-nine (29!) active, gas and ash spewing volcanoes on earth as I write this. This is actually an historically low number.

Multiple simultaneous volcanic eruptions are one fact alone that makes the entire "human-caused global warming" issue very questionable. In one week these twenty-nine volcanoes account for more air pollution than all the cars and power plants on the planet do in a year! No one has proven otherwise. Sorry Greenies, you can't legislate away a volcano.

And there are at least seventy (70!) other volcanoes on earth that are known to have the real potential for eruption much sooner than later, not including those deep beneath the oceans. Indonesia alone is said to have over four-hundred potential future major eruption sites.

We never hear about these events because they are only newsworthy if you happen to live near one. The "Morning News" from Vanuatu or Papua, New Guinea, let alone the Sangihe Islands, doesn't often make page one of your local newspaper or TV news lead story. We tend to think of these events as every-day earth-happenings. No big deal, right? And for the most part, air pollution aside, they are not a major issue. Usually.

On May 8, 1902 about 30,000 people died at Saint-Pierre, Martinique, when the Mount Pelee volcano erupted unexpectedly. A huge flow of hot gas, rock and mud, burst from the summit and flowed outward with devastating consequences. To this day similar eruptions are generically dubbed: "Palean Eruptions".

The beautiful island of Montserrat in the Caribbean was known for years as "The Emerald Isle". No longer. That was so until in 2007 when a massive inactive volcano erupted in the Soufriere Hills. It renderied most of this beautiful island uninhabitable to this very day. This event was neither predicted nor expected.

Every rare so often something different and even more violent happens, such as the Mt. St. Helens event mentioned above. Even this violent event was puny compared to at least two we know occurred in the relatively recent past, geologically speaking.

About four-thousand years ago a massive eruption occurred near Santorini, Greece. What scientists say is extraordinary about that event was that the volcano had been virtually dormant for 180 *centuries* before. Surprise!!!

Far greater even than the Santorini event was the eruption of Mount Krakatau, (better known as "Krakatoa") in the Sundas Strait near Sumatra, west of Java, in 1115 AD. Dormant thereafter for another 768 years, in August 1883 it unexpectedly erupted with the greatest force ever recorded by man's instruments. It is credited with producing the loudest "bang" ever heard by humans on earth before or since! It is known as "the explosion heard around the world".

Its power is said to have been the equivalent of 26 hydrogen bombs being exploded simultaneously! The resulting tsunami, a 100+ foot wall of water, killed 36,000 unlucky coastal dwellers. The resulting pyroclastic flow killed another 1,000 on Sumatra. That is one hell of an explosion! It is still active to this day, spawning "Anak Krakatau" or "Child of Krakatau".

Believe it or not, these colossal eruptions are themselves puny alongside the infrequent "super-volcano" eruptions. These occur roughly once every fifty-thousand years, luckily for us.

Some 73,500 years ago, geologists report that the largest volcanic explosion within the past twenty-million years occurred in Sumatra. It merely deposited a ten feet deep layer of ash as far away as India over 7,300 kilometers away (4,700miles). It filled earth's atmosphere with sulfur dioxide resulting in a rain of sulfuric acid that wiped out most of earth's living creatures. Today's Lake Toba, covering an immense 440 square miles, is all that remains as evidence.

Prior to that event there was a super-volcanic eruption right here in the United States. There is a unique seventy square mile region around Lake Mono in California. It shows geologists that back a million or so years ago, an eruption almost as large as the one that formed Lake Toba occurred here. Then over the past 40,000 years, and as recently as 1300 AD, this potential future-mega-disaster super-volcano continued to erupt periodically. After a thousand quiet years it may well be overdue to erupt.

This area, plus the bulging dome under Yellowstone Park in Wyoming, present the greatest real and present dangers to human life on the planet today. Should there be massive crustal plate shifts, or massive earthquakes caused by whatever, it is almost a certainty that the unimaginable fury of either or both of these two super-volcanoes would be unleashed.

What's the point of all this? Well, for one thing, although volcanologists today have all manner of sensitive instruments both on the ground and on orbiting satellites all used in an effort to predict eruptions of dormant or prospective volcanoes, it is far from an exact science. It is known for certain that there are many other massive domes of magma close to earth's surface worldwide just itching to burst the surface.

Some say when, not if, one of these blow, it will make Krakatoa and Santorini look like firecrackers. It could even exceed the Lake Nomo and Lake Toba events. Bye bye life on earth.

EARTHQUAKES & TSUNAMIS (aka "TIDAL WAVES"):

The earth is estimated to be four billion years old. Over time, what was basically a molten ball of rock slowly cooled. In the process, it formed a crust of solidified rock. The crust under the oceans is three to five miles thick, while under the continents it averages twenty-five miles thick.

That sounds pretty thick, but if the earth were the size of an apple the crust would be about the thickness of the skin.

As the plates cooled they broke into sections. There are seven major "crustal plates" and eight smaller ones. These plates are not fixed. They slowly move about and when they slip over or under an adjacent plate we have an earthquake.

When one of the under-ocean plates slip under or over another, the entire water column above is lifted up. This is how tsunamis form.

From the time I was a child I always heard about how California was in danger of a major earthquake. They have had dozens of smaller ones, but to date not "The Big One". The threat is due to a crustal plate crack known as the San Andreas Fault. Before they cause a disaster the adjacent plates move and create incredible stored-up energy.

Geologists believe this pent-up San Andres Fault energy could be released in a massive quake event sooner than later. The extent of destruction in such major cities as Los Angeles and San Diego could be catastrophic. Millions of lives could be lost. The 2015 movie "San Andreas" should scare the crap out of anyone living in Southern California. It may have been understated!

Northern California had one of the worst earthquake

disasters in modern history. In 1906, a large quake wiped out eighty-percent of the standing structures in San Francisco and killed three-thousand people.

Buildings today throughout California are built to specific "earthquake codes". They are supposed to resist even strong earthquakes. But when "The Big One" hits no amount of special construction will avoid massive destruction.

Every day, small earthquakes occur somewhere on earth. If you have never experienced one yourself, it is pretty scary. One night while in bed, during the time my wife and I lived in Hawaii, we felt the entire house move up and down and side to side. It lasted less than a minute, and caused no damage, but to say we were terrified would be an understatement! It is a very weird feeling,

In April 2024 a relatively small earthquake centered under Lebanon, northern New Jersey, caused very little damage but a disproportionate amount of panic! Cell-phone videos of frightened people running around the streets of New York City give a frightening hint of the chaotic panic that would occur in the event of a REAL catastrophe. The problem was not the severity of the quake but its rarity.

It is amusing to note that on that very same day Southern California suffered THREE earthquakes each much stronger than the one that freaked out New Yorkers. No one there even blinked! Small earthquakes are extremely common in that area. Everyone keeps their collective fingers crossed hoping they will never live to see the inevitable "Big One".

Earthquakes are rated in strength by a one to ten scale, known as the Mercalli Scale. Is a 3.0 scale quake about the same as a 5.0? Very far from it. The scale goes by tenths, 3.0, 3.1, 3.2, etc. Each tenth equals five times greater destructive potential than the previous tenth! Thus a 5.0 quake is 100 times stronger than a 3.0. This fact is easily overlooked when we read the news of quakes of various intensities.

One quake in March 2011 had the potential to destroy all life on earth. The quake itself was bad enough, but the collateral damage was almost earth-destroying. A 9.1 strength quake occurred under the ocean off the east coast of Japan. It generated a one-hundred-foot high tsunami. This wall of water crashed into the Fukushima Nuclear Power Plant. The resulting damage came extremely close to causing a total plant meltdown and a potential global catastrophe.

Historically there have been many devastating earthquakes. In 2023 a quake in Turkiye killed an estimated 80,000 people. Chinese history records a quake in 1556 that killed 830,000! A quake there in 1920 killed 273,000. More recently, in 1976, 655,000 Chinese died in a yet another massive quake.

Closer to home a quake in Haiti killed 346,000 in 2010. In 1960 the most powerful quake ever recorded, a 9.5, devastated Chile.

Other notable massive quakes occurred in Russia in 1952, Alaska in 1964 and Sumatra in 2004.

Massive earthquakes have been known to cause a minor shift in the earth's axis, and actually slightly shorten the length of a day!

As mentioned above, earthquakes under the sea are a major cause of tsunamis. The worst tsunami ever recorded was caused by a 9.1 magnitude quake on the ocean floor near Sumatra in December 2024. Over 230,000 people were killed across fourteen countries. It had taken less than fifteen minutes for the ninety-foot wave to first reach land.

Aside from earthquakes there are two other ways a tsunami can be created. One is minor, one not so. Coastal cliffs erode and crash into the ocean below. The waves created are never extremely large, but anyone in a nearby bay in a boat could easily be swamped.

The most dangerous of all tsunamis originate in outer space. The dinosaurs and most other life were extinguished by a large meteor hitting the water near Yucatan, Mexico, sixty-six million years ago. Any city-size meteor striking any body of water anywhere on earth can create a "splash" that would generate a massive tsunami killing millions. Fortunately this is not a common occurrence.

We only need to look back at recent past history, to Indonesia and Japan, to get some idea of what devastation a relatively small tsunami can cause.

The general cause of most tsunamis is the up-thrusting of earth's crustal plates as they slide and grind across each other in the endless re-positioning of earth's land masses.

Sometimes when a crustal plate beneath the ocean slips by another, creating an earthquake, there is little or no uplifting of either crustal plate and no tsunami results. When the plates slide side by side, you'll get an earthquake, but no big tsunami. If one plate thrusts upward a bit, however, you create a tsunami.

But what if, just once, and for whatever reason, one plate decides to blast almost straight up a long way into the miles-high column of water above it. The resultant tsunami would surely equal or far exceed Noah's flood! One author has even suggested that civilization's only hope is to build huge waterproof ships to ride out an end-of-the-world tsunami.

Another possible cause of a mighty tidal wave is the collapse of a large chunk of solidified lava into the ocean. For example, the lava shelf being added to daily off Hawaii Island by Kilauea Volcano is a perfect example. A thick layer of solidified lava forms above the water as the lava oozes past the edge of the island. It usually collapses after it projects a few hundred yards or so from shore. In theory it could extend much further. In that case, it is not a matter of if but when it cracks off and makes a massive splash. How large a wave will occur? No one knows, but some scientists believe it could be catastrophic over a wide area.

Of course huge volcanic eruptions such as Krakatoa, with water rushing in to fill the hole left behind after a few cubic miles of terra firma are sent skyward, can create unimaginably high waves that can travel entirely around the globe.

Lastly, should a major piece of space rock, asteroid or comet or whatever, strike water and not strike land (which is quite likely since most of earth's surface is water), the resultant tidal wave is incalculable. It would simply be a matter of how big a piece of rock, at what angle it struck and where.

For those who would find a biblical reference relevant, let's look at Matthew 24: 36-39. It speaks of the *suddenness* of the last great flood:

"No one knows about that day or hour, not even the angels in heaven nor the Son but only the Father. As it was in the days of Noah so it will be at the coming of the Son of Man. For in the days before the flood people were eating and drinking and giving in marriage up to the day Noah entered the ark. And they knew nothing about what would happen until the flood came and took them all away. That is how it will be at the coming of the Son of Man."

HURRICANES AND CYCLONES:

There is a prevailing school of thought among "climate gurus" that all storms are much more frequent and powerful than they were at the start of the horrible Industrial Revolution starting in the late 1800s. Statistically significant scientific data across many centuries does not appear to support this theory,

Since the scale of intensity, the "Category" of a storm was created, it rated wind by category from one through five. A Cat5 storm was considered to be the ultimate in strength and devastation.

Because of the belief that these storms are getting even more intense, we now have considered creating a shiny new designation: "Category Six"! We have not had one yet, but stay tuned. Apparently one is expected in a neighborhood near you sooner than later. Is this perhaps simply "Climate Crisis" propaganda?

In 2023 only a single hurricane made landfall in the United States. It hit the west coast of Florida. The resulting twelve-foot-high storm surge caused massive damage inland. Flooding caused by the rain associated with a hurricane almost always causes much more damage than the wind itself.

Hurricanes, cyclones and typhoons are massive wind and rain events. The only difference between the three names is the geographic location where they occur.

These storms also spin in different directions depending upon location. They are called "**cyclones**" when they occur over the South Pacific and Indian Oceans. They are referred to as "**typhoons**" when they develop in the Northwest Pacific Ocean. Storms formed in the Atlantic Ocean, as well as in the Central and Eastern Pacific Ocean, are called "**hurricanes**".

In the Northern Hemisphere storms spin counterclockwise. In the Southern Hemisphere they spin in a clockwise direction. This is due to something called the "Coriolis Effect", an explanation of which is far beyond the scope of this Chapter.

There have been some horrific storms in recorded history.

My wife and I often visited Hawaii and eventually moved there for five wonderful years. On one vacation we spent several nights on the island of Kauai at a hotel called The Cocoa Palms. We arrived without a reservation.

There were no rooms available, EXCEPT The Presidential Suit on the upper level. This hotel is where Elvis Presley filmed the 1961 film "Blue Hawaii". Of course he stayed in The Presidential Suite.

The desk clerk for whatever reason gave us a bargain rate. The opulence of that suite cannot be adequately described! The bathroom sinks were genuine giant clam shells a few feet across! There were countless expensive features and wall display cases. Overall the room looked more as a small museum than a bedroom!

Five years after that visit, in September 1992, a very rare Category 4 hurricane struck the same Island of Kauai It was named Iniki. It's peak wind was clocked at 143 miles per hour.

Pictures of the aftermath were beyond belief. Not one single leaf remained on any tree or bush anywhere on the island. The storm turned a tropical paradise into a barren wasteland. Virtually every structure on the island was leveled. Six people died and many were injured. At a cost of $1.8 billion to rebuild it was one of the most expensive storms in American history.

The Cocoa Palms Resort sustained massive damage, and never reopened. It was very sad to visit the dilapidated remains of the buildings during our later tenure in Hawaii.

Because of the tropical rain and temperature, the vegetation on Kauai recovered quickly. When we visited the island a few years later one would be hard pressed to remember Iniki's devastation. That is, except for a bizarre situation.

Apparently almost every household on Kauai raised chickens. Iniki freed them all. The 2000 movie "Chicken

Run" on steroids! To this day, *almost a half-million* feral chickens are encountered literally everywhere across the island! They have become a primary tourist attraction.

TORNADOES AND WATER SPOUTS:

Tornadoes are far more dangerous than hurricanes. Hurricanes are tracked for weeks and monitored closely. Satellite radar tracks them continuously. Special airplanes fly into them. More recently drones are employed. Landfall can be predicted with some degree of accuracy, usually within a few miles. The intensity of the hurricane is continuously monitored.

Not so with tornadoes. Meteorologists can determine the "possible" development from within a strong storm system. They can provide a "best guess" as to where one might touch down. Until one drops from the shy and touches the ground, no one can predict exactly where that might occur.

Once on the ground the track of the tornado is very erratic and unpredictable. The actual area in contact with the ground is hard to determine except by suicide-jockey storm-trackers in cars!

While residents often have many hours to flee a hurricane, tornado victims often only have minutes. No time to escape by car. Just crowd everyone into a bathtub and pray.

Tornado tracks can be really strange. There are well documented cases of tornadoes flattening entire towns, but leaving a few houses, or even just one single home standing with no damage whatsoever!

Tornadoes have their own "scale" just as do hurricanes. In 1971 a University of Chicago Professor named Ted Fujita collaborated with a climatologist named Allen Pearson. They devised a scale of tornado intensity. Until 2007 it was called "The Fujita Scale". It rated tornadoes from F0 through F6 depending upon damage done to structures and vegetation. F0 started at 73 miles per hour, mild, through F5 which ended at 318 mph.

The Fujita Scale was refined by meteorologists in 2007. They created the scale used today, "The Enhanced Fujita Scale". The range of EF0-EF5 also takes into account a tornado's path width and length. Ninety-nine percent of all tornadoes are EF3 or less in intensity.

I have actually experienced two tornadoes, but have actually never been in one. Back in the 90s I was driving through central Texas and came upon a large area that had been wiped out just the day before by a very powerful tornado. As far as the eye could see on either side of the road there were hundreds of destroyed homes.

The second was an actual sighting. I was driving south in central Ohio back in the '60s. Off to my right, perhaps a mile away, a funnel cloud was obviously touching down. Quite a scary sight. Later on the news I heard that it had touched down in a schoolyard, but no injuries were reported.

Whether tornadoes are worse today than in the past is subject to debate. It seems not. By far the most destructive tornado in United States history occurred in 1925. In mid-March it tore a wide path across southern Missouri, Illinois and Indiana. Although not nearly as populated an area as today, it killed 751 and injured thousands. Known as "The Tri-State Tornado", it is the second largest in history anywhere on earth.

In fact, seven of the eight worst recorded tornadoes in American history all happened *before* 1948. The earliest of these was in Natchez, Mississippi in 1840. A big twister hit St. Louis, Missouri in 1896. Besides the 1925 biggie, there were destructive tornadoes in 1908, two in 1936, and one in 1947.

If you Google the twenty-five worst tornadoes in America's history ALL occurred before 1955! Perhaps today we offer citizens a slightly larger window of escape, minimizing deaths. The most recent large American tornado was in Joplin, Missouri in 2011.

Tornadoes do not always occur as a single entity. In 1974, the United States recorded the worst outbreak ever. One-hundred-forty-eight (148) tornadoes touched down in thirteen different states on the same day! The most destructive were in Alabama and Tennessee. Eighty-six were killed and about a thousand injured. Fortunately only a few of the twisters were really large.

Tornadoes are actually a very common American weather phenomenon. There are over one thousand each year in the United States. Texas gets the most, followed by Mississippi, Alabama and Kansas. While property damage is often extensive, deaths are relatively few.

Ninety-nine percent (99%) of all tornadoes worldwide occur in America. They are caused by warm wet air from the Gulf of Mexico hitting cool dry air from the Rocky

Mountains or the High Southwestern Desert. These same exact conditions exist nowhere else on earth.

Although almost limited exclusively to the United States, a few occur elsewhere. In fact they are recorded on every continent except Antarctica. History's worst recorded tornado hit Adulator and Asturias in Bangladesh in 1989. It killed an estimated 1,300 and injured 12,000. No fewer than 80,000 were left homeless.

The third largest tornado worldwide was just sixteen years earlier, also in Bangladesh. This one killed almost seven hundred and injured thousands. Bangladesh seems to be a tornado magnet. As recently as 1977, yet another killed over five hundred.

In 1951 in Sicily, Italy, a very rare double-tornado formed a waterspout, then traveled inland killing around five hundred. Back in 1555, a rare tornado hit the Island of Malta killing six hundred.

Water spouts are tornadoes over the open ocean, seas, and bays. They are seen by passengers on boats and by observers from shore. They seldom travel inland. However, in February 2024 a water spout came ashore in south Florida. It did some major damage. No injuries were reported.

FLOODS:

By far the greatest danger that mother nature can conjure up is FLOODING. This is most often the result of passing hurricanes, typhoons and cyclones, and can be very widespread. A steady prolonged rain can be an equal problem. Short but violent thunderstorms can cause damaging flooding, but generally only in a local area.

When we think about hurricanes we envision houses being blown away and people being crushed to death by debris. In fact, although the heavy wind can cause injuries in various ways, there are relatively few deaths from the wind itself. The vast majority of hurricane-relate deaths are from drowning in the resulting floods.

Floods can actually be caused by a number of natural forces. Huge amounts of rain from a hurricane, or from any heavy rainstorm, can cause flooding. Hurricanes can push water onshore, called "storm surge", causing inundation of low lying areas.

Melting mountain snow can cause flooding. Ice jams in rivers can cause water to overflow their banks flooding surrounding areas.

Ocean water pushed ashore by an approaching hurricane can inundate coastal cities. In a 500 year period from 1074 to 1570 the city of Rome, Italy suffered ten such events killing 100,000 citizens.

In 1900 in Galveston, Texas, a fifteen-foot storm surge drowned 8,000 residents. This was twenty-percent of the total Galveston population at the time!

Surprisingly, some of the worst deaths-by-flood have been caused by dam or levee failures. This cause of flooding has more than Mother Nature to blame. Human built dams can be destroyed by earthquakes. Dams can also be destroyed because they were not built properly to withstand a worst-case scenario.

There have been some huge natural dam failure disasters. The most famous in America is referred to as "The Johnstown Flood". The South Fork Dam collapsed in 1889, and 2,200 people drowned. The city of Johnstown, Pennsylvania was almost totally destroyed. There have been about a dozen other dam related floods in the United States over the years, but none killed more than a few hundred unlucky individuals.

China, on the other hand, has seen an unbelievable dam disaster. In 1975 massive rain from Typhoon Nina caused The Banquiao Dam in Henan to fail. It is believed that as many as 250,000 may have drowned, though "only" about 150,000 were confirmed.

In 1979 in Gujarat, India, the Machchhu II Dam collapsed and killed an estimated 5,000. This dam was actually built in a dry region essentially for irrigation and was not designed for the massive rain that flooded it.

River flooding is a very different matter. China has seen four major disasters relating to their two great rivers, The Yellow River and The Yangtze River. In 1887 The Yellow River flood killed at least *two million souls*! In a historic seven-year period, from 1931 to 1938, three additional river floods killed over *five* million! That's seven million dead in one generation.

The United States is far from immune from river flooding. Our Missouri River and Mississippi River are the major problems. Although loss of life from river floods is historically low, property damage can be enormous. In 1927 the Mississippi flooded 27,000 square miles in seven states. Drowning's totaled 246. Damages totaled $4 billion.

Midwest floods in 2011 in the Missouri River basin inundated 4,000 homes, killed 48 and cost $30.2 billion in damages.

Is mother nature alone in the flood-creation category? Not according a scholarly article I read recently. It was postulated that if everyone who has a toilet flushed it at exactly the same time it would collapse the entire waste-water collection system countrywide and result in massive local flooding. Was the author actually serious, or drunk?

EXCESSIVE HEAT:

In the unlikely event that we actually do have runaway heating across the planet, humankind will have to find a creative way to survive, or perish. To date, there have been just a few prolonged hot periods in localized areas that did actually cause many deaths.

In 1901, in the United States, 9,500 died. Of course, this was before we had widespread air-conditioning in our homes. Fourteen years later in France it was reported that 41,000 deaths were heat related. More recently, in 1936, 5,000 died from heat related issues in Canada and America.

The worst recorded mass heat casualties in the last two decades were in 2003 when a reported 72,000 died throughout Europe! Then in 2010 Russia reported deaths of up to 56,000 from a prolonged heat wave. If in fact we do ever have nature-induced severe global warming, it can be expected that these numbers will be exceeded.

In April 2024 a severe heat wave occurred across much of Asia. In Thailand thirty died from heat stroke. In Myanmar temperatures rose as high as 45 degrees Centigrade (113 degrees F!). In The Philippines thousands of schools were forced to close. In Bangladesh 33,000 students stayed home for weeks as temperatures there approached 110 degrees F. These areas are all relatively humid, and lack widespread air-conditioning, This trend began in 2023 and shows no sign of stopping.

Global Warming as such does appear to be accelerating. The cause is difficult to establish scientifically, See Chapter TEN for a full discussion of this topic.

WILDFIRES:

There is no question that warming temperatures have dried out forests and grasslands. They apparently are more susceptible to wildfires than in the past.

In February 2024 a massive wildfire consumed over a million acres in the northern panhandle of Texas.

In August 2023, a massive wildfire totally destroyed the historic coastal town of Lahaina on the Hawaiian Island of Maui. Over one-hundred were confirmed dead. The cost to rebuild this town will be in the billions and take years. The fire was apparently caused by a downed power line.

In 2023 and 2024 millions of acres of "bush fires" have devastated southern Australia. Many millions of animals were killed, including countless koalas and kangaroos.

In Canada over that same period, millions of acres of forest have burned. Above ground the forests suffered total devastation. Beyond the loss of trees, so called "zombie fires" continue to burn and spread *underground* beyond the perimeter of the initial fires. Roots and other vegetable matter burns during the winter under the ground and the snow pack above. Come Spring, it is expected that many more new fires will be ignited above ground by the zombie fires an endless cycle.

The existential threat from wildfires is not the loss of life. Although there are often massive property losses, the number of deaths is general very low. The biggest threat is from the emissions of particulates and gasses that enter the atmosphere. It is impossible to quantify these emissions, but clearly they may be far greater than those created during our very useful Industrial Revolution. There is no practical way possible to compare wildfire emissions (as well as volcanic emissions) to emissions from fossil fueled power plants, automobiles, backyard barbecues, cigarette smoke, and cow farts.

There is a very real threat of large-scale fires from enemy attacks. During WWII we dropped incendiary bombs on Japan. We even tried dropping live bats that had tiny attached incendiary devices! A determined enemy could start tens of thousands of fires and in theory destroy much of our country.

The recent influx of illegal aliens and their potential terror cells makes this ugly scenario more likely. A few hundred pyromaniacs could coordinate nationwide, setting massive fires at strategic locations. This could overwhelm our containment resources. Not a comforting thought.

A firestorm is a blaze so hot and intense that it not only reduces physical matter to ash but it also literally eats up the atmosphere. Bye bye oxygen, bye bye life. Every so often we have a massive blaze in a forest somewhere that can level tens of thousands of acres, destroy homes, and kill wildlife and a few humans who didn't get out of the way fast enough. A firestorm does not always happen, but it can. Here again, let's play "what if".

Should a nuclear exchange occur, the resultant firestorm could well be its most destructive feature. But it would not necessarily take a nuclear war to fry the planet. If the massive storms predicted by some "pole shifters" were to occur globally, lightning alone could set enough fires to toast us all (or at least suffocate us all) in massive firestorms.

We also have to contend with our sworn mortal Islamist enemies. They hope to eliminate "The Big Satan." It is known that they are seriously working on plans to send out just a hundred or so trained fire-bombers across our land. They would be "heavily armed" with a BIC lighter and perhaps a can or two of gasoline! That is all they would need to cause chaos.

Their mission? To torch hundreds of millions of acres of American forests and grasslands simultaneously. This would create firestorms so unimaginable that total victory over the infidels will be assured. What is scary about this plot is its simplicity of execution and its potential to destroy America.

OCEAN CURRENTS:

"Ocean currents" are distinct cohesive rivers of water flowing within and on the ocean. The best known is The Gulf Stream. They play **the key role** in the regulation of our climate. In fact, they have by far the greatest potential effect on Climate Change. Humans can never compete.

There are two basic types of currents. Ninety percent are "deep water currents". These are driven by temperature and salinity that together govern the pull that gravity has on them. The other ten percent are "surface currents" that move through the top quarter-mile of the ocean.

Winds can account for currents in about the top three-hundred feet. Lunar-caused tidal forces also affect currents. So do earthquakes and storms. The spin of the earth itself has a major effect. **Currents are a complex dynamic and are far beyond the capability of human intervention.**

Currents carry heat, oxygen, nutrients and critters. Some are classified as "warm", others "cold". Currents to the west of continents and from the polar regions tend to be cold. Those from the equatorial regions are warm.

They can be truly massive in length, dwarfing terrestrial rivers. The largest current is the "Antarctic Circumpolar Current" which actually connects the Atlantic, Pacific and Indian Oceans! It is also extremely strong, moving one-hundred-fifty cubic meters of water per second.

We are a water planet. You can actually turn a desk globe in such a way that the half you are looking at is virtually land-free. Almost three-quarters of earth's surface is water. The oceans contain all but a tiny three-percent of all the water that exists on the entire surface of the planet.

Oceanographers classify our oceans into five major "Gyres". These are the North and South Atlantic, North and South Pacific, and Indian Ocean gyres.

Each one of these five separate and distinct oceans is defined by "boundary currents". On the western side there is a strong narrow current, "the Western Boundary Current". On the east side is a wider weaker current, "The Eastern Boundary Current".

The entire subject of the interplay between currents and their effect on global temperatures are the subject for a PhD curriculum, very far outside the scope of this Chapter. The subject is extremely complex.

Suffice it to say that scientists are becoming concerned to learn that overall the oceans and currents are not behaving as they have in the recent past. No one is quite sure why. They do believe that there is a one-thousand-year cycle and that we may be entering a new one.

Greatly oversimplified, the basic dynamic process is for warm surface currents to carry less dense water away from equatorial areas towards both poles. Simultaneously, cold deep ocean currents carry more dense water from the poles to the equatorial regions.

The greatest existential threat at the moment relates to The Gulf Stream. The melting of glacial and sea ice is reducing the salinity of the ocean. This is contributing to the disruption of the entire ocean/current cycle relationship and could actually cause the Gulf Stream to greatly diminish or disappear entirely! This would cause all of Europe to enter another ice age, killing millions.

While ocean dynamics are not an immediate existential threat such as super-volcanoes, or nuclear war, over the coming decades it could be the single problem most responsible for destroying civilization. **And there is absolutely nothing we can do about it.**

ROGUE WAVES:

These baddies are only an existential threat to vessels on the high seas. Ocean liners, cargo ships and fishing vessels are all prime targets.

Do you recall the 1972 movie "The Poseidon Adventure"? A large cruise ship is hit by a massive rogue wave and overturned! It was a fun movie, but the concept seemed impossible. The movie was, however, based on a real event thirty years earlier.

In 1942 the famous HMS Queen Mary ocean liner was hit by a ninety-foot high rogue wave. It came extremely close to capsizing. Had this wave been slightly larger, a real possibility, the loss of lives would have made the Titanic disaster look like a pool party.

Rogue waves hitting ocean vessels are a rare event. In modern times there are only seven recorded instances.

In 2022, the Viking Polaris was struck, causing multiple injuries and one death. The ship did not overturn.

In December 2023, a relatively small cruise ship, the MS Maud was hit by a succession of thirty-six-foot storm-driven waves. The ship came dangerously close to capsizing. The many cell-phone videos available on the internet would give me pause to ever set foot on anything larger than a row boat on a local pond!

Actually, many years ago, I was in a rowboat bass fishing on a large lake in upstate New York. A violent wind-storm came out of nowhere. No warning. Although my buddy and I were only a few hundred yards from shore the frantic trip to safety was terrifying. It was more so for me because at the time I couldn't swim a stroke! And there were no life rings on board. Obviously we were not Boy Scouts.

Because the odds of a rogue wave sinking an ocean liner are very low, any plans to take a cruise should be left on your calendar. Just not on mine.

I see pictures of the newly launched "Icon of the Seas". This monster is basically a floating city. At any one time over ten thousand people could be on board. I hope the engineers who designed this ship took into account when all ten thousand crowd to one side looking at a pod of whales. Simultaneously, a hundred foot rogue wave hits the opposite side head on. Flip time? Just looking at pictures of that ship it appears to be sort of top-heavy. Nothing could get me to board the Icon. Remember, The Titanic was unsinkable. It sank.

THE OZONE LAYER:

Ozone is an invisible gas. Solar radiation creates it in our upper atmosphere. It forms a barrier that protects us from the sun's deadly ultraviolet radiation. Sufficient exposure to UV rays can kill humans. If there was no ozone layer above-ground life on earth would be impossible. If the ozone layer were to disappear completely, deaths from skin cancer and blindness from cataracts would increase exponentially.

Starting in 1928, an inexpensive, colorless compressible gas called chlorofluorocarbon gas (CFC) was invented and used in those newfangled machines called commercial refrigerators. Unless you are as old or older than I, somewhat unlikely, you would not remember "ice boxes".

Before CFC-cooled home kitchen refrigerators were affordable and commonplace, perishable food was kept cold in a large metal case with an ice chamber at the top. They were called, not surprisingly, "Ice Boxes".

One of my most vivid childhood memories is taking my little red wagon to Grogan's Ice House in Rockaway Beach, Queens, New York. There, my grandfather would buy two large blocks of ice from an ice-storage warehouse. We'd wheel it a mile or so home to my grandma's house, and he'd put the blocks in the chamber at the top. Those were the Halcyon Days of Yore.

In the 1970s, it was discovered that we were losing our invaluable ozone protection layer at an alarming rate. Fortunately scientists discovered the reason. The chlorine component of CFCs was destroying our ozone.
Modern industrialized societies had invented spray-cans! Starting around 1950 in everything from deodorants to shaving cream to whipped cream and paint were shot out of cans using compressed CFCs. No one thought twice about releasing it into the atmosphere.

With uncommon international cooperation worldwide, CFCs were eventually 100% banned in all countries by

2010. Better late than never. Industrialized countries had already ceased use by 2000. The ozone layer immediately slowly began to recover. The so called "ozone hole" got smaller. Life on earth was saved.

Although we can manufacture ozone here on the surface, it would be too costly to create enough ozone to matter in a remediation attempt. The sun's radiation creates it for us in just the right place. Even if we could, injecting it into the atmosphere exactly where needed would be prohibitively expensive and mechanically almost impossible. The ozone we do produce is used primarily as a bactericide in the purification of bottled water.

We replaced CFCs with HFCs, hydrofluorocarbons. These do not contain the chlorine that was destroying the ozone layer. HFCs are, however, a potentially bigger problem than CO_2 as far as global warming is concerned. I'm not sure why our focus is always on CO_2 as THE existential threat.

Even though the ozone hole has shrunk, it is estimated that it will take until 2040 to return to pre-industrial levels. The sun continuously creates ozone, but we still have CFCs in older appliances and in landfills that leak out and slow the healing process.

The use of CFCs is a prime example of modern technology creating unexpected collateral damage. This is the great fear of many scientists as it relates to various "Climate Change" remediation proposals. We might find a magic cure for global warming that turns out to be a global death sentence.

POLE SHIFTS:

Geologic records have convinced scientists that the earth's axis wobbles over a twelve-thousand year cycle. It is a slow, harmless wobble. It is the reason that the "north pole star" and "south pole star" differ in their positions over time. Directing a line north or south from anywhere on earth places different stars in the "pole" position. A powerful telescope can detect this change literally daily.

There is one serious school of thought among geologists, (not a conspiracy theory) that beyond the normal wobble the magnetic poles could suffer COMPLETE REVERSAL. Geologists have determined that such a total magnetic field reversal averages one every 360,000 years. None have happened since humans evolved. In fact, none have happened in 760,000 years and scientists are not certain why. One could conclude that we are 400,000 years overdue!

This is an extinction-level event, an existential threat on steroids. There is a wealth of scientific papers discussing this possibility. There is no consensus on the potential timing for the total destruction of civilization, but it could happen at any time without warning. Stay tuned.

Whether it is a massive super-volcano, a massive tsunami, a massive earthquake, a massive hurricane or a massive firestorm, the operative word is "massive". In theory any of these could occur at any time. They could occur tomorrow, next month, or in a thousand years. Or never. The odds of any one happening tomorrow are probably pretty low. But so were the odds of the USA Olympic hockey team beating the Russians!

Of all the Mother Nature's bitchiness described above only one *really* worries me. Perhaps it is my relative geographic proximity, not that it would matter. **<u>The Yellowstone super-volcano is earth's greatest imminent natural existential threat.</u>**

We can only live day to day as best we can. No one is promised tomorrow.

In Sean Hannity's daily words, "Let not your heart be troubled." It isn't easy.

CHAPTER EIGHT

BROKEN EDUCATION

"The power and salvation of a people lie in its intelligentsia." Anton Chekhov, writer, physician, (1860-1904).

"I am always doing that which I cannot do, in order that I may learn how to do it." Pablo Picasso, artist, (1881-1973).

"The more things you read the more things you will know." Theodore Geisel, (Dr. Seuss), (1904-1991).

"Human history becomes more and more a race between education and catastrophe." H. G. Wells, (1866-1946).

"The cultivation of the mind is a kind of food supplied for the soul of man." Marcus Tellies Cicero, Roman lawyer, (106 BC – 43 BC).

"When I get a little money I buy books, and if any is left I buy food." Desiderius Erasmus. educator, theologian, and philosopher, (1466-1536).

"I will study and get ready and some day my chance will come." Abraham Lincoln, 16th President of The United States, (1809-1865).

"The secret of success in life is for a man to be ready for his opportunity when it comes." Benjamin Disraeli,

(1804-1881).

"Free people read freely." From a lapel button distributed by my local library, authored by The American Library Association, Freedom To Read Foundation.

"What the mind can conceive and believe men can achieve." Andrew Carnegie, (1835-1919).

"The human brain is the most powerful tool in the universe, but it comes without an operating manual." Buckminster Fuller, (1895-1983).

"....pain, loss and failure, the three greatest teachers in life." George Murdoch, (Tyrus), (1973-   ).

"Tyrants must infantilize their people to maintain their hold." Aristotle, (384BC-322BC).

"In the new order socialism will triumph by first capturing the culture by infiltration of *school*s, *universities*, churches, and the media by transforming the consciousness of society." Antonio Gramsci, Italian Communist, (1891-1937).

Education today is a very serious existential threat to our freedoms and to the very fabric of America. It is not by accident.

There was a great movie from 2006 called "IDIOCRACY". It was intended to be a comedy. Perhaps unintentionally, it closely describes where America is headed. Perhaps we already have arrived!

I choose to open this Chapter with an article I read some years ago in the *Hunterdon County Democrat* newspaper (New Jersey). It shocks me to this day. It gives excerpts from a 1905 EIGHTH GRADE local public school exam. Passing this exam with 90% correct was required to move on to High School. Almost everyone passed.

I seriously doubt whether any eighth grader today could answer a single question correctly. In fact, acing this exam would be a challenge for most college seniors, even post-graduates! This is only a small part of the test, and was not chosen to illustrate only the more difficult questions.

CIVICS: 1. What is a census and when will the next one be taken? 2. Name three Constitutional restrictions on the powers of Congress.

HISTORY: 1. What were the terms of the Treaty of Paris in 1783? 2. What is the Monroe Doctrine and under what circumstances was it set forth? 3. Describe the Battle of Gettysburg.

ARITHMETIC: 1.What number subtracted 88 times from 80.005 will leave 0.013 as a remainder? 2. Divide $4.14 between Thomas, Richard and Henry in such a way that Henry shall receive 3 cents for every 5 cents that Thomas gets, and Richard shall receive 2 cents for every 5 cents that Henry gets. 3. A man agrees to dig a cellar 30 feet long, 24 feet wide, and 6 feet deep. What percentage of the work remains after he has removed 144 cubic yards?

GEOGRAPHY: 1. Locate the Philippine Islands, name the

two largest islands, the capital, and the two leading exports. 2. Where are the following: Saigon, Budapest, Niger, Scandinavia, Bass, Hood, Winnipeg and Hatteras?

SPELLING: Words read by the teacher to be spelled included: Cincinnati, malleable, chagrin, and mischievous.

PHYSIOLGY: 1.How is bodily heat regulated? 2. Name the organ and function of respiration.

PENMANSHIP: 1.Write all the small letters, all the capitals, and all the figures. 2. Write the small letters and capitals in cursive.

GRAMMAR: 1. Students are given a stanza from a poem and asked to select and classify all of the clauses. 2. Write four sentences illustrating four case relations of the pronoun. 3. Use the infinitive in five sentences, each illustrating a different construction.

READING: Students are given five stanzas from a poem. They must read it aloud, give the title and author, and explain what the poem is about.

AGAIN, THIS IS AN *EIGHTH GRADE* FINAL EXAM!

Can you even imagine the depth of the curriculum behind an exam this comprehensive? We've come a long way in 119 years, progressively backwards!

I was a WWII child, having been born in 1938. I attended Public School #139 in Brooklyn, New York. It happened to have been the same school my mother attended decades earlier! I attended from kindergarten through eighth grade, before attending the then-academically-acclaimed famous Erasmus Hall High School, also my mom's.

In PS139, every day we said the Pledge of Allegiance. At least once a week we sung The Star Spangled Banner. We saluted the American Flag. The academic focus was on cursive writing, spelling, grammar, reading, geography, American history, arithmetic, elementary economics, civics, and in later grades language of our choice including Latin.

I was taught the tools of good citizenship.

Music appreciation was taught around the third grade and thereafter. In the later years we had "shop", and learned all manner of creative manual skills. We were challenged to think and be creative.

We had an hour a day of play-yard time. We played a variety of competitive games, the kind where the result is a winner and a loser. One gains a certain understanding of life when not accepting a Participation Award for finishing last! I occasionally finished last. It taught me valuable lessons.

I have no recollection of being asked if I was happy being a boy, or by what pronoun I wished to be addressed. I probably still believed storks dropped off babies! I knew girls were different but I had no idea how and could not have cared less. I never heard of the Kama Sutra!

We were mixed whites and blacks, Christians and Jews, Irish, Italians, Russians, Poles and everywhere else imaginable. NO ONE CARED. We all got along. Fights were not along ethnic or religious lines. There were <u>no</u>

"lines".

We were just kids growing up in a free society and collectively being scared shitless until WWII came to an end. I vividly remember "Air Raid Drills" where we all had to hide under our desks and face away from the windows. Ah, those were the good old days! Viva Oppenheimer.

I absolutely LOVED America!!! My father was a WWI Navy veteran. His sister's husband was wounded in Italy in WWI and had a shoulder wound that never healed. My family were all proud Americans. I knew someday I would be a soldier and I became one.

At 86 I am a proud member of American Legion Post #66 in Green Valley, Arizona. Our members are all loyal Americans happy to have served to help preserve our precious freedoms. Many carry the physical and mental scars of battle. All are underappreciated heroes.

By the time I got to High School I could read and comprehend any adult material, could add, subtract, multiply and divide in my head, and could write an intelligent essay. I could name every state capital, locate any state on a blank map, and locate most countries on a blank globe. So could all my friends.

I knew the names of dozens of American Indian Chiefs and their respective tribes. I knew about the Founding Fathers, and had been exposed to the Declaration of Independence, The Constitution and The Bill of Rights. I knew who my state and local representatives were.

I understood slavery, abolition and the race-relations

advances on which we were just beginning to work. As far as my home town of Brooklyn, New York, Jackie Robinson was the turning point. (No thanks to Harold "Pee Wee" Reese the Brooklyn Dodgers' openly-racist shortstop.)

I was no different in my knowledge than were most of my schoolmates. Back then if you were not up to par in the fourth grade (or any grade) you were embarrassed to be required to repeat it. Some repeated twice. Some were shaving before they got to High School!

As medieval as it might sound, up until the fifth grade we even had a "dunce corner". Here, one would sit, for whatever transgression, with a conical hat on one's head. Embarrassing, yes, but I don't recall anyone committing suicide over it. Even the victims often found it amusing.

There was even an occasional well-deserved whack on the ass with a ruler! Those were the forgotten days that produced proud Americans and good hard-working citizens.

My beautiful wife of forty years attended public school in rural New Jersey. Her education, two decades later, was not nearly as comprehensive as mine. Her eighth grade exam, from that same New Jersey school was unrecognizable by comparison to the earlier version above. She suffered through "New Math", and by the time she graduated from High School she was truly innumerate!

Fortunately "New Math", along with the equally-failed "Ebonics" experiment, was deep-sixed decades ago.

Fast forward to today. I have two daughters who are school teachers. One teaches first through third grade. The other is a college professor. My wife's brother, his wife, and their son and daughter are all schoolteachers. They are all under the all-knowing thumb of the George Soros influenced United Teacher's Union.

Today our schools turn out mindless, unhappy, confused children who keep psychiatrists busy and rich. One (of many) new branches of psychiatry focuses on treating "climate change anxiety". Others treat "gender confusion". Irreversible gender-altering procedures are becoming commonplace often without parental knowledge.

The internet and social media are the filter through which young people see the world. Last time I checked, social media was not a bastion of truth. Our modern culture is almost totally devoid of moral education. The decline of the two-parent family, horrific education, and a serious lack of moral heroes have led to a culture of anger, hate, and hopelessness.

Our colleges mostly produce clueless left-wing indoctrinated individuals with no ability for critical thinking. Recent anti-Jewish protests are a sad testimony to where we have devolved since WWII. Anti-Christian protests are not far behind.

Shortly after the October 8, 2023 Hamas attack on helpless Jewish citizens, there was an interview with the relative of one of those who was taken hostage. Speaking to a Christian interviewer he ended with the profound warning: "You're next".

For many years, TV has shown "man on the street" random live interviews. The roving reporters ask seemingly ridiculously simple questions: "Who was our first president?" "Who is president today?" "What countries border the United States?" (That one is always a stumper!)

The answers are hilarious and seldom even close to correct! As a follow-up, the reporter will ask: "What do you do for a living?" After identifying Abe Lincoln as our present-day President, the interviewer might expect: "McDonald's burger-flipper"? "Custodian"? "Homeless? Jobless"? "Quit school after third grade"?

Shockingly many reply that are college seniors and post-grads, and not just a few are schoolteachers! Our schools simply turn out masses of mindless clueless morons.

Clearly some manage somehow to slip through the cracks and become aware citizens and successful businesspersons, entrepreneurs, scientists, doctors, lawyers and such. But we have critical shortages in all of these areas. Nurses are in very short supply. Teachers are even more so.

A case in point is the recent proposal by the Teachers Union to greatly reduce the academic requirements of teachers to make up the deficit!

Are you aware that our military, every branch, falls terribly short on recruitment quotas? Sadly, many applicants cannot pass the EXTREMELY EASY basic entrance exams. I've seen copies of it. I recall taking it many years ago and considered it a joke. A well-schooled sixth grader should be able to ace it. We are in deep doo doo. We are no longer the great military power that won WWII. We need tens of thousands of recruits, soon.

Perhaps many of today's real achievers are taught in religious schools, Charter Schools, or home-schooled. Apparently we are intentionally, becoming an Idiocracy. Uninformed individuals, our majority, can be fed false propaganda, especially political. They simply do not possess the critical thinking ability to recognize truth from fiction.

A video recently showed a group of kindergartners repeatedly chanting a slanted political slogan aimed against a particular candidate. They could not possibly have had a clue of the meaning or implication of what they were taught to chant by their trusted teacher. Political indoctrination starts very early in the good old USA. We've learned a lot from China and North Korea.

Critical thinking is simply not taught from kindergarten through college. I was amused by a profound cartoon I saw recently. A corporate Marketing Manager was speaking to his Board of Directors in front of a display sign. He said: "With critical thinking and mathematics so out of fashion our net profits will double!" His sign read: **"FOR A SHORT TIME ONLY: TEN FOR THE PRICE OF A DOZEN!"**

Have the last few generations been "infantilized" as Aristotle cautioned? So it seems.

Low information voters are a serious threat to our American Democracy. Rejection of classic Judeo-Christian values, on which this country was founded, is rampant. Parents who complain about their white children being taught that they are racist, and Black children being taught that they are helpless victims doomed to be failures, are branded

"Domestic Terrorists" and could be subject to arrest.

In 1786 Robert Burns wrote a poem "To A Louse" (don't ask!) His most famous line was: "O wad some pow'r the giftie gie us to see ourselves as others see us." Did you ever wonder how our worldwide allies see our education system? If you get your news from TV stations such as NBC, CBS, ABC, Fox, PBS or CNN, it is unlikely you would ever know what other countries think of our failed education system.

I occasionally check out England's BBC, or Australia's Sky News. They always have an interesting take on all things American, especially politics. I recently watched a PPV show on Peacock that was live from Perth, Australia. It was a **W**orld **W**restling **E**ntertainment (WWE) special.

As a youth, when TV was in its infancy, the World Wrestling *Federation*, WW**F** (which it was known as until the **W**orld **W**ildlife *Fund* got pissy) was one of the very few shows available. Virtually everyone watched these wrestling shows religiously.

Only old poops like me will remember the wrestlers Verne Gagne, Lou Thesz, Bruno Sammartino, Stan Hansen and Antonino Rocca. I never lost my love of watching professional wrestling. The strength and athleticism of these people is beyond understanding, and I find them fascinating to watch to this day. The "story lines" created by the WWE are sheer genius and addictive. I could not care less that it is all scripted.

One story line today involves the son of the late wrestler Dusty Rhodes, Cody Rhodes. Cody's dream was to become

World Champion, something his father never quite attained. He constantly spoke of "finishing his story" of becoming World Wrestling Champion. It was an obsession.

In Australia there is a beloved wrestler and interviewer ring-named Grason Waller (real name Matthew Farrelly). As part of this pay-per-view event Waller interviewed Cody Rhodes about "finishing his story".

Waller joked: "Thanks to your <u>American Education System</u> you'll *never* finish your story!" Of course Rhodes "story" had absolutely nothing to do with his American education or its broken system. It was a very telling comment from a notable celebrity of one of our allies. Our education system apparently is a well-known International joke. **Very sad.**

Cody finished his story on April 7, 2024 by winning the WWE Universal World Championship at "WrestleMania XL" in Philadelphia. That two-night event was actually attended by over 140,000 fans! Apparently I'm not the only one who enjoys pro wrestling!

Even professional athletics in America has been dumbed down. When I was growing up, there were four prestigious football "Bowl" Games: Rose, Sugar, Orange, and Gator. The eight teams with the best winning records qualified to play in them. A season of excellence properly rewarded.

Today there are <u>forty-one</u> bowl games with eighty-two teams qualifying! (Such as the famous "Pop Tart Bowl"). Any crappy team with an equal won-loss record qualifies. This year they ran out of these mediocre teams, so they included a team with a *losing* record!

No longer is merit required in football to be a year-end hero. Mediocrity is equally rewarded. Sadly this is true across all aspects of American culture today. We have gone from a Meritocracy to an Idiocracy in my lifetime.

Can we possibly recover from our horrific education system? Do we not wonder, or care, why we spend vastly more per child on education compared to all other developed countries? Yet we rank far behind China, and behind all other developed countries in every academic discipline.

In a recent study among eighty-one developed countries the United States rated a poor 26th in math achievement. We lag very far behind China, Japan, South Korea, Taiwan, Hong Kong, Macao and most European countries.

South Korea is far ahead of us in technological advancement, followed closely by China. We are not even close.

We spend more per student than almost any country, a staggering $16,000 per year per student from kindergarten through twelfth grade. Korea spends about the same, but achieve far better results. Japan, also far ahead of America, spends about two-thirds as much for much better results. We spend thirty percent more on math studies than the average of all developed countries.

Incredible as it may seem, The American Mathematical Association has declared mathematics to be ***fundamentally racist!*** What is wrong with this entire picture? Our country has slipped into being an "Idiocracy".

The combination of terrible K-12 education and an all-pervasive social media, has left many teenagers drowning in lonely despair. The suicide rate among young teens is appalling. Our kids have stopped living normal lives by constantly watching others live theirs. They never develop a sense of personal reality.

The're taught that they are either oppressors or oppressed. They are taught to question their birth sex. The're not taught America's greatness or to think critically about anything. Most cannot read, write or do math anywhere close to their grade level. They feel minimal self-worth and meaninglessness. **THESE TEENS ARE THE FUTURE HOPE OF AMERICA!** I find this very concerning.

Why is China so far ahead of us in hypersonic offensive missile development? Their missile *defense* system is considered far superior to ours as well. One reason is that every Chinese youth MUST study mathematics at least fifteen *hours* a week. I doubt whether our kids spend fifteen *minutes* a day. Their students are also subjected to intense training in artificial intelligence programming, all computer skills, and physics.

In other recent studies, the United States ranks seventeenth out of twenty in reading, and twentieth out of twenty-five in science. Our students are lost on the world stage. We are very fortunate that so many brilliant Asian students choose to work in our tech industries. Left to our present-day students alone, we are doomed.

The only logical conclusion that one can draw is an absence of political concern that is *entirely intentional.* Sheep easily follow a leader. Baaaaa! No matter how evil their leader might be or how badly intentioned, they simply are unaware they are being dumbed-down and led along a predetermined path. Hitler's Germany is the classic example.

Many of our once-proud colleges of higher learning have become left-wing propaganda mills turning out prejudiced, America-hating, Jew-hating, religion-hating Neo-coms. It is a known fact that billions of dollar flow into these colleges not only from the American taxpayers' at $45 billion annually, but from foreign countries, most not exactly our friends.

China, Russia, Kuwait, United Arab Eremites, Egypt, Saudi Arabia and Quatar have sent many billions of dollars to American Universities over the past decades. They literally *own* our colleges and Universities. Is it any wonder that anti-Semitism is rampant on American campuses? These institutions and their administrators are simply paid puppets of foreign powers.

Outraged parents appear at School Board meetings. They express their anger that their kids are being put into two groups, "oppressed" and "oppressors" based on skin color. They are angered that their kids are encouraged to consider whether they might really be a different sex from what GOD and biology dictated at birth.

In one instance it was reported that enraged parents were threatened with arrest. Why? Because they were beyond upset over the rape of their daughter in the girls' bathroom by a transgender male student.

ALL OF THESE PROTESTING PARENTS ARE

LABLED "DOMESTIC TERRORISTS" simply for the "crime" of loving their children.

Wake up, America! Poor, hyper-liberal education is a very serious existential threat to our future as a nation. Anti-American education is the worst iteration of this apparently-deliberate decline. Worrying about addressing kids by some pronoun they find offensive should be replaced by worrying about teaching the old-time basics of reading, writing, arithmetic and civics. The whole aim of "Newspeak" is to narrow the range of though. Saul Alinsky along with Cloward and Piven would rejoice.

It is going to take decades to reverse this decline, if it is even possible to accomplish. It is going to take a **Great Awakening** of America-loving citizens to somehow reverse this nightmare. It may well be too late.

There are a few obvious ways we could return to our once-highly educated populace. While unfortunately these are pipe-dreams, hope springs eternal.

For starters, daily singing of the National Anthem, and pledging allegiance to the American flag, must be mandatory for every student in every grade through college. Refuse to participate? Go home and stay home. Move to China or Russia. We'll buy the plane tickets,

Eliminate any mention about gender identity. Let boys be boys and girls be girls, and leave it to the parents and psychiatrists to sort out the others. Eliminate all focus on "correct pronouns". No one ever died from being addressed incorrectly.

Teach the classic "three Rs": **r**eading, '**r**iting, and '**r**ithmetic. Teach *cursive* writing. Teach simple math in kindergarten, increasing in complexity grade by grade. Put a focus on civics, Teach at least one foreign language as they do in Europe and elsewhere.

Return to strict academic grading. Remember A+ to F? The concept of passing everyone so as not to hurt the little darlings' feelings sets up one thing: No one makes any attempt to achieve anything at all. It's right up there with "participation trophies". They really MUST go.

Teach the exceptionalism of our Founding Fathers. Teach a study of the key founding documents. Teach the truth about how our unique country has evolved from slavery through the civil rights movement. Focus on our faults discussed in contrast with our progress and greatness.

The late radio host Rush Limbaugh created his wonderful "Rush Revere" series of childrens' stories. His intention was to teach our kids basic true-history lessons that unfortunately are no longer taught in school. We should have all kids listen to these stories. They just might accidentally learn something.

Basic economics should be taught early in grade school. Teach the geography of the United States, and teach world geography.

Teach the difference between a wrench and a screwdriver. It was called "shop".

Teach respect for individuals of all races and religions. Eliminate teaching "Critical Race Theory" as the racist concept that it is.

The problem? I doubt whether we have many teachers today who could do anything other than follow the curricula they must follow at present to keep their jobs.

Perhaps we must start by educating future teachers in all of the above disciplines. It may take many decades, if it is not too late. If we don't, we are doomed to be relegated forever to the world of the "Banana Republics".

The United States today is a puny pretense of the America about which our Founding Fathers dreamed. Our children are taught only what the controlling forces want them to know. They are never taught those concepts these "leaders" *don't* want them to know. It's called "thought control."

To be taught the real cost of freedom, institute school class trips, in all age groups, to VA Hospitals. Participation should be mandatory. This up-front-and-personal albeit unpleasant experience might shock some into fully understanding how precious our taken-for-granted freedoms really are.

Throughout the entire Industrial Revolution, America was a Meritocracy. You got a job based on merit. You rose up in a company through merit. No longer are the best qualified most likely to be hired.

The key today is to "check the correct boxes". These boxes might be race, ethnicity, sexual orientation, physical appearance, or whatever qualities the hiring entity might value most. ***"Qualifications" is no longer a box to be checked!***

Education is the foundation of a free people. There must be a focus on critical thinking. As an existential threat to our freedoms I can think of no other more important one facing our Nation today than America's BROKEN EDUCATION SYSTEM.

CHAPTER NINE

BRICS
AMERICA'S FINANCIAL SURVIVAL

"It's ALL about money." Michael W. Crolius, musician, real estate developer, author, (1958-), [My business partner 1999-2005].

In 2023 and 2024 there were four Republican Presidential Debates. There have been many televised "town halls". During these many hours not a single question such as: "If elected how do you plan to deal with BRICS"? has ever been asked. It seems to be an important question.

The entire topic of BRICS is tied intimately to international trade in *everything*. The topic is so complex that in the near future there will be entire books written to explain the implications. This Chapter will offer the basics.

The primary goal of our many Global enemies is to eventually create a major financial panic in America. They intend to convince all of our trading partners worldwide to shun the U.S. dollar in favor of their new currency, the "R5", with a much more trustworthy store of value as its backing.

So what exactly is "BRICS"? The acronym stands for: **B**razil/**R**ussia/**I**ndia/**C**hina/**S**outh Africa. These are the first countries involved in this very brilliant multi-national scheme. Their leaders decided to challenge America's decades-long domination with the United States Dollar as the "World Currency" in trade and banking.

The Heads of State directly involved were: Luiz Inacio Lula da Silva, President of Brazil; Vladimir Putin, President of Russia; Narendra Modi, Prime Minister of India; Xi Jinping, President of China and Cyril Ramaphosa, President of South Africa.

When did Brazil, India and South Africa stop being our close friends? Were they ever?

The United States dollar has been the "Global Reserve Currency" since 1945, after WWII ended. Over the following decades, even today, our robust economy allowed Americans to freely buy an endless amount and variety of foreign goods. We paid in dollars, frantically printed by The Federal Reserve.

Eventually, as other world powers emerged, they saw that it would be to their advantage to distance themselves from the American currency. They believed, with justification, that the deck was always stacked in favor of American outcomes.

Two key financial factions, The "Shanghai Cooperation Organization" and the "Eurasian Economic Union" believed that they suffered from the weaponization of the US Dollar. They feared that their dollar-denominated reserves could be frozen at America's will. They do not exactly trust us.

In 1944 James Maynard Keynes, English economist and philosopher, suggested a new world currency he called "The Bancor". It was to be based on a basket of many different essential commodities. He eventually realized the incredible complexity of that approach. He concluded that a *single* commodity, GOLD, would be the best anchor for the new currency. Fast forward sixty-two years.

BRICS was first conceived in 2006. The concept of a "World Currency" was seriously debated in 2014 at a key summit in Brazil. The BRICS nations decided to create a "New Development Bank" with $100 billion at its disposal. In a meeting a year later they created a "Contingent Reserve Agreement". This opened a lending mechanism to help any members needing cash for any reason.

Literally as many as 160 BRICS meetings were held yearly. This was not just a financial group. They had sub-groups on topics as diverse as defense, sports, natural resources, infrastructure and agriculture. The *hypothetical* discussions ended in August 2023. Reality and finalization set in.

In South Africa, the final groundwork was laid. BRICS became a reality. It didn't take long for a number of other countries to come on board, creating "BRICS+": Algeria, Bahrain, Egypt, Indonesia, Iran, Saudi Arabia and the United Arab Emirates just couldn't wait! They're all in.

It docsn't stop there. At least SEVENTEEN additional countries have expressed *immediate* interest in joining the BRICS+ juggernaut: Afghanistan, Bangladesh, Belarus, Kazakhstan, Mexico, Nicaragua, Nigeria, Pakistan, Senegal, Sudan, Syria, Thailand, Tunisia, Turkiye, Uruguay, Venezuela and Zimbabwe. And it is reported that *forty* other nations are studying whether BRICS+ is in their best interest. Want to take a guess?

Argentina, originally committed to joining BRICS+,

appears at this writing to have changed their minds. Their peso had become so worthless that the country was now using only American dollars locally. Their newly elected President Jevier Milei seems conflicted about BRICS, and has agreed to his full cooperation therein without formal membership.

The BRICS+ consortium now boasts $45 TRILLION dollars in the collective coffers, _far exceeding our G7 Group's total assets._

I am certain that by the time you are reading this many additional countries, probably including some "friends", will have joined. It seems inevitable that over time virtually ALL countries not part of our "Group of Seven" will join the BRICS+ nations.

The basic idea is to out-compete and ultimately replace the "G7" on the World stage. The all-powerful G7 includes The United States, United Kingdom, Canada, France, Italy and Japan. Both Australia and Switzerland also adhere to the principals of the G7 "Washington Consensus". Don't be too shocked if these two countries join BRICS+.

Many economists are terrified. They should be. So should every American politician and citizen. It is a *serious* existential threat. I would say rather a bit greater than gas stoves and double-pane windows!

This BRICS movement didn't exactly happen overnight. It has been in the works for a decade. Apparently our financial gurus have been asleep at the switch. Perhaps with early action, America could have done something to derail or at least delay this international initiative. It is clearly too late now.

Here is the most frightening metric of all: In 2023, the "GNP" (**G**ross **N**ational **P**roduct) of BRICS+ group of America-hating countries _EXCEEDED_ the GNP of our once dominant G7's GNP. Why have I heard virtually nothing about this from our politicians? Why have we heard virtually nothing about this from our TV analysts? Why is there not front-page media coverage?

As more and more hostile nations join BRICS+ the GNP disparity will get greater and greater. America will get weaker and weaker on the world stage.

Another deleterious effect BRICS+ has created is the new camaraderie between nations that were never before friends. India is falling all over itself to ingratiate itself politically to Iran and other America-hating Far East countries.

Back in 1890 a brilliant U.S. Navy Captain named Alfred Mahan wrote a book titled "Influence of Sea Power Upon History". He emphasized the importance of sea power to any nation where their ocean trade is critical. To this day this exceptional book is required reading in war colleges across the world. The concepts in this book were not lost on BRICS+.

The consortium has cleverly created a virtual economic lock on the Global water-trade routes. They now surround all of the key coastlines, straits and waterways through which most of the world's oil tankers and all other goods travel. The Suez Canal, the eastern Mediterranean, and the Red Sea are all controlled by BRICS+ member countries to some extent. Since many OPEC members have joined

BRICS, it is often now referred to as "BRICS-OPEC".

The consortium dearly wants Argentina under their control. Just as BRICS founding member South Africa controls the sea lanes around the south of Africa, Argentina controls the seas around the south of South America. In addition, Argentina has rich resources, and is the best gateway to Antarctica This frozen continent is being eyed by every country on earth as a future minerals mining nirvana.

It is not far beyond belief that one of our G7 buddies might forsake us and hop on the BRICS+ steamroller. G6? G5? Just "US" left as the lonely G1? Who can say?

Over the recent decades three American credit-rating agencies have predominated worldwide: Moody's, Standard and Poor's and the Fitch Group. The BRICS+ nations have always felt the ratings of these United States based credit agencies were slanted against them. So the inevitable has happened.

The dynamics of International Credit Ratings is about to be totally upset! A new complex "World Credit Rating System" is poised to replace America's credit rating system monopoly. The impact of this could be catastrophic for world trade from America's perspective. Time will tell.

What is turning the entire world against us? Why are our increasingly-former friends forsaking us? I can think of a few reasons.

After WWII, the United States was seen as an indomitable force. No longer. We are now perceived as weak and feckless, more of a liability than an asset.

They've witnessed our debacle in creating the now "Socialist Republic of Vietnam". The Afghanistan withdrawal screw up shocked the world. Failure to achieve strategic goals in Libya or Iraq added to our growing aura of ineptitude. Warning Iran "Don't" in regard to attacking Israel was quickly igored.

Recently our troops have been attacked over two-hundred times by proxy groups known to be funded by Iran. At least three of our precious military personnel have died. Many others are said to have sustained traumatic brain injuries. Yet we seem incapable of a definitive response. Direct action against Iran is apparently entirely off the table. Perhaps Israel will strike Iran for us.

Our woke-infested military is vastly understaffed. It no longer has the world's most sophisticated weapons or missiles. Our allies have come to the conclusion that the United States will not necessarily prevail in any future confrontations. They don't want to be on the losing side, namely ours.

They fear that we will turn our backs on any ally if we find some political excuse for doing so. They simply no longer trust us. It is hard to blame them. The Israel/Iran conflict certainly provided additional cause for distrust,

They certainly no longer trust "The Full Faith and Credit" of the greatest debtor nation on earth. Thirty-five trillion and counting! No one wants to hold American dollars anymore.

Since 1974, oil has been priced in American dollars, referred to as "petrodollars". It has given the U.S. first crack at the countless oil suppliers worldwide. It has allowed us to freely acquire crude oil with our rapidly diminishing dollar. The petrodollar will be no more. The overwhelming strength of the BRICS+ currency cannot fail to reign supreme.

Allies once joined America without question in whatever cause we asked, whether or not it was entirely in their best interest. No longer. Against our wishes Japan, South Korea, India and Egypt happily purchase Russian oil. Nor do they see it in their best interest to support military efforts in The Ukraine. Our interests are now irrelevant to them.

Many nations fear, as do many in our country, that our endless woke culture and civil unrest will turn the United States into a banana republic or worse. This is clearly the goal of the ultra-left neo-coms. The radical ideas if Saul Alinsky and Cloward/Piven are winning the day. We are being slow-boiled as a frog, without noticing what it is that's killing us slowly.

World Leaders laugh at our relative standing in education and our abandonment of a meritocracy. They are convinced we would leak any critical international secrets. In short, they simply choose to step away from American dominance worldwide and create a "New World Order" one especially *without* The United States as head honcho.

What exactly is the idea behind BRICS+' currency? Over-simplified, it is an international digital currency or group of digital currencies, tied to gold's value, but not backed by physical gold The object is to eventually replace the U.S, dollar in **_all_** international transactions. The dollar simply will not be widely accepted.

A recent example was a huge transaction between China and The United Arab Emirates paid in UAE's newly created "Digital Dirham"!

The long-range plan is to have a single BRICS+ currency for all world commerce. It is expected to be released sometime during 2024 or 2025. It will be a digital currency on a ledger maintained by a BRICS+ financial institution. Message-traffic will be heavily encrypted to record participant transactions.

Various names have been floated for the new BRICS+ digital currency but as of this writing there has been no mention of a final choice. Most often mentioned is calling it "R5" as a nod to the original five BRICS countries, It is unlikely they will call it "Bancor"!

Do not confuse this BRICS+' digital currency with crypto currencies such as "Bitcoin", Unlike cryptos BRICS+ is not decentralized, nor are any "blockchains" involved. Another difference is that BRICS+ is not open to all without prior approvals. These are *huge* differences.

One must wonder just how secure this system will be from hacking. Artificial intelligence is going to arm bad actors with tools that will quickly surpass what brilliant teenagers in their garages seem to be able to easily accomplish today. This same problem will be inherent in any attempt the United States makes to digitize the dollar (see Chapter One).

This entire movement away from the American dollar will inevitably have a very negative effect on your wealth in the short, medium and long term.

The United States is rapidly losing its grip on the world economy. It is too soon to evaluate the full effect BRICS will have on our currency and inflation, but it could be a calamity unlike any we have ever experienced in our financial history.

In the immortal words of the late, great Queen Elizabeth II: "Keep calm and carry on." That was easy for her to say!

CHAPTER TEN

THE FEDERAL RESERVE

"I am a most unhappy man. I have unwittingly ruined my country." Woodrow Wilson, (1856-1924), 28th President of The United States of America, expressing his regret over signing the Federal Reserve Act.

"There's no free lunch." Milton Freidman, American economist, (1912-2006).

"The way to crush the bourgeois is to grind them between the millstones of taxation and inflation." Vladimir Lenin, Soviet Union Leader, (1870-1924).

"Every government interference in the economy consists of giving an unearned benefit, extorted by force, to some men at the expense of others." Ayn Rand, American author and philosopher, (1905-1982).

"If the American people ever allows private banks to control the issue of their currency, first by inflation, then by deflation, the banks, and corporations that will grow up around them, will deprive the people of all property until their children wake up homeless on the continent their fathers conquered. The issuing power should be taken from the banks and restored to the people, to whom it properly belongs." Thomas Jefferson, 3rd President of the United States, (1743- 1826).

This is a plagiarized Chapter! Perhaps you'll recall reading it if you are one of the two people besides my wife who read "Whitewash Y2K". Sadly I published that book far too late in 1999 to bankroll a trip to Tahiti!

If you are searching for an existential threat to our freedoms and present way of life, look no further than The Federal Reserve and our massive **Federal Debt**.

There are probably more misunderstandings and misconceptions about the American banking system than anything else connected with our unique American government.

Banks have done an amazing public relations job over the years. Although banks have gone out of their way the past few years to alienate their customers with annoying charges and high credit card rates, they are still trusted and held in high esteem by the majority of our citizens. How else could one possibly explain the *trillions* of dollars of free loans given to banks by their depositors through non-interest bearing checking accounts? I'm as guilty as anyone.

How else do you explain the *trillions* of dollars in savings accounts and certificates earning paltry rates compared with other investments? (Did I hear you say: "Yeah, but it's safer in the bank." You *can't* be serious). Those are **trillions** of dollars folks (See Chapter ELEVEN).

There are also many billions of dollars entrusted to banks for management in Trust Funds. This often contributes to missing opportunities for growth, in the interest of "decreased risk". Banks are often thought of as benevolent societies with a directive from GOD to protect the public's money. Nothing could be further from the truth.

Banks are businesses, exactly like any other profit-minded business. Their bottom line, their profit and loss statement, are far more important to them than how much interest you earn or how available your money is when you need it.

Many books have been written to explain our banking system. I would not be so pretentious as to even attempt complete coverage of the topic in a single chapter. I believe I can explain in plain language why the banking system is one of the weak links in our financial health, and a serious existential threat.

A number of years ago a professor of mine at Baruch School of Business revealed some facts that startled everyone in the class. We were learning about the Federal Reserve System. I had always assumed, as most people do, that "The Fed" is part of the United States government, thought of in the same breath as the Treasury Department. *Well, it isn't.* Not even close.

What I am about to tell you may not be easily believed, so I suggest you verify it through your own research. No discussion of the banking system could begin without discussing the **"Federal Reserve System"**. I was reminded by my professor of the fact that it is in no way "Federal nor does it have any "Reserves".

In the 70s there was a popular folk song by Carl Klang (1953-2009) that went:

"Oh the Federal Reserve isn't federal at all,
It isn't even close to being Constitutional.
It's fraudulently shoved this country up against the wall,
Oh the Federal Reserve isn't federal at all.

Would you like to know the reason why your taxes are so high?
Would you like to know what fuels inflation every time you buy?
Would you like to know who takes the biggest slice out of your pie?
It's the Federal Reserve, and I'm here to tell you why!

It's not that complicated to explain in layman's terms,
When something's really rotten it is sure to crawl with worms,
And that something really rotten happened in our Nation's past,
It's been feeding on our prosperity until now we're sinking fast.
Oh the Federal Reserve isn't federal at all.

How'd you like to print some money on your very own printing press,
Then loan it out to all your friends at staggering high interest,
Bet it wouldn't take too long 'till you owned the whole neighborhood,
Well that's what the Fed's been doing since our Congress said it could.

Now our Congress shirked its duty back in December nineteen thirteen,
That's when the value of our money changed from gold to inky green,
And when they shrugged the Constitution they damned the Nation's fate,
It was a violation of Article One and Section Eight!
Oh the Federal Reserve isn't federal at all."

It's a very catchy tune that can be easily found on the internet.

To begin to understand our banking system we must go back to the late 19th century and the flowering of our truly-great Industrial Revolution. At that time all of the wealth in the world was controlled by a very few individual family dynasties worldwide. They accomplished this through monopolistic practices that stifled competition and controlled the prices of everything.

The only real competition was between the dynasties themselves! These wealthy individuals became collectively known as "The Robber Barons". The title was quite appropriate.

The wealth of some of these men was so great that there were occasions when they literally bailed out the U.S. Treasury! This group of perhaps twenty individuals collectively represented almost one-third of the total wealth of the planet!

Today's wealthy individuals, such as billionaires Bill Gates, Jeff Bezos and Elon Musk are paupers by comparison. J. Pierpont Morgan was one of these twenty hyper-wealthy individuals. The United States Congress spent endless hours trying to "bust" Morgan and the monopolies. Politicians were elected on "trust buster" platforms.

Now realize, these Robber Barons did not get to the point of controlling much of the world's wealth by being stupid. Over time they decided to stop competing with one another, and divided whole industries dynasty by dynasty. One group of magnates would control the railroads, another would control steel production and so forth. This division of industry was known as the "cartel system".

These cartels worked sort of like the Mafia. One family rules drugs, another prostitution, another trash collection, etc. But the Robber Barons still had the United States government to contend with, so they devised a ***truly brilliant plan.***

There is an island off the coast of Georgia named Jeckyll Island. Back in 1910, the island was owned by millionaires J. Pierpont Morgan (the inspiration for the little mustached man in the board game *Monopoly)* and William Rockefeller. The island was a private playground for them and their Robber Baron cronies, many of whom had "modest" (hundred-room) "cottages" built on the island.

Jeckyll Island had a huge, beautiful clubhouse, which still stands today. On the door to one of the rooms of that clubhouse there is a simple brass plaque which reads: "The Federal Reserve System Was Created In This Room". The story isn't as simple as the plaque.

Over a nine day period in November 1910, a top secret meeting was held in this room. It was so secret that the attendees used code names and traveled there by separate routes. Some wore disguises! There were seven men involved. One of two government officials at the meeting was Senator Nelson Aldrich, Republican whip and not coincidentally father-in-law of John D. Rockefeller, Jr.

Mr. Aldrich was Chairman of The National Monetary Commission, which was established to make recommendations to Congress for banking reform. There was just too much money in the control of too few for the government's comfort. The Robber Barons collectively became known as "The Money Trust".

Aldrich was also, not coincidentally, a business associate of J. Pierpont Morgan. You think we have dirty politics and corrupt politicians *today*? Ours are angels by comparison.

The other government official present was Abraham Andrew, Assistant Treasury Secretary. The most powerful financial personality present was Paul Warburg (inspiration for Daddy Warbucks of *Little Orphan Anne* fame), an influential European banker connected to the powerful Rothschild dynasty and representing the powerful Kuhn Loeb Company.

The three most powerful American banks at the time were Morgan's Bankers Trust Company, headed by Benjamin Strong, present at the meeting; First National Bank of New York, headed by Charles Naughton, also at the meeting and National City Bank, controlled by William Rockefeller, with ties to Kuhn Loeb. The latter was represented at the meeting by its president Frank Vanderlip. Also present was Henry Davidson, senior partner of J. P. Morgan & Co.

In just nine days in that room the legislation that was intended to <u>break</u> the Money Trust was formulated <u>BY the Money Trust!</u> Were these guys slick or what? Here were all of the key financial giants of the day, men who truly hated each other, fierce competitors, devising a scheme to control all of the wealth in America for all time, with the blessing of the United States government!

No word of this meeting *ever* leaked out at the time. Years later a number of the participants wrote books about the secret meeting and its consequences.

Vanderlip drew up the legislation **creating** The Federal Reserve System. It was, in effect, a creative banking cartel to be run in partnership with the Federal Government, as conceived by the Robber Barons during that infamous week on Jeckyll Island. ***The foxes had designed the hen-house and were living in it!***

No one in our government quite understood all of the nuances of Vanderlip's "Federal Reserve Act". It was incredibly complex by intention. (Remember Nancy Pelosi: "To understand the bill you will need to read it after it is passed.")

Because the need for banking reform was so pressing and was so universally acknowledged, the Act was passed by Congress with very little opposition. It was signed into law by President Woodrow Wilson in 1913.

Guess who was named as the first head the new Federal Reserve System? None other than Benjamin Strong, head of Morgan's Bankers Trust Company!

Wilson, not long thereafter signing the Bill, was quoted as saying: "I am a most unhappy man. Unwittingly I have destroyed my country." Apparently he finally read the bill! We had lost our economic sovereignty. Sadly, we have been asleep at the switch ever since *and have never gotten around to repealing this onerous and unconstitutional legislation.*

So just what exactly *is* the "Federal Reserve System"? It is in fact a sovereign power structure separate and distinct from the Federal United States Government. Technically, the Federal Reserve is a "maritime lender", an insurance underwriter to the Federal United States government operating exclusively under <u>Admiralty Maritime Law,</u> **<u>not</u>** **<u>United States</u>** **<u>Law</u>**!

The Federal Reserve System is independent of the United States Congress. It doesn't file a tax return or pay any taxes. It has never been audited. It is not subject to the United States Code or to the scrutiny of the General Accounting Office!

It has never filed a statement of assets or any other information form for the U. S. government. It doesn't have to! ***It is a private joint stock trust corporation.*** *It is sovereign with respect to the Federal United States.* It is not a part of our government, and it is not representing "We the People". It is a fraud perpetrated on every American citizen, and almost no one today knows it. I do not believe most of our politicians have a clue either.

But here is the greatest shocker of all: <u>***ALL***</u> private property of United States citizens, all of **YOUR** property and mine, everything we own now or ever will own, has been "hypothecated", <u>pledged eternally to the Federal Reserve System.</u> Theoretically, you actually own nothing!

In exchange for our publics' generosity, the Federal Reserve Board has pledged to supply <u>***UNLIMITED***</u> funds for any purpose to the United States. There is, of course, a price. That price is called "interest", and this interest, the "debt service", is paid through the income tax that was created just for that purpose! Aren't we lucky? What a deal! Americans were misinformed and totally screwed.

There was no stipulation in the Federal Reserve Act for *ever* paying back the principal and folks, that principal is now thirty five *trillion* dollars, our so-called "National Debt".

The Banking Cartel has it all. Everything we own is pledged to a non-American power, just as it was in pre-Revolutionary War days. The United States has been sold down the river. As a country, we have been in bankruptcy since the Great Depression. Every time we raise the debt limit, we reaffirm that bankruptcy. The Federal Reserve owns us, literally.

Structurally, the Federal Reserve System consists of twelve Regional Federal Reserve Banks controlling 35 million shares of stock in the "corporation". The New York, Chicago and San Francisco branches control about half. The four New York banks formed originally by the Robber Barons, Citibank, Chase, Chemical and Morgan Guarantee, control one-third of *everything*.

Let's now talk a bit about the worthless paper we call "money", "fiat money". The Federal United States Government and the United States Congress have never been authorized by the Constitution to issue paper currency of any kind. That's a fact. A dollar is a measure of *weights,* specifically defined amounts of silver and gold, established by the original Coinage Act of 1792, still in effect today. We are supposed to be on a gold standard, with real wealth backing our money. Sadly, we are not.
The Federal Reserve Notes we call "money" are simply a money substitute. They are "banker's script", a commercial loan, a debt obligation, a promise to pay the Federal

Reserve Bank. They are paper drafts, fiat currency.

And just for the record, the word **"Federal"** was added to the notes in the hope that citizens would not question the *"Federal"* Reserve Act! Clever guys those Robber Barons!

Quoting directly from a report of the Federal Reserve Bank of Chicago published in 1975: "Neither paper money nor deposits have value as commodities. Intrinsically, a dollar bill is just a piece of paper. Deposits are merely book entries." They said it, not I.

How does our "money" come into being? By magic! With smoke and mirrors! Houdini would be proud. When the government needs more money than it receives in taxes, The Fed simply prints more U. S. Treasury notes, bills and bonds. These are all simply "IOUs". Citizens buy them. Foreign governments buy them. Mutual funds buy them. Hedge funds buy them. Insurance companies buy them.

"Why", one might ask? Hot damn, they're backed by the full faith and credit of the United States Government. Sounds great! What could go wrong?

How do they actually cover the face amount of this freshly printed paper? They simply walk down to the Federal Reserve Building and ask for a check for, say, a trillion dollars or so. Then the Federal Reserve literally writes a check to the United States Government for whatever amount is requested. And from what huge bank account does this money come? ***There is no account, just a check book!*** Incredible but true. Check it out. You can't make this stuff up.

What about the famous "Federal Deposit Insurance Corporation"? Well, it was formed in 1935 as a tradeoff for all of the Federal Reserve Banks retaining *all* of the banking profits! And how much of the money in the banking system does it protect? 100%? Nah. How about half? Not a prayer. The figure is actually closer to 10%, which puts trillions of American citizen dollars of deposits at risk throughout tens of thousands of banks. It is a never ending cycle of "funny money", just smoke and mirrors.

What can one of these freshly printed notes possibly end up being worth in terms of buying power? I have a vivid recollection of seeing pictures in the newspapers of German citizens pushing wheelbarrows full of their hyper-inflated banknotes on the way to the grocery store to buy a single loaf of bread!

There is a local joke about a woman who left her wheelbarrow full of cash outside when she went briefly into a store. When she returned someone had stolen the wheelbarrow. All of her inflated cash was left scattered on the sidewalk!

Will our paper currency have any value at all in a financial meltdown? You can believe with all your heart that it will not. This is why you *must* consider owning hard assets.

I know for a fact that a lot of people believe that when they deposit money into their bank savings or checking account that the bank takes the money and puts it in their vault the very day. Of course, these same people assume the bank mixes it with every one else's money in the vault, so if the depositor wants their money back the next week or month they would not actually get the *exact* same bills. It is believed, however, that the money is *always* there, waiting for them whenever they want it.

Do *you* think that is the case? Would you be surprised to know that they keep as little as three cents out of every dollar on hand? We operate on a "fractional reserve system". There is the basic premise that for every dollar one depositor puts into the bank, another draws a dollar out, and everything stays in a sort of balance. If every depositor wanted money on the same day and it was apportioned equally, you and they would each get *three cents* for every dollar on deposit!

Or to look at it another way. If there was a line outside the bank containing all of their depositors, some in the first part of the line would get 100% of their deposits, and at some point in the line (near the beginning) the bank door would be shut in the other's faces after on-hand cash was depleted. This actually happened during the Great Depression. My father told me so. His father, a successful entrepreneur, lost everything. Literally from affluence to poverty in a day.

Are not all of our deposits insured by the Federal Deposit Insurance Corporation up to certain limits? The best research I can find says that in a financial meltdown FDIC could only cover $3 of every $14 deposited, about twenty-two cents on the dollar.

Our fiat currency once was tied to physical gold, "The Gold Standard". Countries worldwide hoard gold. Gold has been a standard of value since pre-biblical times. Gold has never been worth zero. By April 2014 it hovered around $2,300 an ounce. Many economists believe it will go much higher in the next decades, if not the next year or two.

So should you run out and buy gold to protect your assets? Many TV ads would say "YES". In Chapter ONE I discussed in detail the confiscation of private gold by President Roosevelt in 1933. Turn in your gold in thirty days or go to jail! You might also be required to pay a fine which amounts to $230,000 in today' cash. Compliance rate was high.

Could this happen again? Of course it could. Specifically exempted by President Roosevelt were so-called "collector coins". Generally speaking these are coins that are graded as to quality by one of the three major coin grading companies. These coins are heat-sealed in special plastic cases. Of course a future government recall would likely include collector coins as well.

If you do decide to buy gold I have a few helpful suggestions. Do NOT buy from the companies that advertise on TV. Someone, you, has to pay for the expensive advertising. You can check the "spot price" of gold literally minute by minute on many internet sites. I use kitco.com. You should never pay more than 5% or so more than this spot price per ounce for bullion bars or coins.

A Google search will provide many sellers at fair prices. Always shop many sources. I suggest buying bullion *coins*, not bars or ingots. Coins at least have a monetary value in dollars minted right on the coin.

For convenience, I also suggest buying fractional-ounce coins. In a true emergency, it will be more practical to pay for goods in $1/10^{th}$ ounce pieces than with full one ounce coins. There is a premium for the lower weights (one gram, and 1/10, ¼, 1./2 ounce weights), but I believe it is worth paying.

Do NOT buy from companies who hold your gold for you in "secure places". I am sure you could think of a number of reasons why!

Also, don't be tempted to buy silver. Dollar for dollar, it simply takes up too much space. A single one-ounce gold coin is a lot more convenient than a five pound door stop!

Let's talk about worldwide gold. A Google search relates the following major gold holdings, by country, expressed in metric tons: United States 9.0; Germany 3.6; China 2.7; Russia 2.6; Italy 2.5; France 2.4; Switzerland 1.2; Japan 0.9; India 0.88; Netherlands 0.6 and Turkiye 0.5. Virtually every country on earth has some lesser gold reserve. The International Monetary Fund itself holds 3.1 tons.

The United States actually has almost as much gold (reportedly) as the next three countries combined! This sure sounds like a lot of gold. What is that gold actually worth at today's market price? The spot price of gold recently flitterd around $2,300/ounce. That makes our reserve worth about *eighteen percent* (18%) of our National Debt! That's just eighteen cents on the dollar!

In terms of all the dollars in circulation in America ($2.6 trillion), if we sold our entire gold stockpile at today's price it would only cover about thirty-six cents on the dollar!

Feel free to do the math!

There is a conspiracy theory regarding the gold in Fort Knox, our primary repository. There has never been a real audit, bar by bar. In fact, very seldom has anyone connected with our government or otherwise even been allowed entry.

In the only instance that I can find, a single government official was allowed into a single vault and allowed to hold a single bar in just one of the many vaults. Many believe that, as we have done with our Strategic Oil Reserve recently, over the years we have sold off our gold to keep the country minimally solvent. Some believe there is actually NO gold left in Fort Knox. All requests for a full audit have been denied. Suspicious?

Up until 1971, the United States was technically on the "gold standard". There was expected to be enough gold stored in Fort Knox and elsewhere to back our currency. For reasons too complicated for this book President Nixon removed us from the gold standard.

Another hedge against monetary collapse that is often mentioned is diamonds. I see a big problem there. Recently India has developed a high-pressure chemical process. They have been producing over 200,000 carats of diamonds monthly that are said to be totally indistinguishable from mined diamonds.

Real property, land and buildings, have been valuable sources of wealth in the past. In a monetary meltdown it is possible that there would be no buyers! The same is true for valuable art. What has worked in the past will not necessarily do so in our "Future America".

Macro-economics are tremendously complicated. My Master's Thesis was on "Econometrics". I really didn't fully understand it myself! It was graded highly because the professors who reviewed it didn't either!

The United States is technically bankrupt. It is impossible to argue this. Our Federal debt is actually greater that our GDP (**G**ross **D**omestic **P**roduct) for the first time since WWII. At thirty-five TRILLION dollars and counting, the National Debt is beyond the comprehension of most individuals. The following Chapter in this book might help to grasp the enormity of this debt number.

The "National Debt", however, is only the tip of the iceberg. Seldom discussed in the media is the fact the the United States has well over TWO HUNDRED TRILLION DOLLARS in "unfunded promises". These include Medicare, Social Security, government pensions, veterans benefits and public-held debt.

Confiscating all of the monies in IRA and 401K accounts, about $40 trillion, is a tempting idea that has actually been floated in political circles for years. This money would be replaced by some sort of IOU. While this would cover our present National Debt, it would hardly make a dent in the unfunded promises.

Preposterous idea? In Argentina in 2008 citizens with money in retirement funds woke up to find that it had all been confiscated with absolutely no advance warning. With a simple "Executive Order" (remember these?) the government replaced all of their money with IOUs! Believe me, a cash-starved government will do anything to survive. That includes America, the most cash-starved bankrupt nation in world history.

When Cyprus ran out of money in 2013, with European approval, they simply confiscated a large chunk of every bank account large or small. Those Executive Orders can really sting.

When recently questioned about this staggering debt President Biden replied: "We're the United States, the greatest country on earth." Not exactly a comforting or even relevant reply. I read that statement as "This is the United States, I'm the President and I'll take your money whenever I feel like it." He may have no alternative.

Are we great enough to somehow dig ourselves out of this bottomless monetary hole? Time will tell. It seems impossible.

I feel really frightened for anyone born since 2000, and more so those born in 2024 and thereafter. They will inevitably be affected negatively by this enormous financial burden. In some fashion that we can only imagine this debt will be *their* burden. This rotting albatross that would make The Ancient Mariner's burden seem to be as a sparrow!

In Chapter One I discussed the possibility of the Chinese system of "trackable" digital currency coming to America. This Central Bank Digital Currency (CBDC) could be imposed on hapless Americans some time soon. The government under this Draconian system will have total control of all money, and basically your entire life. They can confiscate anything with the press of a few computer keys. It can reallocate money to create "equity" so that no individual has any more CBDC than any other. It works well for Xi Jinping. The question is, do we want to be like China? Let's hope not.

Our massive Federal Debt combined with unfunded promises, is added to daily by the increasing cost to support the massive influx of illegal aliens. Combined, this is as great an existential threat to our survival as a Nation, as any other threat from within, or those existential threats entirely outside our control. Global Climate Change is a useful distraction, but takes a back seat to America's fiscal problems and many other more *immediate* existential threats.

CHAPTER ELEVEN

TRILLIONS & AMERICA'S NATIONAL DEBT

"Blessed are the young for they shall inherit the National Debt." Herbert Hoover, 31st President of The United States of America, (1874-1964).

"Innumeracy is an even greater danger than illiteracy." Sir Arthur Charles Clarke, sci-fi author, futurist, (1917-2008).

I have another admission to make. Much of this chapter, as with Chapter Ten, is almost 100% plagiarized. My apologies to the author. I accept!

This Chapter is excerpted from a book I wrote and published in 1998, "Whitewash Y2K". "Y2K" was an acronym for "Year 2000".

This Chapter was relevant at the time due to the massive number of code-lines that had to be re-written. The world was struggling (and panicking) to prevent utter chaos in every time-related code-based system.

Every power plant, all manufacturing, the entire electrical grid and the entire banking system were at risk of total collapse. Code had never been written to recognize a transition to a new century! Y2K was the greatest existential threat to humanity ever faced in my lifetime.

This was daily front-page news in every newspaper and magazine for over a year. I even had my own daily local call-in TV show for many months. The world dodged a bullet with a massive collective effort and the expenditure of many trillions of dollars.

Worldwide, billions of lines of code had to be re-written. Programmers, most notably in India, got rich! The amount of money spent remediating Y2K has financial repercussions a quarter-century later. But somehow the world survived. Apparently if you toss enough money at a problem anything can be fixed!

A bit of trivia: Do you know who was appointed to be the Y2K czar? It was none other than Hillary Clinton!

I hope this chapter will spark an awakening when thirty-five trillion dollars ($35,000,000,000,000!) of national debt are mentioned as if it were some easily comprehended amount of money. **IT IS NOT. IT IS INCOMPREHENSIBLE**. This is why the amount of our National Debt is not taken as seriously by many as it should be.

That massive amount of debt, which as I point out below, is almost beyond comprehension, has to be held by someone. Before I did some research I thought it was mostly in foreign hands, especially China.

In fact, seventy percent of our Federal Debt is held within the United States. Our own Social Security Fund and government pension funds are holders. Also included are insurance companies, hedge funds and private investors.

Foreign countries account for about 30%, with Japan and

China being the two largest holders. But China owns less than a trillion dollars, under 3%.

Who holds any remaining balance? Why it is none other than our own Federal Reserve, who mop up any debt that no one else wants. It amounts to around 13% of the total.

So, as I see it, the Fed can create all the debt our government wants out of thin air, and if no one wants it we simply buy it ourselves! Pardon me for saying so, but that's nuts! I'm not a macro-economics guru but doesn't this create a rather direct connection to inflation?

If America is good at anything, adding debt has been elevated to an art form.

There are bigger numbers than "trillions" known only to math geniuses. Ever hear of a "googleplex"? To math folk that's a "google" raised to the google power! Are "zillion", "gazillion" and "bezillion" real numbers? No, but they can be useful in everyday conversation!

Mathematicians express huge numbers as the number ten raised to some power. For example ten to the second power is ten times ten (10 X 10) equals 100. A trillion looks puny when expressed in this manner.

A trillion is 10 X 10 X 10 X 10 X 10 X 10 X 10 X 10 X 10 X 10 X 10 X 10. That's 10 to the twelfth power. In math that is the number ten with a tiny number twelve attached to the upper outside corner of the zero. A trillion is numerically: 1,000,000,000,000. $35,000,000,000,000 is our National Debt as of April 2024.

Not having a "feel" for large numbers is one reason why our National Debt's immensity does not cause the degree of public panic that it should. It is a major existential threat, not on a par with CBDC, AI, or the Yellowstone Volcano, but in many was at least as serious. The public can get all worked up over "The Climate Change CRISIS" because they are generally familiar with climate. It is a prevalent a topic heard constantly from our leaders, then greatly exacerbated by uninformed media coverage.

WE DO NOT HAVE AN IMMINENT CLIMATE CRISIS! WE DO HAVE A VERY IMMINENT AND SERIOUS NATIONAL DEBT CRISIS.

Can you ever recall any article or any TV talking head referring to The National Debt as a serious Existential Threat? Was it ever even mentioned in our recent Presidential debates? Does anyone know or care that at the turn of the century, Y2K, about two decades ago, our National Debt was only **three** trillion dollars. Today it is an absurd **thirty-five** trillion and getting larger every day with no ceiling in sight!

A large number of people really fear mathematics. I find this especially true of those trained in the arts, including many teachers and lawyers. As a Securities Principal I worked with hundreds of highly-educated innumerate individuals. Many in the general population suffer from "number numbness" a lack of facility with "street math" regardless of their level of education. The fact that we rate so low internationally (See Chapter Eight) in the math efficiency of our young graduates is one contributing factor.

Being "innumerate" does not necessarily mean that you

cannot count, add, subtract, multiply and divide small numbers, though a surprisingly large percentage of people have some difficulty here as well. Many cannot balance a checkbook, or read and understand their bank or brokerage statement.

What innumeracy refers to is the difficulty most people have in grasping, "feeling", the relationship among really large and really small numbers. We tend to toss around millions, billions and trillions almost as if they were interchangeable. There is a tendency in our society to trivialize very large numbers. The same is true of tiny numbers such as parts-per-million or parts-per-billion, commonly used in discussions of pollution levels.

Mattel's "Barbie Doll", 1992 model, had a microchip programmed to speak phrases. One phrase was: "Math class is tough!" A lot of kids would agree. So would a lot of adults.

Personally, I *love* numbers. I don't think it is genetic because both my parents were innumerate, as were my grandparents.

You know you love numbers when, while you are driving your car, you are constantly figuring idiotic things in your head such as how many seconds it will take to reach a certain distant visible object at a particular speed, and converting to metric units while you're at it!

I know that my love of numbers traces back to my third grade teacher from Public School 139 in Brooklyn back in the 40s, Miss Petrella. I was a pretty awful child at the time. I think I had Attention Deficit Disorder when it was known then as "rotten kid syndrome". Paying attention in class was unthinkable! Anyway, Miss Petrella had a deadly discipline weapon, her dreaded "punish papers". In retrospect, they were a blessing.

For various indiscretions she had the perpetrator (she was arresting officer, judge, and jury) sit in the corner with a pad of paper she had set up with multiplication problems. There were nine columns across the top, and nine down the side, with the numbers one through nine randomly across those two edges. The idea was to do the multiplication, 9 X 7 = 63, 7 X 4 = 28, etc., and enter the answer in the tic-tac-toe-like boxes.

After a few months of that, you could do it unconsciously. Once she knew you had mastered single digit multiplication the numbers across each edge became two digit, ten to nineteen. You would be amazed how quickly you can learn that 14 X 17 equals 198! After a year in her class you dreamed about numbers! You either learned to hate them, or grew to love them. Every child today should have a Miss Petrella.

And in that same school we had a rather benevolent old gentleman named Doctor Nathan Dickler. He had actually taught my mother when she was in the same school some thirty or so years before! He was now the Principal.

Dr. Dickler had the seemingly magical ability to sit in front of our class and have us fire sets of four or five digit numbers at him; "2,375 times 5,699" someone would say. "Thirteen-million,five-hundred-thirty-five-thousand-one-hundred-twenty-five" he'd shoot back almost without hesitation. We assumed he was plugged in to GOD!

It wasn't until rather recently when I saw a TV ad for a speed-math course that I learned that such seemingly amazing feats of mental magic were actually simple arithmatic calculations once you knew the "trick" to it. There are a number of books revealing Dr. Dickler's secret.

When I obtained my degree in Chemical Engineering, all of our calculations were done with a "slide-rule". This was pre-computer. It was an amazingly accurate flat foot-long stick about four inches wide with a thin stick in the middle that slid along while you matched up sets of numbers. We never even *imagined* hand-held calculators, much less computers.

Remember, the entire Industrial Revolution, the invention of trains, cars, planes, electricity, telephones and all else we take for granted were invented *without* the benefit of computers, just pencil and paper, and slide-rules.

Many ordinary Chinese citizens to this day perform incredibly complicated math on the "abacus". It is a wood frame about a foot square with lines of horizontal rods containing many wooden beads. Modern computers are wondrous devices, but they clearly are not necessary for a civilization to survive and prosper for centuries.

Of course, anyone who has suffered through an engineering curriculum was forced to learn "math beyond math". Niceties such as simultaneous differential equations, Fourier Series, and Laplace Transformations required a great deal of study and an ample supply of aspirin. I can't say I ever found a practical use for this torture!

The following two stories may serve to illustrate the wide

disparity between the understandings of numbers among different individuals.

There were two aristocrats out riding one day when one challenged the other to a contest. "Let's see who can come up with the largest number" suggested the first. "Great idea" said the second. There was a pause of a few minutes when one shouted out: "Three"! There was an even longer pause, when, after deep thought, the other shrugged his shoulders and conceded defeat!

Then there is the story of a mathematician who was visiting a sick friend, also a mathematician, in the hospital. He had come by taxi, and casually remarked, trying to make small talk, that he had arrived in a taxi with a very boring serial number: "1729". "No, no", exclaimed his ill friend. "That is a <u>wonderful</u> number! I can see clearly that it is the smallest possible number that is the sum of two cubes *in two different ways*!" (For the record, nine cubed plus ten cubed, and one cubed plus twelve cubed both equal 1,729).

Everyone's understanding of numbers falls somewhere between these two extremes, unfortunately more, I fear, towards that of the two aristocrats.

Personally, I try to relate large numbers to something familiar that I can visualize, such as counting off seconds, or laying one-dollar bills end to end. Let us look at a trillion in terms that one might relate to.

Let's consider counting off seconds: one-one-thousand, two-one-thousand, three-one-thousand. One can, with a little practice, learn the proper cadence and count off many minutes with quite good accuracy this way. If we were to count to one thousand, it would take about seventeen minutes. Ten thousand seconds would take us three hours and tax our patience to the limit!

How about a hundred thousand seconds? Well, that would take us about three whole nine-hour working days. And now we get into some *really* big numbers. How about counting to one million? Here we are talking about counting for two working <u>months,</u> nine hours a day, every day. One would be in a padded cell by then!

But what about a *billion* seconds? Let's forget about sleep, let's just count for twenty-four hours a day, day in and day out. It would take thirty-two *years!* If you started in 1992 you would just be finishing up!

A billion is surely a big number, but what about a <u>trillion</u>? It's just a single letter different, a billion, a trillion, so what? Well, it would take a person, counting at one-second intervals, ever since <u>30,000 BC,</u> a mere thirty-two millennia ago to reach a trillion What was going on then? Neanderthals were roaming through Europe. I doubt whether they could count at all.

How much is the United States national debt? That's <u>*thirty-five*</u> **trillion** dollars folks, one damn big number. Our hypothetical person would have started counting back in the Pleistocene Era!

Let's look at these big numbers a different way, seeing how long a line one could make laying dollar bills end to end. One thousand bills would stretch out almost two football fields. Ten-thousand dollars would stretch a mile, about a six minute walk.

One-hundred-thousand dollar bills would stretch for ten miles, about a ten minute *drive*. But how about a million dollars? Laid end to end, a million one-dollar bills would stretch for a hundred miles, almost a two hour drive.

A billion bills? These would circle the earth four times! That's a long way.

A trillion dollars? Laid end to end, the one-dollar bills would reach from the earth to the sun, some 93 million miles! It takes *light* about eight minutes to traverse that distance. A trillion is a really, really big number. Thirty-five trillion? We could go back and forth to the sun seventeen times!

Numbers can actually be fun. I'll leave you with a little party game that many find astounding. I'll ask you to give me a penny today, and twice as much tomorrow, two cents, and continue to double the amount you gave me every day for a 31-day month (one cent, two cents, four cents, etc.). At the end of the month I'll promise to give you one-hundred thousand dollars. Otherwise, you'll give me the ending balance. Which do you choose?

Take a quick guess of how much the total would be on the 31st day.

Did you guess a hundred dollars? A thousand dollars? Ten-thousand dollars? No, that would be at the end of three weeks. Did you guess a hundred-thousand dollars, your "break even" point? Few guess that high.

How about a *million* dollars? That would come at the end of four weeks. But on the 31st day you would pay me over ten-million dollars! The actual total number, starting with a penny and doubling it every day is $10,798,243! Numbers are really weird. Most people have not a clue

We are no better with tiny numbers. If you drew a line across this page to represent "one-millionth" and at any place along it drew a vertical line, the tiny part of your first line at the spot where it is crossed by the second line would represent "one-billionth".

How small are human cells? Viruses? Atoms? Well, from the viewpoint of a human cell in your body, you are the size of the State of Rhode Island! To a virus, you are the size of the earth! To a tiny atom, you are the size of the entire orbit of the earth around the sun! These guys are *really* small!

Why do I point out all of this trivia? First of all, I hope you might find it interesting. Mostly, I would like you to reflect on these ways to represent very large numbers, and then try to look realistically at the *immensity* of the Federal Debt. We are dealing with an almost incomprehensibly large amount of money.

This explains why the probability of The United States ever digging out of the debt hole is virtually zero.

As an existential threat I would rate our ever-increasing National Debt quite close to the top of the list.

CHAPTER TWELVE

CLIMATE CHANGE (AKA "GLOBAL WARMING")

"That Lucky Old Sun, Has Nothing To Do, But Roll Around Heaven All Day." From the hit recording (1949), by Frankie Laine, (1913-2007), written by Haven Gillespie, (1888-1975).

Those who would give up essential Liberty, to purchase a little temporary Safety, deserve neither Liberty nor Safety." Benjamin Franklin, (1706-1790).

"The urge to save humanity is almost always a false-foe for the urge to rule it." H. L. Mencken, journalist and writer, (1880-1956).

"In building a defense against every conceivable contingency.....so much 'security' that the 'saved' are without resources..... helpless and hopeless." Lonard E. Read, American academic, (1898-1983).

"We have met the enemy and he is us." Early environmental comment from the Pogo Possum cartoon by Walt Kelly, (1913-1973).

"Modern journalism, by giving us the opinions of the uneducated, keeps us in touch with the ignorance of the community." Oscar Wilde, Irish poet and playwright, (1854-1900).

"What is wanted is not the will to believe, but the will to find out, which is the exact opposite." Bertrand Russell, British mathematician and philosopher, (1872-1970).

The remedies are agreed upon but the needed medicine is feared more than the disease." Victor Davis Hanson, American news commentator, classicist, and military historian, (1953-   ).

Samuel Clemens (Mark Twain) said: **"It is very easy to fool the people, but very hard to un-fool them."** This is the most pressing problem we have with Climate Change.

Our President has repeatedly stated that climate change is *by far* the greatest **Existential Threat** to humanity, greater even than a *nuclear war*. I have no idea whether he actually believes this. Perhaps this is a convenient distraction from the many much greater and more frightening threats that exist to our very lives and to our ever more fragile freedoms.

Not long ago the "crisis" was referred to as "global warming". That term has been conveniently dropped. It is too easily forgotten when most of us far-removed from the Equator are freezing our collective asses off during the four-months or so most of us experience. It's called "winter".

"Climate change" is more conveniently all inclusive, summer, fall, winter, and spring. It happens every year. My guess is it always will.

I'm quite certain that the Mongol herders would laugh at the old "Global Warming" terminology. In the past they had brutal winters about once a *decade*. Now it has happened six of the last ten years. This condition, called a "dzud", kills as many as 70% of all the cattle these nomadic herders rely upon for survival. During the 2023-2024 winter, it is estimated that twenty-million cattle will freeze to death, devastating the entire Mongol population. Many will starve, or be forced to find unfamiliar employment in the capital city as unwelcome migrants.

I AM NOT A "CLIMATE CHANGE" DENIER. Far from it.

The evidence is overwhelming that glaciers are melting, perma-frost is no longer "perma", and some ocean waters are getting warmer.

The evidence is equally overwhelming that the earth has undergone cycles of cooling and heating for eons, long before humans evolved from the primordial ooze (or however). Long before the Industrial Revolution endeavored to destroy the planet. Or not.

Are hurricanes getting stronger? Are there more frequent and deadlier tornadoes? Are forest fires worse? There is much real data to show that none of these are fact. These claims by climate alarmists are simply not substantiated by *long-term* historical records.

Do we presently have a "CLIMATE ***CRISIS***"? Not according to many climate scientists who have recently bravely come forward with books containing researched and attributed studies by the dozens proving otherwise.

There is one serious crisis related to climate change, the

damage it is doing to the impressionable minds of our youth. I live in a retirement community. Virtually everyone I know has grandchildren or great-grandchildren in grade school. I also have two daughters who are schoolteachers. I've listened to their stories.

Teachers from kindergarten through high school instruct our youth about the "climate crisis". Apparently that is an approved, or more likely mandated curriculum dictated by the powerful Teachers' Unions.

I hear horror stories about kids who should be thinking wonderful fun thoughts but who are literally terrified over the prospect of being fried or drowned. Terrible nightmares are frequent. Terrifying innocent children is an existential threat that will contribute negatively to the mental state of our future adults. Psychiatrists rejoice!

Recently I read an "expert" article that listed ten American cities that will be *under water* by 2030. That's only six short years from now! Head for high ground folks! I see maps almost daily on the internet showing much of Florida as uninhabitable except by alligators, manatees and pythons. Same for the entire east coast up through Maine!

I know a family who live in Atlantic City, New Jersey, directly on the coast. They have lived there for decades. Their famous "Boardwalk", a major tourist attraction, is a few feet above sea level. It was so fifty years ago. From what anyone can tell visually it still is. Does anyone seriously believe it will be under water in the next six years? These climate alarmists are delusional.

A friend of mine has lived on a canal, with a private dock,

in south Florida for decades. He swears that the water level in his canal is exactly what it was when he bought his home in the '70s. He'd better sell before 2030!

I vividly remember the shocking and scary low-budget ninety-minute documentary, "An Inconvenient Truth". That was back in 2006, about the time today's impressionable teenage climate activists were born. Politician Al Gore was sounding the alarm over greenhouse gas emissions. His focus was on carbon dioxide (CO_2) a minuscule percentage, a tiny fraction of one percent, of our atmosphere.

Gore actually was co-recipient of The Nobel Prize for his misleading alarmist documentary. This gentleman studied *government* at Harvard. When and where did he receive his formal education in climatology? Just asking.

Gore essentially blamed fossil fuel emissions **and** *the entire Industrial Revolution.* Perhaps he prefers horse-drawn buggies and candles over autos and electric lights? Caves to houses? Un-scientific hyperbole.

Learned scientists find more than a few other possible contributing factors. Many brave climatologists today are writing well researched and attributed books that totally debunk the entire premise leading to the "Green New Deal".

Back in 1900, the human population of earth was about 1.7 billion. Today it is estimated to be 8.0 billion, over four times greater.

As I recall from high school biology class, humans breathe in air which is mostly nitrogen, oxygen and argon, with minor amounts of other gasses plus a little tiny bit of CO_2.

They breathe it out with a bit less oxygen and an added dose of that scary carbon dioxide.

All the mammals on earth do the same, except there are probably fewer of them today thanks to our endless human efforts to cause extinctions. Any possible effect on CO2 emissions from all mammal breath worldwide? Who's counting? Perhaps someone should.

Methane is also considered a no-no by climate alarmists. They point to cow burps and farts as a primary source. There are hundreds of different ungulates (cow-like critters) worldwide. In total, we are talking about literally millions of animals. Does anyone seriously think that eliminating these would save us all from climate catastrophe?

There are around eighty potentially-active volcanoes on earth. It is documented that at any given time thirty-five of these are actively spewing out all manner of noxious gases, including CO2, into the atmosphere.

As I mentioned in Chapter Seven, for five years we lived in Ocean View, Hawaii, literally on the flank of an active volcano. It was in an area of solidified lava known as the "west rift zone" of Mauna Loa Volcano. It had been inactive for a few decades. At least the property costs were low!

We had periodic Civil Defense meetings to offer us the comfort of knowing that there were helicopters ready to pluck us off our roofs in the event of an unexpected eruption!

Fifty miles away a sister volcano, Kilauea, had been

spewing lava and gas for over forty years almost continuously! Unless you see it with your own eyes, you cannot imagine the sheer volume of gasses and particulates that are emitted every second of every day from this one volcano alone.

When there was a west wind the air on my deck was opaque! This volcanic fog is known locally as "vog".

The general area around Indonesia has three underlying crustal plates with edges in close proximity to each other. These are the Philippine, Pacific and Australian plates. In April 2024 movement in these plates caused an inactive volcano in the North Sulawesi Province to violently erupt. The Ruang Volcano on Tagulandang Island sent a massive plume of hot ash and dust and gasses 75,000 feet into the atmosphere!

I wish that Climate Change alarmists who believe that power plants and auto emissions are the reversible causes of our "crisis" would actually look at this and the other thirty or so volcanoes erupting at any particular moment. These emissions contribute so much to "Climate Change" that trying reversing the Industrial Revolution is a waste of time, effort and money. Mother nature is in total control. Human activity is not a factor that matters.

Today, massive volcanoes in Italy and Iceland are spewing out incalculable amounts of atmospheric pollutants. You can add to this the unimaginable amount of CO_2 and other pollutants that were spewed out in 2023 by the huge forest fires in California, Canada, Australia and Greece. Also add the intentional deforestation fires in the Brazilian Amazon.

Considering all of this it is hard to believe that our auto emissions and power plant emissions are worthy of costly and unpopular elimination. Will being blessed with electric vehicles and double-pane windows and super-efficient expensive appliances as proposed actually accomplish something useful? Ask mother nature.

If we spent as much money planting trees as we plan to spend on replacing gas kitchen stoves and various other home appliances, and making sure all homes are blessed with special windows, we might actually make a positive contribution. Even Al Gore mentioned the need for planting forests to remove CO_2. So let's plant lots of trees. Uncle Al knows best!

All of this present climate hysteria points to CO_2 as the primary culprit. This is not the place for detailed scientific counter-arguments. Reading the two climate-related books I suggested at the end of this book might offer you some reason for suspicion as to whether we are even looking in the right directions. Many climatologists today understand that CO_2 is NOT the major culprit or perhaps not even a culprit at all.

I am a scientist, by both education, and for thirty-years by vocation. I am neither a climatologist nor meteorologist. My first degree was in Chemical Engineering. If I learned one *absolute* truth: **SELECTIVELY CHOSEN DATA CAN BE MANIPULATED TO PROVE *ANYTHING*!**

Consider this extreme hypothetical example: Say we had a tornado last week. Based on this select data it is quite mathematically correct that over a four-week month we averaged four tornadoes. Continuing, in a twelve-month year that gives us around forty-eight per year. Further, that amounts to 480 per decade. That's a hell of a lot of tornadoes! Silly? Yes, for tornadoes. But NO for manipulation of statistics.

When one really looks at ALL of the scientific data on any particular topic, over a _statistically-significant_ time frame, and not just that select short-term data which proves a desired point, conclusions might be totally opposite. Food for thought.

Reading is my passion. I read scientific papers one would have difficulty even locating. I also read books on scientific subjects. I recently came across three on climate change. These books are based on a huge number of cited peer-reviewed papers by REAL climate scientists, those with no agenda other than facts.

I challenge anyone who is even mildly frightened by our "greatest existential threat" to read the two climate-related books added to the list near the end of this book. Actually delve into the long lists of referenced scientific papers. It would be impossible to not come away come away with, at the very least, serious doubt as to whether we have a "climate _crisis_", or an Existential Threat at all.

There is one fact that seems to be well documented and accepted by climate scientists. Since 1900 the annual rise in sea level has been **one millimeter** (1mm). Since 1900 that is a total rise of around five inches (5"). Does this qualify as a "crisis"? Perhaps it does to someone who lives four inches above sea level!

Here are two totally unscientific stories from my actual life experience. I find them interesting, albeit proving nothing.

First story: I was born in 1938. From the time I could write an intelligent sentence, around age seven, I kept a daily diary, which I still own. I lived in Brooklyn, New York. At the end of each day I carefully recorded the high and low temperature for the prior day as reported in our local paper.

My last diary was written in 1952. I guess I was too busy being a teen-ager, and the diary was abandoned. I wish more than anything that I had kept writing a daily diary for the next seventy or so years!

The point of the story is this: Recently I carefully summarized the temperatures from the diary. Then with some difficulty, I accessed the daily Brooklyn temperatures from 2015 to 2022. I compared them with my childhood figures in every way I could conceive. Averages, means, daily, weekly, monthly, yearly, highs, lows. Result: I could find NO evidence whatsoever of any warming over the ensuing seven decades! If anything it was warmer in Brooklyn way back when I was a kid!

Second story: My first wife's family built a tiny home directly on the shore of the Atlantic Ocean, in 1921. It is now over a hundred years old! They don't build them as they used to!

It was built in a small town called Breezy Point, at the southern tip of the Borough of Queens, New York City, New York. It was built on pilings about two feet high, so the deck was about two feet above mean sea level. I spent thirteen summers there between 1959 and 1972. I hated the place because clothes were always damp, and my job was to paint the deck every year!

The bungalow still sits there today, inhabited by my youngest son. It is clearly no closer to being inundated by the rising Atlantic Ocean waters than the day it was built over a hundred years ago. In that hundred years there appears to be no noticeable rise in ocean levels. Can a five inch rise be noticeable? Perhaps no perceivable rise at all is true only in front of that one home? Maybe by 2030?

There do appear to be some places on earth where a small rise in sea levels is becoming a problem. One such country is Vanuatu. Their highest mountain is six inches! There are plans afoot for relocation of the entire population of 300,000+ if matters worsen. Most of the island is only a half-foot or so above high tide sea level at this time. A few inch rise actually matters to them. They are a rare exception.

Huge rogue waves have been a nuisance to seafarers since sailing ships were invented. It does seem that recently there has been an increase. In January 2024 a luxury ocean liner was almost swamped, a very rare occurrence. The cell phone photos taken by passengers would discourage many from ever considering setting foot on an ocean liner!

A month later the entire military base on a Marshall Island was hit by two consecutive rogue waves creating massive damage. Whether this is a new threat caused by climate change or just a coincidence has yet to be determined. Of course the Greta Thunbergs of the world will say a resounding "YES".

Climate change is almost <u>infinitely complicated</u>. There are many complex moving parts in constant interplay. **Blaming climate change on human activity is scientifically absurd.**

As discussed earlier, we did manage to save life on the planet by closing the ozone hole a few decades ago. Ozone in our upper atmosphere protects us from deadly ultraviolet rays from the sun. The entire world got together, identified the problem, and banned the use of chlorofluorocarbons (CFCs) in pressurized containers. Problem solved.

This was, however, **one** discrete problem with one identifiable solution. Climate change is **a vast number** of different problems seemingly without any possible conclusive human-devised solutions.

Shakespeare wrote a play called "Much Ado About Nothing". Looking at the decades of conferences and meetings attended by tens of thousands of scientists, world leaders, business leaders, and activists, one cannot help asking: "WHY"? Has any actual climate change remediation been accomplished as a result of decades of talking? Have we actually reduced any measurable problem contributing to our life-threatening Global Climate "Crisis"?

The biggest air pollution problems our planet faces are directly caused by China and India. China, classified somehow as a "Developing Nation" is said to put one new coal fired power plant on line *every week!* American politicians are trying to shut down all of *our* fossil fueled plants as quickly as possible. What's wrong with that picture?

India? Apparently in 2024 their population actually surpassed that of China. I have frequent contact with two computer gurus in different parts of India. Both say that air pollution is so bad they frequently can't see the length of a soccer pitch. Green initiatives do not appear to be a very high priority in that massive country.

My point is that no matter what tiny climate change progress America and other countries worldwide might achieve through Draconian climate remediation efforts, until China and India come on board, it is all totally pointless rhetoric and any money spent is wasted.

All of the talk began with the creation by The United Nations of "The UN Framework Convention On Climate Change". It was convened in Brazil in 1992. There were one-hundred-sixty five (165) signatories, including The United States.

Their stated goal was: "Stabilization of greenhouse gas concentrations in the atmosphere at a level that would prevent dangerous anthrapogenic human-induced interference with the climate system." Say what?

Since then, The Framework was built upon by the 1997 "Kyoto Protocol" (192 signatories). This required only that *developed* countries set emission standards. It was further amended in 2012 by the "Doha Agreement" convened in Qatar in 2012.

The "final" 2015 "Paris Agreement" (197 signatories) recognized that *every* country should participate. The Paris Agreement was a *legally binding* International Treaty on Climate Change.

The basic idea was, by various measures, to limit the increase in average global temperature to a specified number of degrees above pre-industrial levels. The many and complex means for implementation can be found with a Google search for "How Does The Paris Agreement Work"? The complex details are far too long and complicated for this Chapter. I wonder whether any of our politicians actually ever read it.

In 2017, President Trump removed The United States from The Paris Agreement. He believed that the restrictions would put America at a permanent economic disadvantage. In January 2020 President Biden re-established our full participation on his first day in office.

In August 2020 President Biden signed "The Inflation Reduction Act". This environmental-focused legislation allocated billions of dollars for electric vehicles, solar panels and wind generation farms. It also funded "environmental justice", whatever that means.

There is also something called the "**C**onference **O**f **P**arties". or "COP". It convenes under the above mentioned "United Nations Framework On Climate Change". The most recent, COP28, had this stated goal: "Boosting climate action and elevating climate ambition through gender-responsive climate financing." Say what, again! Who writes this gibberish?

The most recent major conference took place in Davos, Switzerland from January 14-19, 2023. This was "DAVOS 54", the annual meeting of "The World Economic Forum". It was attended by literally thousands. The tickets to attend cost more than tickets to the Super Bowl!

Who attended? *Sixty* Heads of State, including Isaac Herzog, President of Israel, Volodymyr Zelenskyy, President of The Ukraine and Li Qiang, Premier of China. Did our President or even Vice President attend? We sent two Cabinet Members and a few Congresspersons. Apparently we don't take global trade and economics and climate change as seriously as others do.

One-quarter of this COP was devoted entirely to Climate Change. The topic was: "A Long Term Strategy for Climate, Nature and Energy". Aside from the sixty world leaders, present were climate scientists and over a thousand CEOs of Fortune 1000 companies. All major International Organizations were represented.

Also present, focused on elimination of all fossil fuels and promoting other Climate Change "Green New Deal" matters were "over two hundred Social Shapers, Civil Society Leaders, young Change-makers, Social Entrepreneurs and young Global Leaders". No comment.

The great British statesman Sir Winston Churchill once said: "It is better to jaw, jaw, jaw, than to war, war, war." That sounds great for wars, which can be prevented when negotiations work and sanity prevails. But decades of "jaw, jaw, jaw" on a nonexistent Globalist-promoted "crisis" that human intervention has no chance of affecting would be comical if not so tragic.

Let's look at "Social Engineering". "ESG" is a corporate principal encompassing ideas relating to the issues of "**E**nvironmental, **S**ocial and **G**overnance" matters. Of course it has its roots in our precious USA-funded United Nations Organization. Back in 2004 the UN invited huge financial organizations to create a joint initiative called "Who Cares Wins". ESG was hatched.

ESG was not particularly successful. "Governance" was supposed to be total transparency of all operations. Many investment firms do not subscribe to transparency.

Opponents of the ESG principles evolved among the most powerful financial institutions and investors. They pointed out that ESG creates a bias against "environmentally unfriendly" industries such as oil and coal. It clearly puts political goals ahead of investor interests.

The world's largest fiduciary investment bank is the massive 70-office/30-country worldwide BlackRock. They have ten *trillion* dollars of financial assets under management. That's more than the GDP of any country on earth except China and the United States!

BlackRock has been widely criticized by environmentalists because of their intensive support of fossil fuel companies such as ExxonMobile, ConocoPhillips and Marathon Petroleum. They even hold a fifteen billion dollar stake in Saudi Arabia's Aramco. They have also invested billions in coal industries worldwide. BlackRock's financial input is a major thorn in the collective skin of the movement to save us all from climate change. Thank you, BlackRock.

In his recent State of The Union Address, President Biden reiterated something he proposed some months before. He plans to create "The Civilian Climate Corps". This would be similar to the "Civilian Peace Corps" created by President Kennedy back in 1961. President Biden stated that they would start with 20,000 young adults, with an ultimate goal of 60,000. That's a small army!

Recalling proposals when this idea was first proposed, this army of climate activists will be instructed to visit (read "invade") every peaceful suburban neighborhood. Their mandate will be to evaluate every home in America for its level of "greenness". Are there double or triple pane windows? Insufficient insulation? Inefficient appliances? Thermostats set incorrectly? Roof coatings not sufficiently reflective? Lack of solar panels? Heaven only knows what else they might be instructed to find fault with.

The Corps results will be collected and analyzed by a "Central Government Authority". One can only imagine what penalties could be imposed on "non-compliant" homeowners who just want to be left alone. Surely reports from these snoops will impact our "social credit scores" (see Chapter ONE). I find this Orwellian proposal <u>FAR MORE FRIGHTENING</u> than Climate Change.

How soon could you expect a Climate Corps cop to knock on your door? Sixty-thousand, of these young adults inspecting four single-family homes each day would take just ONE YEAR to inspect every home in the country!

I would like to mention something here about the negative publicity fossil fuel power plants are constantly given in the press. It really irks me. Virtually every photograph ever seen in the media shows a line of huge conical shaped buildings spewing out massive amounts of a visible gas. Massive pollution. Very scary. They must be eliminated at all cost. Nasty, dirty fossil-fueled power plants.

The super-scary visible emissions, the huge "gas" clouds

portrayed in these "proof of pollution" photos is good old harmless water vapor, condensed steam. These giant buildings are totally harmless but essential "cooling towers". This phony scare tactic is serious enough to convince the public over time that it is the best interest for the survival of humanity to eliminate all coal and oil fired power plants.

Of course that will include the corollary disaster of eliminating millions of jobs in the coal, gas and oil industries. I pray that someday sanity prevails and we drill and frac, and tap all of our precious reserves, which far exceed those of any country on earth. Drill baby drill!

For over ten years, I personally visited dozens of fossil fuel and nuclear power plant across the country. This was neither out of curiosity nor a hobby! I was employed by an air and water pollution control company as their "Director of Special Projects". It was a fascinating job.

The company sold a wide variety of very effective chemical concoctions designed to minimize air and water pollution emitted by all manner of power plants, including nuclear. My job was to assess needs and offer solutions, then send in the salespersons.

The fact is that for decades these power plants modified their operating procedures at very great expense. This has brought all emissions down to a tiny fraction of what they were in past decades. To vilify these essential power generating plants to the degree that Americans universally see them as a threat to our survival is unfortunate and very unfair.

As a side note, if you have ever quickly hopped on a very rapid continuously-moving foot-wide vertical-stairway up to various levels of an earsplittingly noisy coal-powered power plant you would never find any amusement park roller coaster scary again!

As reported in "Smithsonian Magazine" (one of my faves), The University of Copenhagen in Denmark did an annual physical checkup on our "pale blue dot" (Aptly named as such by astronomer Carl Sagan.) They evaluated nine criteria that are an environmental "call to alarm". The only one that passed muster was the ozone layer. Other than that we are in deep doo doo.

The six pressing dangers named are climate change, biodiversity, land use, fresh water availability, nutrient runoff and miscellany (such as micro-plastics and radioactive waste). Two other benchmarks close to "pressing" status are air pollution and ocean acidification. We have indeed met the enemy and it is indeed homo sap.

Is climate change an immediate and by far GREATEST existential threat facing humanity today? Is is even in the top ten existential threats? Human beings have always *adapted* to whatever was presented to them. Will our scientists find ways to reverse whatever threats are perceived to be most critical? Will Artificial Intelligence find a creative solution before whatever actual threat or that of AI itself wipes us out?

More likely mother nature will continue doing what she has for eons, far beyond the capacity of humans to interfere.

A classic story of adaptation can be found today in the

country of Holland. If I recall my High School geography correctly, twenty-five percent (25%) of that European country is BELOW SEA LEVEL. They adapted and manage quite well to this day. No one drowns.

Is it possible that ALL of this climate worry is very simply a matter of that ball of incredibly hot gas we call the sun. There is strong evidence old sol is getting hotter. If it decides to cause havoc on earth, there is very little we can do about it other than to adapt, or die.

The Paris Climate Accord Conference made a point that once we hit a 1.5 degree Celsius rise in worldwide temperatures we are doomed. Guess what? It was recently discovered that we passed this point a decade ago! We're still here.

In the 1960s a friend introduced me to a brilliant young folk singer named Jon Batson. He wrote protest songs about the VietNam war and many other issues that he saw as un-American. One song he wrote and recorded was about the biased American media which he considered to be nothing but a mouthpiece for the government bureaucrats spewing out whatever lies they were directed to publish.

Batson aptly referred to them as **"The Chaos Merchants Of The Mind."** I never forgot that song. It is more true today than ever.

Since 1990, the amount of climate-scientist-generated media-reported misinformation on "Climate Crisis" has **totally misled the American Public.** We have been lied to for decades. We have been indoctrinated to believe that we have an impending life-threatening crisis due primary to both the burning of coal and oil that generates our critical electricity, and gasoline-fueled automobile emissions.

As pointed out in the above quotes, Samuel Clemens (Mark Twain) is credited with saying: **"It is very easy to fool the people, but very hard to un-fool them."** The Climate Change "Crisis" has been burned into the brains of our school children and adults for many years. Can they ever be convinced of the true scientific FACTS? Can they ever be "un-fooled"?

As the evil Nazi Joseph Goebbels said: **"If you repeat a lie often enough it becomes accepted as the truth."** It worked for Hitler. It works for Climate Change Alarmists.

Why has this untrue media indoctrination happened? It is not a mystery. Consider this scenario: You are a climate scientist working for a prestigious University or Liberal think-tank. For decades these climate scientists were threatened with loss of tenure, loss of grants, loss of employment, and eternal black-listing *if they published what they knew was the scientific truth.* If your very livelihood was at stake if you were to report honestly what you knew to be the true proven scientific facts about global warming and climate change, what would *you* do?

With these life-destroying events hanging over them, they simply could not publish or offer the clueless media the truth in peer-reviewed journals. Report the truth, lose everything. Your life, your family, is ruined. Fortunately this is changing today, albeit slowly.

The truth about climate change and its causes has become so well documented over the past five years that today many climatologists are bravely writing papers and even publishing books exposing the "Green New Fraud". CO2 is NOT the enemy. Mankind is NOT the enemy. Mother Nature is a *bitch*, always was and always will be!

For decades climate scientists were fully aware of the truth. We may have global warming, but humans cause only a relatively-small contributing fraction of dozens of different causes. And there is no *"crisis"* as such.

It is well documented that there was a warm period during early Rome and a later one around 1,000AD. Vikings were happily growing all manner of crops in presently-frozen (though now slowly melting) Greenland! They might be back to growing crops again in no time. Believe it or not, a warmer climate would be a blessing to millions worldwide.

Then the earth entered a "Little Ice Age" that lasted from about 1475 to 1875. Rivers such as the Hudson, Thames and Seine were frequently frozen over allowing people to walk or take horse-drawn carriages across at will. Then we slowly returned to more temperate times, read "today".

We often hear about the "Heat Index". The formula used by climatologists to calculate this number takes into consideration temperature, humidity, sun angle, wind, degree of shade and level of physical activity. It is a *very* complicated formula that you can find with a Google search.

The National Weather Service publishes a useful Heat Index Table. Along the top is temperature. Along the left side is humidity. By choosing a given temperature and humidity and tracing down and left you get an approximation of the

"Heat Index" under those specific conditions. What this does not specifically mention is that this graph assumes light shade, slight wind and zero motion. How a human is affected depends upon a host of varying factors at any given moment in time.

The government recently published a statement that the absolute limits for a human to survive is a temperature of ninety-five degrees Fahrenheit and a one-hundred percent humidity. If global warming ever gets to this point they say we are all doomed. Not sure how they came up with this idea but I wouldn't want to test it.

Realistically, nowhere inhabited on earth *at this time* reaches this extreme combination of temperature and humidity. Here in southern Arizona we often hit one-hundred-fifteen degrees in the shade in mid-summer, but the humidity hovers around five percent. Cooling-sweat dries instantly. We stay cool. As humidity rises the body cannot cool itself as efficiently.

My grandson is a permanent resident of Germany. What I have learned from him I have not seen reported in our media.

Germany has always been an industrial power. When my grandson moved to Germany, Angela Merkel's "Green Party" was in power. These environmental extremists were screaming "CLIMATE CRISIS"! Germany must do its part to save the planet from certain doom.

So, in lockstep with The "Green New Scam" they decided to shut down ALL electricity-generating power plants, both fossil fuel and even nuclear. These were replaced by countless wind turbines and solar arrays. Hurrah for planet earth! Germany has helped save all humanity. Whoopie!

The result? In conjunction with absurd restrictive regulations on electricity-dependent manufacturers, hordes of German plants were forced to close their operations and relocate to other countries. Renewable energy wasn't quite so renewable! Their modern power grid could not be supported with wind and solar.

This had three major results: Germany's GDP dropped, serious unemployment in the manufacturing sector resulted, **AND THE REOPENING OF COAL POWERED POWER PLANTS IS UNDERWAY!**

Bureaucrats seldom consider collateral damage issues. Take our government's obsession with electric cars. Aside from the rather high purchase price and low resale value, lithium batteries have a relatively short life before they need to be replaced. A recent quote I saw for a replacement was $7,700!

Disposal of the old dead lithium batteries is a very serious pollution concern. More important is the fact that lithium mining is very unfriendly to the environment. In addition, we need to import this critical mineral largely from China. It is estimated that, if all of the insane EV dreams are realized, even China will not have enough lithium.

But wait! Great news. The largest lithium deposits ever seen on earth have been discovered right here in Nevada, USA! General Motors has committed $650 million to develop one mine. Our Feds are lending $850 million for a different mine and are contemplating a one-*billio*n-dollar further investment in yet another project. In my opinion, this will insure that lithium will be the EV standard forever.

There are many fabulous alternatives to lithium battery powered EVs. For example, between 1902 and 1924 the Stanley Steamer company built 11,000 automobiles that ran on *water*. The small boiler could be heated with any non-polluting fuel, such as propane or natural gas. It could go 127 miles per hour, unheard of back in those days.

It sounds bizarre, but with today's technology and Artificial Intelligence could we not develop a modern water-powered vehicle? If we can plop men on the moon this should be really easy.

It *is* 100% possible *today* to use non-polluting hydrogen or propane gases instead of liquid petrol. All existing gas guzzlers can be easily converted to use hydrogen or propane. Why MUST the focus be on expensive lithium-powered Electric Vehicles?

Up until recently, extreme pressure from big-petrol squashed any advancement of autos powered by anything other than good old liquid gasoline. Now, however, with industry and government pouring billions of dollars into Nevada lithium mines, you can be 100% certain we will be stuck with lithium batteries forever.

Other types of auto batteries are in various experimental stages. Sodium-ion technology is promising. We sure have enough sodium from sea water to last forever. It is also possible to create solid-state batteries using various chemicals such as sulfur.

As an aside, Hertz Auto Rental just scrapped its entire fleet of six hundred EVs due to customer indifference. Perhaps when we build the 600,000 charging stations promised by our President, rented EVs will become more popular.

Need a job? "Bloomberg Businessweek" just reported that the most sought after job applicant at this time in America is for the position of *"Wind Turbine Service Technician"*. The job pays up to $100,000 annually and requires NO college degree.

The only requirements are no fear of heights, ability to rappel down from a high tower and be able to carry fifty pounds up a three-hundred foot ladder and not die from exhaustion. I would not have applied for this position for *any* wage!

We had an acronym in the Army that fits Climate Change perfectly: "VACA". It stands for **V**olatility, **U**ncertainty, **C**omplexity and **A**mbiguity. We had another good acronym, "BOHICA" that was uttered when an angry-looking NCO entered the barracks. I'll leave it to my readers to guess at the meaning of that one! It could also apply to ALL government edicts.

Remember, "Climate Change" is by far the greatest Existential Threat to human existence, greater even than nuclear war. Our President told us so.

CHAPTER THIRTEEN
COSMIC THREATS

"Do not take life too seriously. You may never get out of it alive." Elbert Green Hubbard, author and philosopher, (1856-1915).

"....you do not know what your life will be like tomorrow." Christian Bible, New Testament, James 4:13-15.

"The universe is not required to be in perfect harmony with human ambition." Carl Sagan, (1934-1996).

The National Aeronautics and Space Agency (NASA) launched its space program in 1967. They eventually made six moon landings. Twelve astronauts actually walked on the lunar surface. A total of twenty-four astronauts were directly involved in the landing missions.

During these missions, astronauts reported strange flashes and streaks of light *outside* their windows and visors. Guess what? The lights were not outside, but *inside* their eyes! What was happening was that the most energetic and dangerous of cosmic particles were damaging the tissue in their eye lenses and retinas.

NASA had a perfect opportunity to study the effect of space on a human. The vital signs of the Kelly brothers, genetic twins, were compared after one twin spent time in space. The changes were startling and very concerning.

"Cosmic Rays" are not actual rays as from a flashlight. They are tiny sub-atomic particles with actual mass, traveling at very close to the speed of light. How close? It is estimated to be 99.999+, with a total of twenty-two nines following " percent of light speed". You can't get much closer than that!

These cosmic bullets are very tiny, but very fast. They pack a lethal wallop when they strike anything. Inertia, the culprit, equals "mass multiplied by speed".

A baseball might hit a bat at a hundred miles an hour. The baseball is a lot heavier than a cosmic ray particle, but it is a whole lot slower. Its inertia is infinitesimal compared to a tiny particle traveling near light speed.

Cosmic rays come in three "flavors" depending on their origin. **Solar Cosmic Rays** emanate from our sun. **Galactic Cosmic Rays** come from the vicinity of our Milky Way Galaxy's central black hole. **Universal Cosmic Rays** come from outside of our home galaxy.

Our sun sends out the solar cosmic rays that are slowed down by other solar particles. Then they are mostly defected by our earth's weak magnetic field and then our atmosphere. Those slowed-down particles that hit atoms in our atmosphere are reduced to "muons" that rain down harmlessly to earth. Solar cosmic rays by themselves are not a problem for space travellers.

Billion of stars all over our Milky Way Galaxy emit these cosmic bullets. They are shot out in every direction. These *"Galactic Cosmic Rays"* are the ones that damaged our astronaut's eyes and to some extent altered their very DNA.

Something called the "solar wind", particles emitted continuously by the sun, offers some protection for astronauts traveling through the solar system. The *frequency* of cosmic bullets is the single greatest limiting factor to future space missions.

It seems intuitive that the solution to astronauts' safety is thick metal shielding on all space capsules. For starters, thick shielding adds too much weight for economical launches. More important, these Galactic Cosmic Rays travel so fast that they go straight through shielding as if it wasn't there. In the process the released kinetic energy smashes their entry points into countless other deadly particles. How NASA is going to solve this problem is still uncertain, especially for months-long flights to Mars.

Astrophysicists believe that Galactic Cosmic Rays are particles spun off the large black hole at our Milky Way Galaxy's center. This black-hole-interaction cannot account for the speed of the third, the Universal variety.

Cosmic rays that originate from stars outside our Milky Way Galaxy are called "*Universal* Cosmic Rays". These travel incomprehensible distances across billions of light years of space. Astrophysicists are not certain how these sub-atomic particles can travel so far so fast, or their actual origin.

Fortunately these death particles are few and far between, but in theory *can* arrive at earth, penetrate our sun's solar wind, penetrate earth's magnetic shield and atmosphere and kill anything they hit on the ground. As far as our space-faring astronauts, there is apparently no way they could be protected. NASA will just have to rely on good luck.

Since I was first able to read adult books, science fiction and astronomy have been a passion. As a pre-teen I had read everything ever written by Edgar Rice Burrows, H.G. Wells and Jules Verne. Over the years, I have immersed myself in Heinlein, Clark, Asimov, Stitchen and von Dainiken. Everything ever written by Carl Sagan fascinates me. It is a shame that he could not have been born a few decades later. Some of what he wrote has come into question because of modern knowledge of the cosmos.

For example, commenting on Mr. Spock from Star Trek, Sagan remarked, in his great 1979 book "Boca's Brain", that: " there is no more possibility of a human Vulcan hybrid than a man and a petunia." Had he lived to see the "CRISPR" gene-editing technology evolve to where chimeras are easily created with gene splicing, his opinion might be different. Of course "a man and a petunia" is a bit of a gene-splicing stretch, but "Human-Vulcan" would surely be possible. Of course that would require a Vulcan.

Sagan tells an amusing story. It relates to ignorance of the possibility that a child could be interested in something as deep as astronomy. He went to his local library and asked the librarian to direct him to the book section about stars. She promptly took him to the large selection of books about Clark Gable, Gregory Peck, and other Hollywood "Stars". Sad.

Sci-fi TV and movies are among my most treasured memories. I think I have seen all seventy-nine episodes of the original "Star Trek" series at least three times. Many are truly profound. Over the years the "Star Trek" animated series and thirteen movies, plus the many great spin-offs ("The Next Generation", "Deep Space Nine", "Voyager" etc.) have excited my imagination.

There are three excellent archaeology periodicals that I read from cover to cover. I have tried to watch every episode of "Ancient Aliens" on TV. Many of these episodes should be required course content for every Grade School, High School and College student.

What I have learned beyond question is that our present civilization was preceded by at least one, and almost

certainly many more, pre-Adamic technologically advanced civilizations.

"Conventional wisdom" still adheres to the belief that modern humans became "modern" roughly six-thousand years ago. This is clearly incorect, based on archaeological finds of the past decade. There is very real indisputable physical evidence of human technology far more advanced than ours going back ten thousand years or more, possibly hundreds of thousands of years.

It is impossible to study recent archaeological finds of ancient constructions that cannot be accomplished today with any modern machinery and not come to this conclusion. This is covered in greater detail in my Chapter FOURTEEN. If you are curious, I suggest you research: Gobleki Tepe and Kerahan Tepe. These ruins contain T-shaped stone columns weighing a hundred tons each that were somehow moved from quarries miles away! Baalbec in Lebanon has architecture with blocks of granite weighing up to 150 tons each!

In Japan there is a stone structure containing two carefully-placed massive blocks, each weighing over a hundred tons each! We have no machinery on earth today that could transport these blocks from where they were quarried miles away.

In Bolivia the ancient mountain top site of Puna Punku is constructed of massive blocks from a quarry located thousands of feet *below* the mountain top! We simply do not have the technology or machinery to create this site today.

The island of Malta has building sites constructed of huge blocks that could only be moved with massive cranes. No such cranes existed in prehistoric time.

There is also a massive underground city called Derinkuyu

in Turkyie that apparently housed a population of 20,000! How this city was cut from solid rock, leaving no apparent debris behind, is another wonder that cannot be explained in terms of today's technology.

All of these ancient sites and dozens more across the globe defy explanation.

Carl Sagan made an omission in his "Cosmos" TV series. He showed a four-billion year calendar, representing the age of the earth. It was divided into 365 days. He then CORRECTLY showed that our Biblical Adamic civilization was created in the last few minutes of December 31st.

What many scientists point out is that after, say, 100,000 years, if all of today's modern concrete and steel buildings were abandoned there would be no trace for a future archaeologist to find. A million years? *Surely* not a trace. Consider how many hundred-thousand-year periods, or even million year periods there have been during our four-billion year old earth's history.

Many of these time periods were as habitable as earth is today. Why could not one or more highly advanced technological pre-Adamic civilizations have come and gone without a trace? Sagan's calendar does not even hint at the possibility of one or more earlier human iterations (or possibly extraterrestrial) that may have existed on planet earth eons ago.

My interest in space-science was first kindled when I was about eight years old. I lived in Brooklyn, New York, about ten miles from the famous Coney Island Amusement Park area. In the summer, once a week, there was a fireworks show. A barge stationed a few hundred feet from shore put on a spectacular hour-long presentation. One could stand on the beach at the water's edge and feel as if the fireworks were almost touchable!

My parents and I traveled to Coney Island on the local BMT (**B**rooklyn **M**unicipal **T**ransit) "subway". Most of the fifteen minute ride was actually over tracks that were above ground. The walk from our destination station to the shore was about a half-mile.

One night we walked past a large flat-bed truck on which was mounted a massive tube pointed towards the sky. For $0.25 a lady offered passersby a look through this tube, which was actually a large telescope! Though this was only four dollars in today's money, it was wartime and my parents were poor. I really had to plead with my folks to allow me to take a look at the marvels this lady promised. They relented.

What I saw was this gleaming yellow ball surrounded by rings! It was the most beautiful sight I had ever seen! I was breathless! Right then and there I decided to become an astronomer!

Well, that didn't happen, though I did immerse myself in other branches of science. What did happen was that I saved every penny I could. I delivered laundered dresses and suits slung over my shoulder for a local laundry. Seeing a little kid burdened with hangers containing many pounds of laundry and gasping for breath inevitably evoked a nice tip!

Within a year I had saved enough to buy my first telescope. Compared to what is available today there was virtually nothing "telescopic" one could buy. There were binoculars and mariner's draw-tube scopes, but no real astronomical instruments. That is, EXCEPT *"Skyscope"*.

This was a simple "Newtonian reflector" with a mirror at one end that sent light to a second mirror which then sent cosmic images up through an eyepiece. It was 4 1/2 inches in diameter, had a black cardboard tube and brass fittings. I believe it cost $150.00 (about $2,500 today).

At that particular time in my life I kept a daily diary, which I still have! Looking back at the record of the days that transpired until my treasure finally arrived almost brings me to tears. Maybe tomorrow. Maybe tomorrow. Please GOD tomorrow! And then it arrived! It came slightly dissembled, with three thin but heavy iron legs and a weird contraption that linked the tripod to the scope. I could not wait to start my journey to the stars.

I lived in a very large six-story tenement apartment building. The roof was freely accessible to all, after an elevator ride and a few steps. The flat tar-paper roof was quite large, many thousands of square feet. I was soooo anxious. Only problem? It was raining! It rained the next day and the next.

Finally a clear night! I had bought the only star book I could find: "A Beginner's Star Guide", so I had a vague idea what to search for. New York City light pollution was only a tiny fraction of what it is today. You could actually *see* the beautiful bright streak of the Milky Way on a clear night!

So I pointed my scope towards the brightest star in the sky. Shock! There was a small striped marble with four tiny bright dots around it! I had discovered Jupiter! Of course it was four-hundred years after Leonardo, but in that moment I WAS Leonardo!

I became quite popular in the neighborhood because my friends, who were frequently invited to the roof, were astonished! Remember, this is before TV, and long before fantastic printed detailed images of the cosmos were even imagined. I became a local legend!

In the ensuing months I found other planets and double stars. The moon was my favorite target. Believe it or not, I still own my now-antique SKYSCOPE. It turns out that it actually had excellent optics, far better than any beginner's scope today.

Over the years I have built two large rotating-dome observatories, one in New Jersey and one in Arizona. Each had a 16" fully automated "catadioptric" Celestron-brand scope. Because of technological advances today, $1,500 will buy you a scope capable of sights that only massive observatories enjoyed when I was a child. For the $2,500 my SKYSCOPE cost in today's money you can buy an exceptional professional-quality telescope from many different manufacturers.

So what does all this blather have to do with existential threats to our very existence. WELL, INDIRECTLY, MY LIFE-LONG STUDY OF THE COSMOS HAS MADE ME FULLY AWARE OF THE VASTNESS OF THE UNIVERSE AND **THE <u>ABSOLUTE FACT</u> THAT EARTH WILL NOT BE AROUND FOREVER!**

I have studied and learned all of the ways that the Universe wants to destroy us and it's pretty scary. Am I an "apocalypticist:? Jesus apparently was. "End Times" are a certainty. Resurrection? Heaven and Hell? Who can say?

Astrophysicists are generally in agreement that everything began with a "Big Bang", instantaneous creation of the known universe out of a tiny point of energy containing everything. The Hand of GOD? That, to me, is as good an explanation as any. I do not see science and religion as being mutually exclusive.

Apparently two kinds of matter appeared at first: regular

matter and anti-matter. When a particle of regular matter meets a particle of anti-matter they annihilate each other! So why wasn't this Big Bang a zero-sum event leading to nothingness? It is believed that there was a very tiny imbalance with one atom in a million (1 PPM) more of regular matter being created. No one can explain this initial disparity, but here we all are to prove it!

Albert Einstein's magical simple equation, "E=mc squared" explains it all. Don't ask. Just accept that all life is created from death, the death of stars exploding and sending the various elements for life out into the universe. These elements eventually coalesce into stars, planets, and us. A bit oversimplified, but essentially accurate.

The earth is a minuscule ball of rock in a massive galaxy in an unimaginably large universe. We're just a tiny spec in our own Milky Way Galaxy, and there are many millions of other galaxies. We are a target for all manner of events that could wipe out all life in the blink of an eye.

Planet earth and we feeble beings, cosmically speaking, are very fortunate in one way. *We are a very tiny target whirling about in an incomprehensibly large universe.*

We have learned all we know about the universe in the past few hundred years. In fact, what has been learned in my lifetime alone is huge. I have in my library, among hundreds of more-recent astronomy books, the "Beginner's Star Guide" mentioned earlier. It was published in the 1940s. The information, and photos contained in that book are so outdated as to actually be comical! We knew almost nothing about the Universe, or our own local Galaxy, our moon, or our local neighborhood, the planets and *their* moons.

Galileo is credited with creating the first simple telescope.

Through his small crude instrument he was the first to see the four brightest moon of Jupiter! Earth-based telescopes got larger and more powerful over hundreds of years. It was not until our two amazing space telescopes were launched that the true nature of the universe was revealed to astronomers and astrophysicists.

First was the "Hubble Telescope", placed in orbit in 1990. Initially it was a shocking flop! Somehow the designers had incorporated a flaw in the design that resulted in blurred images. The scope had been placed in a relatively low earth orbit, just above our atmosphere. By a near miracle it was possible to send astronauts up to do repairs. They did, and the scope worked flawlessly thereafter. It expanded man's knowledge of the heavens exponentially.

Then it was decided to create a much larger and more sensitive instrument. This complex telescope was to be placed at an altitude of 1.5 million kilometers by an Ariadne 5 rocket in 2021. The distance from earth to make a space mission to repair it would be impossible. It had to be flawless.

It took over a decade to build. It was so large it had to be folded to get it into the rocket and launch it. Once it arrived at its space destination it had to unfold perfectly. It was the greatest engineering feat in modern history! It performed perfectly from day one. It is called "The James Webb Space Telescope".

Quite different from the Hubble, it sees in the infrared and can peer back through the universe almost to the moment of the Big Bang, some fourteen billion years ago. It is much more sensitive than Hubble and has produced hundreds of thousands of amazing images. Webb has photographed distant galaxies, the births of stars and planets, planets around distant stars and our own planets and their moons.

Webb is hoped to have a useful life of five to ten years. Yet it would only take one single hit from some tiny fast-moving space-nasty to disable it permanently.

Based on the geological record, scientists believe that earth has seen two mass-extinction events in its history. They also believe that we could be long overdue for a third. We are said to be in "an extinction quiet period". The most imminent virtually-certain extinction event is not, however, from The Cosmos, but from right here on earth. Discussed in Chapter SEVEN is the Yellowstone Park Super-Volcano.

We have a large neighbor galaxy called "The Andromeda Galaxy". It is actually visible to the naked eye, and spectacular looking through even a small telescope. Our Milky Way Galaxy and the Andromeda Galaxy are on a direct collision course! Approaching at a snail's-pace of seventy-miles-per-second it will take four billion years before our mutual black holes collide and destroy everything. But it will happen.

Items much smaller than colliding galaxies are a far more present existential threat to humanity. I am referring to asteroids. These are called meteors as pieces of all sizes fall to earth. They streak through the atmosphere every minute of every day. We only see their streaks at night. Most are sand grains that burn up upon entry through our atmosphere. Some land. These are called meteorites. They are avidly collected by individuals such as me.

I've actually seen a large meteor impact crater. Right here in Arizona is "Meteor Crater". This large hole was created by a meteor that fell some 55,000 years ago. At that time (The Pleistocene Era) Arizona was wetter and cooler and covered with grasslands and forests. Woolly Mammoths and Giant Ground Sloths were the predominant land mammals, with man slowly evolving elsewhere, probably in Africa. Rattlesnakes and Gila Monsters came much later.

This meteor left a large hole 3,900 feet in diameter and 560 feet deep. It has become a worldwide tourist attraction, with a museum and viewing platform on one rim. Back in the 1960s one could even buy pieces of the recovered meteoric crust. I own a lovely five-pound chunk among the dozens of other meteorites in my extensive worldwide-falls collection.

Had this meteor hit a modern city it would have obliterated it.

Asteroids are space debris, located in orbit between Mars and Jupiter. They are either the remains of a destroyed planet, or a planet that never formed. There are billions of them, from the size of sand grains to massive city-sized behemoths.

We have sensitive instruments that track the larger asteroids. One such, "Asteroid ft3" was first discovered in 2007, and it looked large and dangerous. Then it was lost from our instruments for a while. It has been recently re-discovered. We had better watch it more closely. It is large and has a very real possibility of colliding with earth in October 2924. But that is very far in the future. Plenty of time to prepare?

Asteroid "Bennu", a loose agglomeration of rock and ice is due for a close encounter with earth in only five years. We recently sent a successful probe there to return samples. We are tracking this asteroid closely. A collision with earth could result in an extinction event. There is a real possibility it will hit earth in 2182, but unlikely sooner.

The dangerous biggie is "Apophis". This is a total-extinction-level asteroid about the size of Manhattan Island in New York. It was first discovered at the Kitt Peak Observatory near my present home in Arizona. Apophis will cross earth's path on Friday the thirteenth in April 2029. Will we be in the same place in our orbit at the same time? NO ONE KNOWS FOR CERTAIN!

When first discovered, Apophis was estimated to have a 3% chance of destroying all life on earth in 2029. That's soon! That estimate has been updated recently to something much more unlikely but still **not zero**. My fear is that as usual we are not being told the whole truth to prevent wide-spread panic.

As recently as 1908 a small space-something exploded over a sparsely-populated area of forest over the Tunguska area of Russia's Siberia. The sonic shockwave flattened hundreds of miles of forest. There was some debate as to whether the object was an asteroid or a comet. Recent expeditions to the forest failed to find any space-rock particles. This led to the conclusion that the object that exploded was most likely an icy comet.

Even more recently, just eleven years ago, another untracked meteor exploded without warning over the city of Chelyabinsk, Russia. The shock wave broke windows for miles around and caused 1,600 injuries. Scientists believe that had this meteor come in at a different angle or been a bit larger it would have stuck the ground and killed tens of thousands.

You see, astronomers can track the orbit of any large asteroid with some degree of precision, once they actually find it. All asteroid orbits change literally every second of every day! Orbits are affected by our sun's solar-wind particles. They are affected by the gravity of other asteroids as they pass by. Their orbits are also affected by the orbits of the giant planets Jupiter and Saturn. So for all intents and purposes it is virtually impossible to make a 100% accurate orbital prediction. There are simply too many variables.

Astronomers make their "best guess" at the possibility of an exact timing of the orbits of earth and a particular asteroid being at the same exact point in space at exactly the same time for a kablooie event. I hate "best guesses" when the extermination of civilization lies in the balance!

We have many proposals for changing the orbits of dangerous asteroids. One solution involves focused lasers powerful enough to deflect an asteroid just enough to change its orbit. We're not there yet but it is theoretically possible. Present military work on laser weapons could speed up development of the asteroid-moving process.

We recently proved beyond any doubt that we can deflect an asteroid's orbit by crashing an object into it. This was NASA's "DART" Project (**D**ouble **A**steroid **R**edirection **T**est.) We did this in 2022 aimed at a small moon named Didymos. Didymos orbits a minor asteroid named Dimorphos. Our small impactor deflected Didymos slightly. We also blew off a huge cloud of particles out the opposite side from the impact. Each particle would then have its own potentially dangerous orbit. Good try. Definitely showed promise. Deflection, "Yes." Problem solved? Not quite.

The common suggestion that we could just send up a hydrogen bomb to destroy an asteroid sounds great. But what happens to the pieces that result? Any guesses?

An interesting and possibly useful solution is to send a

spacecraft to an asteroid and anchor it just off the surface. Then the tiny gravity of the space vehicle could, over time, move the asteroid's orbit just enough to prevent a catastrophe. As a last resort we can just do nothing and hope earth continues to remain lucky!

Asteroids are the most obvious existential threat. There are millions of them and we can track the big dangerous ones. That is, except the sneaky ones we may not see coming.

Aside from the relatively small one that landed in Arizona, it is well documented that big space rocks have impacted earth in the past. There is a huge crater in South Africa. The most famous is the biggie that landed near Yucatan in Mexico. That space-pebble is credited with killing off the dinosaurs and just about all other life as well! The really big ones cause mass-extinction events.

In addition to asteroid worries, there are comets. These millions of balls of mostly ice are located far out beyond the dwarf planet Pluto, in what is known as the "Oort Cloud". Occasionally one is barfed out of the cloud and orbits the sun, ultimately reaching the general area of earth.

Within recent decades I was been fortunate to spend many nights on the roof of my home in the Arizona's High Sonoran Desert watching the beautiful naked eye comets Hyakutake in 1996 and Hale-Bopp.in 1997. Neither was a collision threat., but beautiful to behold and photograph.

Was the "*Star* of Bethlehem" a bright comet? Many astronomers believe so.

Depending on its initial size, any comet will eventually be stripped of all its ice by solar particles and disappear. Big ones, such as "Halley's Comet" orbit the sun in relatively short predictable time periods. This famous comet has a "period" of about 76 years. This has been unchanged over and over for centuries. It is the only bright naked-eye comet that in theory could be witnessed twice in a single lifetime.

First recorded in 240BC, it was English astronomer Edmond Halley in 1705 who first predicted the periodic nature of the comet that bears his name. My wife and I were fortunate enough to view Halley's Comet from the Australian outback in 1986. I doubt whether I will be around to see its next fly-by in 2061.

If you ever care to experience REALLY dark skies go to Australia and drive between Alice Springs and Ayers Rock. When you step outside your car, the "closeness" of the stars is absolutely breathtaking. It is a life-changing experience one never forgets.

Are comets a danger to life on earth? Yes, in the same manner as asteroids. Collision with a big one could easily destroy the earth together with anything living on it at the time.

What about the many other dangers lurking in the cosmos that we can't actually see, such as the cosmic rays discussed earlier?

For starters, astronomers believe there are rogue "black holes" drifting about in space. These nasties have gravity so intense that even photons of light cannot escape. If earth happens to encounter one, the result would not be pretty. And we'd never see it coming, because it is invisible!

There are also rogue *planets* floating around aimlessly throughout the Universe. These have somehow escaped their parent stars. It is estimated that within our Milky Way Galaxy alone there are many thousands. They are virtually undetectable. Direct encounter with one would have the same effect as bumping into a black hole: Oblivion!

Has a rogue planet ever hit earth? The answer appears to be "yes"! During earth's early formation, a Mars-size object collided with earth and is credited with creating the moon from the resulting splat.

There are even thousands of rogue *stars*. These have been ejected from their galactic centers, including our own, and travel in totally unpredictable directions literally out of their galaxies and into space. We don't know of any headed our way. Yet.

Light can kill. Have you ever taken a simple magnifying lens and focused the sun on a small stick? It bursts into flame from the focused intensity of the light. Consider this focused beam of light on super-steroids. What you have are gamma rays. And earth is the stick!

As an aside, one should NEVER look at the sun through binoculars or a telescope. Your retina will burn and you go blind. This is why a young child should never be gifted a telescope.

Commercial "eclipse glasses" have a special coated lens that makes it safe to view the sun at any time. Many people choose to bypass them and attempt to view the sun directly. It only takes a second or so to cause irreversible eye damage. This explains why ophthalmologists' offices were swamped by new patients after the April 2024 solar eclipse.

Apparently many "eclipse glasses" sold over the internet were not the quality needed for full protection and caused eye damage. ALWAYS buy these glasses *only* from reputable companies that advertise in the major astronomy magazines.

Flashes of super-intense light, called "gamma rays", spawned from cosmic explosions, can destroy the earth in a flash (bad pun).

Stars are formed from dust within nebula. Depending upon many complex factors, stars can become various sizes and live various lives. Their final demise can take many different forms.

Every day somewhere in the immense universe a star will burn up all of its fuel. It then collapses upon itself and becomes a "neutron star". These can explode in what is called a "supernova". The amount of energy spit out into space from these supernova explosions is beyond comprehension.

Because most stars are very far away from earth, any one exploding would have little effect on us. But any supernova occurring within 500 or so light years could send us a dose of intense light, gamma rays, that could strip away our atmosphere and kill all life on earth.

Are we aware of any nearby star about to go "boom"? YES WE ARE! Right here in our Milky Way Galaxy, Betelgeuse, in the constellation Orion, is one such star. It is a "red giant" star. It is so large that if it were in place of our sun its surface would extend out to the orbit of Jupiter! That's really big.

It is located just 640 light years away. And it may have already exploded! If it went supernova today we wouldn't know until 2664. BUT, if it exploded back in 1384 during the Siege of Lisbon by the Castillian Army, we could all be dead from that gamma-ray burst sometime soon! Not a comforting thought.

How far away could light from a supernova actually be seen? In 2016, an observatory in Chile saw a supernova explosion that occurred 4.6 billion miles away! In 2008 earth took a harmless direct gamma ray hit. Fortunately it was from an event that occurred before the formation of our solar system, and had lost its potentially deadly energy.

Our own mid-aged sun itself will eventually destroy the earth. It cannot be avoided. As it burns off all of its fuel in five billion years or so, it will expand until the orbits of Mercury, Venus and Earth are INSIDE the sun! Mankind had better find another home planet, sooner than later, or we become crispie-crisps.

Our nearby star, "That Lucky Old Sun", is somewhat predictable. Every eleven years it decides to get really nasty. We are nearing one of these solar-cyclic nasty periods. Recent particle-outbursts from the sun have disrupted radio communications and harmed satellites. The aurora borealis (northern lights) caused by the interaction of solar particles with our atmosphere, have recently been visible well into the northern tier of States.

A solar super-flare has been known to actually warp earth's magnetic field. This field normally protects us from cosmic and solar radiation particles. It is theoretically possible for the sun to literally destroy the magnetic field and end all life above ground almost instantly in what is called a "Mass Coronal Ejection."

A mass coronal ejection of sufficient intensity to destroy civilization actually hit earth back in the 1860s. It destroyed telegraph communication. Fortunately it happened pre- Industrial Revolution, pre- electric grid and pre-communication satellites.

What other horrors of the universe are lurking out there? The Universe is an incredibly violent place. Stars are born. Stars die. Cosmic explosions beyond comprehension occur daily. Our good fortune is that the Universe is rather large compared to our Milky Way Galaxy, let alone compared to our private third rock from the sun.

There are events known to astronomers and astrophysicists that are violent beyond human comprehension. In 2013, a collision between two neutron stars was detected. It was called a "kilonova". The amount of energy released had no scientific means of expression.

Colliding neutron stars create theoretical particles called "singlets". So, it is believed, does the collision between a neutron star and a black hole. Think of singlets performing as anti-matter. Are any singlets headed towards earth from the far reaches of the universe? Astronomers hope not but cannot be certain.

Astrophysics is an incredibly complex field of knowledge and understanding. If by some weird accident an astrophysicist is reading this chapter PLEASE excuse my very elementary understanding and explanation of cosmic events. I am aware that my discourse is far from perfectly accurate.

We are helpless passengers on a tiny rock hurtling through space. We are in the cross hairs of countless possible entities that can kill us all in an instant. This planet will die. It is not if but when.

To reiterate, we are a very tiny target in an immense universe. Almost all of the many potentially lethal cosmic bullets miss us every day. Whether our good fortune will continue until we figure out how to get off the earth and colonize a safer place before something lethal hits us is anyone's guess.

My arthritic fingers get cramps from crossing!

CHAPTER FOURTEEN

LITTLE GREEN MEN – UFOs & EXTRATERRESTRIALS

"The most important encounter of all is yet to come." Erich von Daniken, author, (1936-   ).

"I saw an immense cloud with flashing lightening and surrounded by brilliant light. The center of the fire looked like glowing metal, and in the fire was what looked like four living creatures." Bible, Old Testament, Ezekiel 1:20.

Are extraterrestrials real? Are they a serious existential threat to humanity? Are we alone in the universe? Are UFOs Chinese experimental craft? Russian? Our own? These are matters of endless speculation, discussion, argument and a lack of hard evidence.

DATELINE NOVEMBER 2011, WHITE HOUSE, WASHINGTON D. C.

"The U. S. Government has no evidence that any life exists outside our planet, or that an extraterrestrial presence has contacted or engaged any member of the human race. In addition, there is no credible information to suggest that any evidence is being hidden from the public's eye."

They go on to acknowledge that the existence of alien life is *possible*, but the vast distances throughout the Cosmos make alien contact with humans impossible. This report simply continued sixty years of denials and cover-ups.

In a shocking turnaround in 2021, the Government issued a report based mostly on two recent years of U. S, Navy pilots' reports. They studied radar images of strange objects that were often sighted and photographed. They admitted that out of hundreds of events studied they could only state with certainty that *one single sighting* could be explained! While the report did not mention the possibility of "extraterrestrials", they never excluded the possibility.

The most significant outcome provided by this report was the blessing of Uncle Sam for any and all service members of all Branches, and any government employees, or any private citizen, to report **any** unusual sightings! For decades, individuals coming forward were excoriated. Some were fired. All were labeled as liars or kooks. Most simply learned to keep their mouths shut.

I have heard it said that only morons, the naïve, and the uneducated believe in UFOs and extraterrestrials. I've been called all of these and worse. I can assure you I am none of the above.

When I was in my thirties I read Erich von Daniken's 1968 book "*Chariots Of The Gods*". Thereafter, I was a true believer in extraterrestrials. His reasoning made a lot of sense. Since then he has written a mere thirty-one more books and is credited with selling sixty-three million copies overall, in many different languages.

In his more recent 2010 *"Twilight of the Gods"* he predicts the **return** to earth once again of extraterrestrials. I do not doubt it for an instant.

In Shakespeare's *'Hamlet*", Act III, Scene II, he penned the phrase: "Methinks the Lady protesteth too much." It referred to a torrent of contrary statements that were clearly made for the purpose of hiding a truth.

The classic case in point of denial is of course America's "Area 51" in Roswell, New Mexico.. In July 1947 a disk-shaped craft came to a one-skip crash in the desert. The debris from the ship was seen physically by those first on the scene. After initial media reports of a crashed "Flying Saucer", once the authorities took control it was announced to have been a weather balloon. Weather balloon? Really? The media promptly retracted the original accurate account.

Since that time a number of "whistle-blowers" have come forth with additional information about Area 51. These are individuals who can prove that they were physically there during the incident. They confirm that it was **not** a weather balloon. It was a disk shaped craft, as reported by the few ranchers who were first on the scene. It contained two dead alien beings, and one that was quite alive and captured without incident. The damaged craft was spirited away to an unknown location for study and reverse-engineering.

Autopsies were performed on the two bodies. The surviving alien mysteriously disappeared. To this day the government denies that this incident was other than a non-event. Who do *you* believe?

In 2012 an event occurred that to me is equally suspicious. It relates to a live streaming video from the "**So**lar and **H**eliospheric **O**bservatory" known as SOHO. This is a satellite launched in 1995 as a joint NASA/European Space Agency venture specifically to study our sun and its activities.

On two occasions the SOHO video images appeared to show a mysterious, huge, rectangular object in the immediate vicinity of the sun! This rather fuzzy image is, of course, subject to viewer interpretation. The image certainly shows "something" there. As soon as this object was reported NASA suspiciously disabled the video stream. Talk about food for conspiracy theorists!

The mysterious "something" of course was explained away as either a natural phenomenon or a glitch in the imaging system. How about an alien spacecraft? Just asking.

If you accuse me of being a devoted "Star Trek" fan I'd say: "Guilty as charged." I have been a science fiction enthusiast since I was a child. I haven't read everything written by Isaac Asimov, but I've tried! A fellow MENSAN, I believe he is credited with writing over *six-hundred* sci-fi books and short stories.

Though less prolific as writers, Ray Bradbury, Arthur Clarke and Robert Heinlein are my other favorites. All really great reads. Decades earlier, Jules Verne, H.G. Wells, and Edgar Rice Burroughs wrote amazing science fiction books as well.

Movies such as "2001 – A Space Odyssey", "Avatar", and "John Carter", along with the "Star Wars" and "Star Trek" movies, have always captured my imagination.

The death of Carl Sagan affected me deeply. His "Cosmos" TV series and book should be required viewing and study by everyone before they are granted even a High School diploma. Most Americans have received almost no astronomy education.

There was one point Sagan made almost in passing that impressed me more than anything I have ever contemplated. **He stated that there are more stars in the cosmos than there are grains of sand on all of the beaches on earth.** That's one hell of a lot of stars!

Each galaxy contains hundreds of billions, if not trillions of stars. Our own Milky Way Galaxy, a rather medium sized unremarkable galaxy, is said to contain around a half-trillion stars itself. These numbers are very hard to
comprehend. They *almost* approach our National Debt. (See Chapter ELEVEN).

The brilliant visionary writer Arthur C. Clarke said: "Innumeracy is an even greater danger than illiteracy." Once we started teaching social, sexual, and environmental-"crises" to the apparent exclusion of fundamental math and language skills and civics, we became a country on a downward spiral compared to other developed countries in all academic areas. Astronomy is certainly one of them. We are, in the words of one-time Tucson AM drive-time radio announcer John Justice, on "an endless parade of stupid."

Professional astronomers are finding that almost every star they study has a planetary system of some kind. Our Milky Way galaxy, which in itself, with its half-trillion stars, is a collection of those tiny sand grains of which Sagan so eloquently spoke. **It appears that planets are the rule, not the exception. It is estimated that there are hundreds of millions of planets in our home galaxy, perhaps one in ten of those capable of sustaining life as we know it.**

That's a lot of planets, and ours is just our one of trillions of galaxies. The point is, we can be quite certain that the number of planets in all of the galaxies in the universe is a number so large that it in itself is almost beyond human comprehension.

<u>With so many planets, how can anyone possibly believe that we are alone in the Universe? It is inconceivable.</u> In *"COSMOS"*, Carl Sagan, the greatest astronomy-communicator of all time, stated: "To me, it seems far more likely that the universe is brimming over with life."

Some planets are too close to their parent stars to be habitable due to solar heat. Others are to far and so cold that atoms virtually cease to move. But there is an ill-defined "Goldilocks Zone" where a theoretical surface and atmosphere would be "not to hot and not too cold" as with Goldilocks' porridge.

We also focus, not necessarily correctly, on planets where we believe liquid water exists. We insist that, because life on earth is based mostly on water, no water, no life. Probably a very bad assumption.

We cannot exclude the possibility of life developing elsewhere that thrives on something other than water. Ammonia based, sulfur based, silicon based? Why not?

One thing we have learned in the past decade is the existence of "extreme beings." These are known as "extremophiles." These are living creatures that have evolved on earth to withstand, heat, cold, radiation, absence of light, extreme pressure and vacuum. It seems hard to believe but these are real creatures, with dozens of well documented examples.

At the bottom of the ocean, at depths that would crush almost everything, there are colonies of complex creatures, even fish, that thrive. There are specialized creatures that live near "smokers", undersea vents that spew out hot water and toxic chemicals. Before we actually photographed these creatures oceanographers never believed them to be possible.

Let's look at space. No air. Near absolute zero temperature. Scientists sent up colonies of tardigrads, also known as "water bears", cute little microscopic critters, to the space station and left them *outside* for days. They were exposed to extreme radiation, cold and no air. When returned to earth many of these exposed tardigrads survived and prospered!

Even more amazing is that fact that plankton-like tiny critters called "diatoms" have been found on the *outside* windows of a space station. These are a unique form of algae, each having a shell of silica. When collected and returned to earth these tiny beings thrived!

Let's look at glacial ice. Much of it was formed eons ago, during the great "Ice Age" when the planet was covered with meters of frozen water. Scientists recently extracted cores of ice from thousands of years ago from deep caves in Iceland.

WHEN THEY THAWED THE ICE CORES THEY WERE ASTONISHED TO FIND TINY CRITTERS SWIMMING AROUND! SOME WERE AS COMPLEX AS LITTLE WORMS. These had been frozen solid for eons, yet somehow returned to life.

Scientists have studied the steam vents and bubbling mud pots in Yellowstone Park. Sure enough despite incredibly hot conditions and a sulfur environment many little critters were found living and thriving.

Astronomers have concrete reason to believe that organisms can live within the ice of comets and within the ice and rocks of asteroids. Particles from these bodies rain down on earth in quantities estimated at thousands of tons a day!

This is the world of extremophiles. It is not too great a stretch to believe that somewhere extremophiles have found a way to evolve even to the point of sentience. Earth-like environments may not necessarily be a prerequisite for life to evolve.

So, where *are* the aliens? Are they monitoring humans for some reason? If so, I can imagine that their stand-up comedians, whether standing on two, four, eight or hundreds of legs, will never lack for material!

Scientists theorize many reasons why we have not physically encountered them in recent history. Of course if you study the ancient Sumerian tablets, Hindu Vedas, Indian and Chinese manuscripts, Egyptian ancient history, Australian Aboriginal beliefs, Japanese ancient writings and Hebrew scrolls it seems irrefutable that aliens *did* visit earth in the far distant past. Just apparently not *recently.*

That is, unless you consider a weird object that cruised past earth and around the sun in late 2023. This long, cigar-shaped object was confirmed as not being from within our solar system. Its orbit showed that it was clearly from interstellar space! It was named "Oumuamua", in Hawaiian meaning: "A Messenger From Afar Arriving First".

Anyone familiar with the four great sci-fi novels by Arthur C. Clarke , which debuted with "Rendezvous With Rama" in 1972, recognized this object immediately as an alien spacecraft! Scientists do not agree on what Oumuamua was, or its purpose. It is a mystery for the ages.

The most obvious reason aliens have not been met face to face is the vastness of space. We measure astronomical distances in "light-time", the time it takes photons of light to traverse a particular distance.

Light travels about 183,000 MILES in one second. That seems pretty fast! Our SUN, our nearest star, is on average 8.32 light-*minutes* (about 500 light seconds) away. In astronomical terms, that's a stone's-throw.

We see the sun as it was about eight minutes ago! The next

nearest star, Proxima Centauri, is located 4.2 light YEARS away. That's a tad further than the sun. You view that star as it actually was over four years ago!

Whether an alien species can figure out how to travel near to the speed of light is considered improbable. Can "warp speeds" in excess of the speed of light be achieved? Not according to Einstein. Absolutely "yes" according to "Star Trek".

But there is one theoretically possible way to travel vast distances quickly: TIME TRAVEL. According to Albert Einstein's hypothesis, enlarged upon by Stephen Hawkings, time travel <u>is theoretically possible.</u>

I tried reading Hawking's "A Brief History of Time". Although it was written in English it may as well have been in Greek! I quit after a few chapters. Not recommended reading unless you happen to have a PhD in theoretical physics. I'm just a lowly Chemical Engineer.

There is also the interesting possibility of "wormholes", distortions in space-time connecting disparate destinations at different times in history.

A recent real-life report of a possible time-distortion was by a private pilot flying in the infamous "Bermuda Triangle" from The Bahamas to Miami, Florida. Shortly after takeoff from The Bahamas he flew into a strange haze. His instruments went haywire.

When he flew out of the haze and arrived at his destination of Miami, Florida, he had flown for an impossibly short time. He arrived in less than one-quarter the air time his plane could possibly have achieved! There was no logical explanation except for a time-space distortion. His story was confirmed by ground radar.

There is also the widely accepted theory of parallel universes. Is our known universe the *only one?* Why not two? Why not an infinite number?

A large portion of the scientific community believes that there are many possible other dimensions. Some speculate on the existence of "bubble universes" whose edges occasionally touch and allow occupants of one universe to appear in another. Something called "String Theory" allows for other worlds beyond our comprehension. This, too, is the realm for advanced physicists.

Which brings us to **U**nidentified **F**lying **O**bjects, UFOs. Recently these have been renamed UAPs, **U**nidentified **A**erial **P**henomena.

There is such an overwhelming volume of recorded sightings by military pilots, professional airline pilots, astronauts, private pilots, radar, and countless people on the ground, that it is hard not believe that these craft really do exist But are they piloted by "Little Green Men"? Unlikely.

The forces exerted by many of the observed instantaneous aerial maneuvers would crush anything of flesh and blood, no matter what color the blood might be! These craft are either remotely controlled and unmanned, or manned by Artificial-Intelligence-enabled machines or robots.

Are the inhabitants of these craft an existential threat to

earth? My belief is that if they wanted to do so they could wipe out humanity in a heartbeat whenever they choose. Last time I looked we're still here.

Apparently UAPs exist for surveillance of unknown purposes. Could alien robots be capable of invisibility? Could they be able to assume whatever shape or form they choose, the so-called "shape-shifters"? Could they walk among us undetected? Many believe this is a real possibility. The person walking next to you could be from an Orion or a Pleiades-area planet! Scary.

It is not only the Judeo/Christian Bible and other religious texts that clearly speak of flying saucers and extraterrestrials. Many artworks created by Renaissance artists in the 15th and 16th centuries clearly depict flying saucers! The UFOs are often located rather obscurely up in a corner, but they are unmistakable.

There are many recorded UFO sightings from hundreds of years ago. In Basil, Switzerland in 1644 most townspeople were astonished by the flying vessel they *all* saw in the sky. In Nurenberg, Bavaria, just seven years later, thousands were terrified by the sight of a large flying saucer.

In Japan in 1803 a flying saucer not only washed up on a beach but aliens were seen walking out of it! Were these all simple incidents of mass hysteria as many non-UFO believers would have you believe? I think not.

Hanging in the Palazzo Vecchio in Florence, Italy is a painting attributed to the artist Ghirlandaio: "Madonna with Saint Giovannino". It is known locally as "Madonna of the UFO"! Off to one side it shows a man on a hill shading his eyes looking up towards an obvious flying saucer. Close examination of the painting shows tiny faces looking down from the saucer!

A famous painting by Carlo Crivelli called "The Annunciation, with St. Emibius" depicts the Virgin Mary. In the sky above her is a large flying saucer with a ray-beam coming down to Mary's side. Allegory? Or a depiction of something the painter once witnessed and chose to include it in this religious art work.

Have alien civilizations mastered anti-gravity? Or anti-magnetism? Many physicists believe these things are theoretically possible. Remember, alien civilizations could be millions, even billions of years older than ours. They had a lot of time to learn a lot of good stuff. Humans are mere newborns.

Let us assume for the moment that sentient aliens actually exist. What might they look like? Are they the classic four-foot tall critters with big heads and oval eyes? These are known as "The Grays", as the ones that crashed near Area 51.

There are actual reports that humanoid aliens have had audiences with past American presidents! Are there on-going negotiations with alien civilizations for whatever reason? This all sounds crazy, but we probably will never be told the truth. There are many whistle-blowers who swear that this is all true.

I will only touch upon two well-documented instances. There have been books written about these, and there are volumes of information on the internet.

Three Presidents have reported seeing UFOs: Nixon, Carter, and Reagan. President Truman appeared to be in total denial. He did everything he could to debunk UFOs.

The two reported personal encounters with extraterrestrials on earth were with Presidents Eisenhower and Nixon. In 1954 Eisenhower suddenly disappeared from public view. The AP actually reported that he had died! On February 20th, at a secret location on a U.S. Air Force Base, Eisenhower is said to have had a face to face meeting with extraterrestrials. He was reportedly offered a deal: Give up all nuclear weapons in exchange for humanity-advancing knowledge.

Eisenhower refused, believing that Russia, offered the same deal, would refuse, thus leaving the United States defenseless if he agreed. Once Eisenhower reappeared in public life, he would never discuss the incident but did not deny it.

In 1973 Richard Nixon was invited to a meeting with extraterrestrials at a secret location. He invited his close friend Jackie Gleason, the comedian, to accompany him.

It was rumored that some sort of Agreement with an Alien Federation was reached. The only fact that adds credibility to this story is an account by Gleason's wife. Upon his return home he was apparently so shaken by what he had seen that it took months for him to regain his composure.

The most historic story relates to a totally private meeting between President Ronald Reagan and Michael Gorbachev. It was at this meeting that it was decided to "tear down that wall" as Reagan had earlier requested.

Why did Gorbachev agree? Apparently both leaders concurred that an attack on earth by hostile extraterrestrials was a real threat. The United States and Russia having better relations would open the door for a mutual response should such an attack happen.

Are these stories factual? Needless to say our government will never tell us the truth. We are just too stupid to handle the truth.

Aside from countless Biblical accounts, there are two events that add credence to the "ancient aliens" theory. In his writings none other than George Washington, at a dark and desperate moment in the war at the Valley Forge encampment, writes that he was visited by an alien being.

This "angel from heaven" appeared to Washington and gave him the encouragement and will to proceed against insurmountable odds. Shortly thereafter his re-spirited troops won the war! Score one for "Little Green Men", and the founding of The United States.

Christopher Columbus recorded in his logs frequent sightings of strange glowing lights at sea in the middle of nowhere!

Is there any reason why all alien races should look alike? Is humanoid form the only model for sentient life? Of course not. Just look at the millions of different species on earth. Elephants look quite different from mice. Redwood trees are easily distinguished (by most people!) from petunias.

If there are many, perhaps millions of advanced alien races scattered throughout the universe why could not some have eight legs and four eyes? Four legs and eight eyes? Wings? Purple flesh? Exist as pure energy? Live under water? Live in the vacuum of space?

Astronauts aboard the International Space Station reported "angel like" beings floating about outside their capsule. These were trained professionals and unlikely delusional, especially as a group. They all agreed to what they saw. Mass hysteria? Unlikely. Extraterrestrial beings? Likely.

There are many stories of alien abductions of humans. Most are dismissed as dreams or hallucinations. One recent case, however, is very hard to dismiss. In 1961 a married couple, Betty and Barney Hill, claimed to have been abducted by aliens during a drive along a country road. They were taken aboard a spaceship and had various experiments performed on them. Then they were returned to their car.

Each was placed separately under intense professional hypnotism. Their recollections were *identical*. After years of interviews and study both have remained steadfast in their belief that they were actually taken aboard a UFO.

Hollywood has made millions depicting aliens. I vividly remember the 1951 film "The Thing from Another World". That alien, played by famous actor James Arness, was sort of a living carrot! Then there was the very scary 1958 flick "The Blob." This alien critter could ooze itself just about anywhere. The Blob played itself.

The hilarious 1999 movie "Galaxy Quest" portrayed a friendly shape-shifting alien race that could assume human appearance but were actually octopus-like creatures. In that same movie a different alien race was portrayed as a hostile lizard-people. And let's not forget Star Trek's lizard spaceship captain of "The Gorn" species. Scary stuff!

Other comical alien movies included the 2011 movie "Paul". It depicted a stranded, wise-cracking, dope-smoking, foul-mouthed but very friendly and harmless bipedal humanoid alien.

Most recall the friendly stranded turtle-like creature in the 1982 movie "ET- The Extraterrestrial". He could fly! Or the mute, friendly alien in the 2023 flick "Jules". He possessed other-worldly abilities such as exploding an intruding-burglar's head and turning seven dead cats into flying-saucer fuel! Go figure.

In the 2023 movie "Asteroid City" there are two very brief scenes where a cute skinny bi-pedal friendly alien puts in an appearance. First he is seen climbing down a ladder from his flying saucer to steal the city's prized grapefruit-sized meteorite. He picks up the meteorite. Then, noticing someone with a camera pointed at him he quickly smiles and poses, before returning up the ladder to his flying saucer and disappearing in a flash.

Later on, the saucer returns, and you only see his spindly hands reaching down and gently returning the meteorite, sans a tiny piece he sliced off for study! This guy could not have been less threatening.

Predictably, within minutes of his initial departure, the United States Army descends on this tiny town and quarantines everyone for weeks! Typical expected government over-reaction.

Almost everyone has seen the 1977 movie "Close Encounters of the Third Kind" which depicted friendly aliens conversing through music notes and offering humans a free ride to the cosmos.

But does the imagination of Hollywood and TV writers always make aliens appear benevolent? Far from it!

I vividly recall a great TV program from the 1964 "Twilight Zone" series. A race of tall, human-looking aliens land on earth, professing that they were there to help humanity advance. They were very convincing, and the world rejoiced! The aliens each even carried an instruction book titled "To Serve Man". Turns out it was a *cookbook*!

Or consider the more recent 2015 movie "Jupiter Ascending" where an alien race harvests humans for their genes. All extraterrestrials may not be cute and friendly.

Earlier in the "Twilight Zone" series, in a 1961 episode, a perfectly normal looking farm-woman was in her home and heard terrifying sounds of someone walking on her roof. When she quietly investigated she found this tiny bi-pedal alien creature outside of a mini-spacecraft. The "UFO" had a USAF decal on the side!

The funny little aliens in the 1996 comedy movie "Mars Attacks" (Ack, Ack) "came in peace" and proved quite otherwise.

And of course we have the super-scary aliens in the 1979 and 1986 "Alien" movies and the 1987 "Predator" movie. Not to mention the ground-dwelling aliens in "War of the Worlds". This series of four (the first in 1953) adaptation movies were based on the 1937 radio show narrated by Orson Welles. That show was based on H.G. Wells 1898 book of the same name.

Welles' broadcast, a simulated news cast, was so realistic that it actually caused a country-wide panic! Millions actually believed we were under attack by Martians!

Does this single radio incident explain why governments worldwide are so reluctant to disclose the truth about alien visitors? Are they convinced, rightly or wrongly, that the general populace would panic today as they did from a harmless radio show almost ninety years ago?

The 2008 movie "The Day The Earth Stood Still" portrayed an omnipotent humanoid alien who could suspend time on earth.
His companion was a large robot! He tried to convince humanity that his intentions were peaceful. Humans panicked, and would not believe him, with disastrous results.

Anyone who is familiar with the "Star Trek" TV series is familiar with beings that are advanced far beyond anything we can imagine. Characters such as "Trelane – The Squire of Gothos" are portrayed as beings that could snap their fingers and create any alternate reality, even a planet!

One "Star Trek" Episode portrayed a shape-shifting race of human-appearing beings that showed absolutely no fear when confronted with imminent annihilation. It didn't matter to the Scolosians because they could disarm hostile weapons at will, and create whatever alternative reality they chose.

And again, sticking with "Star Trek's" earliest episodes, a race of benevolent bubble-headed aliens, the Thelosians, were able to create whatever alternate reality *they* desired.

The fascinating character "Q", from the "Star Trek" series, was truly omnipotent. He could create any complex alternate reality scenarios instantly whenever he wished. Could one, or perhaps many, such beings actually exist, the product of BILLIONS of years of evolution within our sixteen billion-year old universe. No one knows. It absolutely cannot be ruled out.

So much for playing "Siskel and Ebert".

My grandmother was born in 1879. I was absolutely fascinated as a child by her stories of life by candlelight, travel by horse and buggy, no running water, and an outhouse! She said life was great!

Such things as automobiles, airplanes and universally available electricity were not even dreamed about during her childhood. Incredible miracles such as telephones, computers, smart-phones and virtual reality devices were beyond imagining. So were flush toilets!

In fact, when I was a kid in the 1940s, jet commercial aircraft, television, computers and cell phones were equally beyond my imagining. In the unlikely event we survive for another hundred, or even fifty years, we simply cannot imagine the advances that will be commonplace in daily life, for good or bad.

Unfortunately, I will never know. Personally, I'm only shooting for 2040! I'd better keep my SCUBA gear handy!

Are extraterrestrials a true existential threat? Will aliens someday take over earth enslaving humans or eliminating us completely? Or will a benevolent race of highly-advanced extraterrestrials teach earthlings about technologies we cannot even imagine today. Could they help us live in peace? Doubtful.

What if they "made us an offer we couldn't refuse"? Such as: "Get along with each other starting today or we will annihilate earth". We'd probably choose annihilation.

There are two curious reports that may indicate that some alien race might want to help humans. In the case of the two prominent nuclear plant disasters, Chernobyl in Russia and Fukushima Daichi in Japan, there were many verified reports of UFOs immediately flying over the disaster sites. Did they in some way prevent these meltdowns from becoming much worse and causing unimaginable damage? What were they monitoring?

Is endless free energy from nuclear fusion, in its very infancy today, a simple reality if one knows how to do it? Aliens probably have already mastered fusion.

Can anti-gravity or anti-magnetism devices be used to move massive objects, as apparently was done on earth in the far-distant past by pre-Adamic civilizations? Did they master the use of sound waves to levitate massive granite blocks?

Can we puny humans be taught how to live healthy productive individual lives for hundreds of years? The Bible and many and diverse ancient texts and Sumerian cuneiform tablets says that conveying extraterrestrial knowledge to humans was commonplace eons ago. We must have missed the lessons on how to peacefully coexist.

The Bible tells us that Enoch, Methuselah's father, "only" lived for 365 years. (Enoch is only mentioned briefly in Genesis 5: "He was not, because GOD took him." The entire "Book of Enoch", included only in the Ethiopian Bible, tells the whole story in Enoch's own words!) His son Methusaleh lived for 979 years, the longest recorded human life.

Methusaleh's son Lamech lived to 777. His great-grandson Noah lived for 950. Moses only made it to 120. Were they all extraterrestrials? Were Biblical-years different from our 365 (or 366) day years?

Is the Bible pure fantasy? If one reads the Bible as a theologian, all of the amazing creatures and events are not accepted literally. They are all considered allegorical. The word of GOD as humans are capable of understanding.

If, however, the Bible stories are read as actual accounts of events that really happened, then these Books can be accepted as the greatest historical accounts of extraterrestrial events ever penned!

As mentioned above, there is a wonderful Bible Text included today only in the 71-Book Ethiopian Christian Bible. It was left out of Jewish, Catholic and Protestant Bibles because it was considered far too controversial for believers to hear. It is "The Book of Enoch".

Enoch wrote eloquently in the first-person. He describes being lifted up into heaven in a loud "Flaming Chariot" (Read "UFO"). He describes in infinite detail what he saw in the spacecraft. He articulated details in the best descriptive words he could have known at the time. He describes seeing the entire globe of the earth below. He was returned to earth, the first recorded alien-abduction in history!

One alien encounter somehow made it past the Bible-censors. In the Book of Ezekiel, he reports a strange craft consisting of "a wheel within a wheel." "Extraterrestrial Spacecraft" were words not in his vocabulary of the day. In the same Book, Ezekiel describes what could be interpreted as a landing spaceship. He describes beings he identified as "Cherubim."

The Bible has countless beings described as Angels, Cherubims, Seraphims, and dragons. Were these imaginary beings? Are they allegorical? Or could they be different races of extraterrestrials?

Who were the "Greek Gods"? They had no fewer than twenty-four of them! The best known are Zeus, Poseidon, Apollo, Ares and Athena. They were giants and possessed unearthly powers. Greek literature certainly indicates that these creatures existed, and came from the heavens to live among and breed with humans.

They created a hybrid race of Demigods called The Olympians, who eventually overthrew the early Gods. Was this all simply a superstitious myth? Or were these real live extraterrestrial beings?

The Sumerian "Kings List", translated from the Aramaic, accounts for rulers each of whom are said to have lived and ruled for many thousands of years! Were they extraterrestrials? Or were they someone's vivid imagination? Or should "years" be translated as "days"?

Who were the "Fallen Angels" of the Bible? The Watchers? Did GOD create the Great Flood (which according to today's archaeologists actually happened) to rid earth of these creatures who bred with humans and produced evil giants? Many theologians believe so.

Do you believe The Bible relates true historical accounts? Do you believe in "little green men"? Or big purple ones? If an alien landed on the White House lawn tomorrow would you freak out? Would our government freak out? We will only know the answers when, not if, we have "first contact". Most likely this will occur sooner than later.

Is it possible that we have actually identified alien creatures on earth! Oceanographers, marine biologists, and geneticists, have concluded that octopuses have absolutely no hereditary lineage. They simply appeared. They did not follow Darwinian evolution at all. Are these creatures with eight arms and nine brains and capable of amazing feats, actually extraterrestrials?

We know far more about the surfaces of Mars and the Moon than we do about the depths of the vast earthly oceans. Might many other extraterrestrials lurk in the depths? Many believe so.

One of the great unsolved mysteries found everywhere on the planet are CROP CIRCLES. They appear to be a relatively recent phenomenon. In 1956 a farmer in Australia witnessed a large metal disk-like object in a field. He saw it take off! On the ground, flattened into a perfect form in the crop, was a circle.

In the decades since scientists have identified over 10,000 "crop circles". It is well within human capability to create relatively simple crop circles. People flatten crops with boards on their feet. There have been many such frauds, easily proven as such by investigators.

Many crop circles are anything *but* circles. They can be *incredibly* complex designs that can cover *acres* of a crop. More important, they appear literally overnight. On some occasions, an extraterrestrial craft has been seen sending down a beam of light to create a complex design. The only possible explanation for the more complex crop circles is extraterrestrials.

What is even more astonishing are the finds archaeologists have made within the past few decades. These have literally rewritten the history of human life on earth.

It was widely believed for decades that "civilization" arose in Sumeria and Egypt, some 5,000 years ago. We had never "dated" anything human-made that was older.

It was also known form the fossil record that humans may have begun to evolve 500,000 years ago. Primitive humans first achieved the ability to draw pictures on cave walls in Africa about 50,000 years ago. For the following 40,000 years or so it was believed that humans were simple hunter-gatherers with slowly evolving stone tools and limited technology. Agriculture and animal husbandry followed later.

Archaeologists have now found hundreds of constructions

that pre-date known human history by tens of thousands if not hundreds of thousands of years. Were these sites built by pre-Adamic civilizations of highly advanced humans?

Or were these incredible constructs created by extraterrestrials with technologies such as powerful lasers, magnetic or harmonic levitation, or anti-gravity? In any event, studying these diverse sites, located all across the globe, certainly provides food for thought. As much food as a huge banquet!

Let's explore a few of these sites which could not possibly have been created by modern humans. Why not? Because even today we do not have the technology or the machinery to build these complex sites. Not even close.

The following is just a small sample of these worldwide marvels.

Let's start with Egypt. Virtually everyone has heard about the Pyramids and The Sphinx. For decades archaeologists believed that the Pharaohs directed their construction.

Recently there is a valid school of thought that believes the erosion on the sides of the Sphinx was caused by heavy rain. In the desert? Well, long before the Pharaohs, that area was a lush plain with lots of rain. If the erosion hypothesis is correct the Sphinx long- predates the known Egyptian civilizations.

The Sphinx was carved in place out of solid rock. It did not require any special tools or machinery. Ancient tools actually could have built it. It is its age that is the subject of much speculation.

The pyramids are a different story. Archaeologists based the dating of these three huge structures on a clever fraud! In the 1800s an archaeologist needed an exciting story to justify the money his backers had paid to fund his expedition. He came back with the amazing tale that within a chamber he created in the Great Pyramid of Giza he found an inscription indicating that the Pharaoh Khufu was the ruler who directed the construction.

Much later an expedition confirmed with absolute certainty that the inscription story was faked! With the Khufu bubble burst, archaeologists today do not have a clue about the true age of the pyramids.

Conventional wisdom for decades was that a large number of Egyptian or possibly Jewish laborers built the pyramids. The massive multi-ton granite blocks were quarried miles away. This was accomplished with crude hand tools. No drills, no dynamite. The blocks had to be precisely shaped and smoothed.

From the remote quarry, the blocks were somehow dragged to the Nile River. Next they were lifted or dragged onto reed barges. The barges themselves had to be extremely well built to carry a multi-ton block. We're talking here about *grass*, hand woven together. That is a major project by itself.

After loading, the reed rafts were hand powered with oars or poles, and floated miles to the job site. Then the blocks were somehow off-loaded from the reed raft and hauled a mile or so inland. This was probably accomplished with rollers created with tree trunks. Once they were rollered across the soft sand the blocks were somehow lifted up and precisely piled to create the pyramid.

By using enough slaves over a *very* long time period, plus enough reeds, plus enough logs, and enough hand-made rope, the Great Pyramid was completed.

With the debunked long-held belief that a Pharaoh was in charge, and with the pyramids now incorrectly dated, there was no logical alternate construction explanation speculated..

The Great Pyramid alone was constructed with 2.3 million blocks estimated to weigh a total of 5.5 million tons! Thinking about this logically makes the "laborer and reed raft" hypothesis look ridiculous.

Try doing the math. It has to take a fair amount of time with *primitive tools* to cut and smooth a multi-ton granite block from a quarry wall. Look at the above trip for a single block. It is hard to believe they could possibly do one block a day, quarry wall to finished block to pyramid. If they could, 2.3 million blocks at one block per day would have taken over six-thousand years! They would have needed to do a hundred blocks a day to finish in one lifetime! It simply makes no sense. Extraterrestrials had to be involved. The only other explanation I can think of is that the pyramids are, say, a hundred thousand years old. In that event a prior pre-Adamic advanced human civilization could have had the time to develop their own extraterrestrial-level technology. Note the following:

Not far from the pyramids is a little known construction called the "Serapeum of Saqqara". This is a massive underground chamber 790 feet long. It is so well made it is absolutely impossible for this to have been cut out of the rock so precisely with ancient tools. The massive chamber contains twenty-four large side-rooms that totally baffle archaeologists.

Each side room contains a huge granite box. Each box is thirteen feet long by seven and a half feet wide by ten feet tall (13' x 7.5' 'x 10'). This is 975 cubic feet of space each! On top of each box is a foot-thick granite lid alone weighing *twenty-five tons*!

The surfaces are smooth as a tabletop. There is no logical explanation for how the ancient Egyptians could possibly have created the underground chambers, and created these massive stone boxes, let alone moving them underground. It had to be a technology either once known by a highly-advanced human iteration, or by extraterrestrials with highly advanced technology.

Is it a stretch to believe that these same beings also built the Pyramids and the Sphinx along the way as a side project? Compared to the Searpeum the pyramids are a "Leggo" project.

Let's look at South America. Across the world from Egypt is a site in Bolivia called Puma Punku. It is high up in the Andes Mountains at a 12,000 foot elevation.

It consists of dozens of massive duplicate pieces that literally fit together as a jigsaw puzzle would to form the walls. Each of these blocks, some being 26' long and weighing 100 tons, has precisely cut glass-smooth sides. They could not possibly be quarried and formed without modern tools and technology.

Cut into the faces of the blocks are perfect rectangles within rectangles. Some blocks have large snaking internal-holes that defy explanation. Some have perfectly spaced deep smaller holes. The exceptional precision of these blocks is absolutely impossible to produce with ancient tools and virtually impossible to recreate today with our latest technology and machines.

The mystery of these perfect, massive, duplicated blocks may have recently been solved. A chemist studied the "granite" material chemically and microscopically. He came to the conclusion that these were actually not made of granite but a type of granite-*plastic mix*! They may actually have been cast in place! Needless to say our ancient hunter-gatherers did not possess this technology either.

Another amazing South American site is Sacayhuaman in Peru. Also high in the Andes Mountains, it consists of a city built of thousands of massive granite blocks. Cutting granite, a mixture of feldspar, mica and quartz, requires at a minimum diamond blades to cut so precisely. These are a modern invention.

What makes the building technique fascinating is the extremely close fit of the blocks. They are not all simple geometric figures. As needed, some were fashioned to fit an intricate irregular space between other blocks. And there is <u>zero</u> space between all of them! No mortar was used to hold it all together.

It appears that the blocks, some weighing 100 tons, were literally *melted* together! This could only have been accomplished with intense heat, as from a laser. A more remote possibility was the use of some super-powerful acid. In either event, we could not duplicate this manner of construction today.

Also worthy of note is the fact that the blocks were quarried at a site thousands of feet *below* on this very steep mountain! Moving them up and into place seems impossible. Local oral legend attributes the lifting of the blocks and the construction of this site to their "Space Brothers", who levitated the blocks into place!

In a remote area of the South Pacific Ocean is a group of 607 islands that form "The Federation of Micronesia". One island in particular, "Pohnpei", is home to an amazing pre-Adamic construction called "Nan Madol". This Island, built upon a coral reef, is believed to be almost entirely artificial!

Known as the "Venice of the Pacific", it is an island of canals. It was built from millions of tons of basalt, beautifully cut into rectangular blocks. The largest block is estimated to weigh fifty tons! The smaller blocks weigh five to ten tons each. They were quarried from a dormant volcano twenty-five miles away.

Local oral Micronesian legend states that the blocks were flown from the volcano "by a giant eagle nesting at the top". The blocks flew into place and were constructed into walls and canals by "Eagle-People". Somehow this sounds to me more like extraterrestrials than birds. Or perhaps extraterrestrials that *looked* like birds, as are many depicted in ancient Egyptian and Samarian wall art.

Throughout the world, whether it be in Egypt, Samaria,

South America, Australia, Japan, India, Mexico, anywhere on earth, or The Holy Bible, "giant birds", "flaming dragons" or "chariots spouting fire" are attributed as bringing knowledge to humans from the Heavens.

Ancients did not have the vocabulary to identify flying saucers or extraterrestrials. They did not have words such as "spaceships", "rocket engines", or any other modern flight technology. If it flew it was a "bird". If it had fire coming out of one end or other it was a "dragon" or a "flaming chariot".

There are also many amazing pre-Adamic sites found in Asia.

Let's swing far over to Turkiye. Here we have two pre-Adamic city complex that defies all explanation. These sites are named "Gobeckli Tepe" and its adjacent "Karahan Tepe". Excavations have continued there for sixteen years. It is believed that only 5% of the sites have been uncovered from the sand. It will take decades before the entire extent of these cities is revealed. They cover many acres.

The two sites consist of dozens of vertical T-shaped granite blocks nineteen-feet tall and weighing fifteen tons each! Many of the blocks are adorned with beautiful depictions of animals. None of these animals are present in the area today, adding to the mystery.

Mount Ararat, 350 miles away, is believed to be the final resting place of Noah's Ark. Could these carved animals be depictions of the diverse fauna *from* the ark? It is an interesting hypothesis.

Also in the Nevsehir Provence of Turkiye is what I consider to be the single greatest wonder ever created by advanced pre-Adamic humans, or by extraterrestrials. It is named "Derinkuyu". It is a huge underground city cut out of solid rock. It has multiple levels, and extends two-hundred feet below the surface.

Estimates are that it could have easily supported a population of 20,000 or more individuals. Even with modern technology one can see no way this city could be built.

Above ground there is not a trace of the millions of cubic feet of debris that would have been created during the construction. Could the material have been vaporized? Archeologists are totally puzzled by this incredible site.

There is also an amazing underground city in Paolia on the Island of Malta in the Mediterranean Sea. It is known as the "Hypogeum of Hal Saflieni". "Hypogeum" is Greek for "underground". "Hal Saflieni" was a long-lost town once located above the underground site.

The massive underground complex has three levels. The limestone stone-work was cut with laser-like precision. It is polished to such smoothness that only the most modern diamond-encrusted blades and drills could have accomplished the construction. Who built it, and when, is uncertain.

The Hypogeum was definitely build many thousands of years before any modern tools we know of would be capable of the task. The only logical explanations are a highly advanced pre-Adamic human civilization, or extraterrestrials.

There are dozens of chambers and connecting passages. It may have been used partly as a necropolis. Over 7,000 skeletons with oddly-elongated skulls were found in one level. Who these people were is also a mystery. Were they the extraterrestrial builders?

In the Armenian Highlands on a high plain near the city of Sisian is the archaeological site of Carahunge. It consists of 203 fifty-ton basalt slabs most buried upright in the ground. Thirty-five of these stones have a perfect hole drilled through near the top. The holes are slanted to point towards the sky in seemingly a random fashion.

Other stones form a massive circle giving the site the local name of "The Armenian Stonehenge".

It is believed that Carahunge was the first astronomical observatory ever conceived. Because the holes do not seem to point towards anything important in the heavens it seems that it may have been built thousands of years ago when the stars were in very different positions.

There is no agreement as to who built Carahunge, or when. What knowledge did the pre-historic builders have directing their efforts? Possible extraterrestrial intervention?

In Honsu, Japan, there is a site estimated to be 16.000 years old! Called "Ishi-No-Hoden", it consists of a single block of stone carved in place weighing 500 tons. It is known as "The Flying Rock From The Heavens". It sits over a pool of water and from no point around the periphery can one see where it is attached to the ground! Local legend attributes it to "Sky Gods".

In Japan's Asuka Park Region is an even larger *800 ton* carved stone! Known as "Masada-No-Infume", it is said to be, or to represent, a spaceship. When one looks from above at the top of the stone there are two large doors cut into it. It is referred to by Japanese archaeologists as a "Sky Boat".

In Sipur, India is the Surangtila Temple. What makes this ancient structure particularly amazing is that it was built in a large city that was once 100% leveled by a massive earthquake. That is, all except this temple. It survived with minimal damage for a very unusual reason.

The millions of blocks from which it is built are literally *glued* together! The glue substance used is called "Ayurvedic Paste". This mortar is twenty times stronger than anything we have ever come up with in modern construction. It has been scientifically analyzed and its complex composition is not understood. Local Indian archaeologists today are convinced the Temple was constructed by beings from outer space.

There are three structures on earth that can be seen clearly from outer space. The "Nazca Lines" in the Peruvian desert, "The Great Wall of China", and the miles-long lines of massive stones in Carnac, France.

Let's turn our attention to Europe.

At Carnac, France, there are over 3,000 massive granite megaliths, roughly pointed at the tops. They are planted in the ground. They are arranged in rows of generally-straight lines. Most are twelve feet tall and some weigh an estimated 350 tons! They are said by many to be 70,000 years old.

No one knows how they got there or by whom. They are said to emit magnetic energy so strong that it can be felt by persons walking by. Could this be anything other than an extraterrestrial construct?

In Ferentino, Italy there is a massive stretch of walls around the city. This city is considered one of the "Five Cities of Saturn". Saturn was one of the ancient Gods. All five cities have similar walls. The architectural style is called "cyclopean". The walls are hundreds of feet high, and were clearly built in three stages, with three defined layers based on the size of the stones.

The upper layer is rubble-like, added by hand since Roman times. The mid-layer consists on large blocks that probably could have been moved with difficulty into place by humans.

The bottom layer, supposedly built by The God Saturn, consists of tens of thousands of blocks *each* weighing over 200 tons. They are beautifully crafted, and fit together so precisely that no mortar was used.

Who were the "Gods" who built the original Italian wall foundations? The written history of the area, including Greece, speak of Zeus and eleven others including Apollo, Hera Ares, Athena, and Poseidon. Are they myths? Were they extraterrestrials?

On Sardinia Island in Italy is found The "Well of Santa Christina". The entire construction defies explanation, from the staircase access to the perfectly-circular deep-well itself. The construction blocks are physically perfect with glass-smooth sides. The most amazing fact is that the foundation of the well is located *below* the water table! How this could have been possible by prehistoric humans with crude tools is a total mystery.

There are simply far too many pre-Adamic sites worldwide to list
more than a small fraction in this Chapter.

For example, there are dozens of massive, scattered, toppled basalt columns in Java, situated above a buried pyramid. The pyramid is estimated to be 80,000 years old and larger than those in Egypt! It was located using ground penetrating radar.

Another "impossible" construction is at Lalibela in Ethiopia. Here we find *thirteen* intricately carved huge *below-ground* churches. What is amazing about these three-hundred foot high (deep) structures is that they were built **from the top down! They are carved out of the existing rock, starting at ground level!** There is no way we could accomplish this with today's modern machinery.

How did workers ages ago actually build these beautiful churches? Who were the architects? Where did they get the plans? Did they somehow have knowledge of lasers or disintegration rays and anti-gravity devices? If so, who taught them? We may never know.

Yet another megalithic structure is found at Baalbec, Lebanon. Here we have colossal Roman architecture, more spectacular than many sites in Rome. One construction contains three 1,500 ton blocks, and dozens of 50 ton blocks. All were somehow removed from a quarry a half-mile away. We don't have machinery today that could accomplish this. Extraterrestrial levitation device? Direct construction by alien beings? Here again, we can only look in awe and speculate at how, when and by whom this was accomplished.

Underwater explorers have discovered stone ruins of cities hundreds of feet below today's surface. Most have been visited and photographed by divers. All have been seen clearly in radar images. There are dozens of such sites worldwide. The most notable are off the coasts of Japan and Cuba. Sea levels were not that low for hundreds of thousands of years! What advanced civilization could have built these?

The amazing constructions discussed above, all beyond even our "advanced" civilization's abilities, point to some sort of extraterrestrial involvement. The following, however, offers what I consider to be ABSOLUTE PROOF POSITIVE.

As previously mentioned, the identity of the actual builders of the pyramids is not known with certainty. The largest, "The Great Pyramid of Giza" was known to the Ancients as "The Mountain of Light". There is a theory that it was actually some sort of power generator. This sounds absurd, but so do two facts outlined below in regard to its exact location. These are facts that defy any possible logical explanation.

First, it can be shown by a cartographer that the Great Pyramid is located at the *precise* center of earth's land masses. It is unlikely this is a coincidence.

The following fact is *absolute proof* of either Devine intervention or someone possessing very highly advanced knowledge, thousands of years before their time.

The precise location of the Great Pyramid, to seven decimal places, is **29.9792458** degrees North latitude. The precise speed of light in meters per second is **299,792,458**! *The precise values with the same seven digits.* **THIS CANNOT BE A COINCIDENCE!** The odds would approach infinity! What possible conclusion can *you* draw from this?
I believe that extraterrestrials must have been somehow involved. It is also possible that a vanished human civilization, far advanced beyond today's iteration, could have developed the abilities to build these structures.

Alien races, with possibly millions of years of evolution more than present humans, certainly had the time to develop construction capabilities far beyond any we can even imagine today. Did alien beings come to earth and teach some pre-Adamic humans these techniques? Did they simply create all of these marvels employing their own knowledge?

The day may come, sooner than later, when a celestial visitor will come to earth and explain the true origins of humanity. Until then, we simply must try hard not to eradicate ourselves so that ET will actually have someone to visit!

Has any extraterrestrial technology ever been employed on earth recently? Apparently "*yes*"! Located in Bradenton, Florida, is an amazing tourist attraction called "Coral

Castle". I've been there twice, and it is truly mind-boggling. My clearest recollection is of a massive coral door about ten feet square and a foot thick, which must weigh dozens of tons. It is so well balanced that a finger-tip can easily open and close it!

Coral Castle was built by a love-starved Latvian immigrant named Edward Leedskalnin who hoped his masterpiece would entice his beloved sixteen-year-old Agnes Scuffs to emigrate from Europe to join him in his castle. Sadly, she never did.

This guy was five feet tall and weighed a hundred pounds soaking wet. What he accomplished on his thirty-two acre property cannot be explained. Over an eighteen-year period starting in 1923 he built this large futuristic sculpture garden out of 1,100 tons of massive coral blocks. He quarried them from his property. Some blocks are said to weigh many tons. He worked alone, and always at night out of sight of anyone trying to see how he managed to cut and move these massive blocks.

Ed's only evident "technology" was a simple wooden tripod and a set of chains and pulleys. These implements were totally inadequate for the task at hand. BUT WAIT! At the top of the tripod was a mysterious black box! It has never been studied because he took it home every night and it vanished after his death. Whatever that box contained apparently was able to do something quite magical.

During his lifetime, he often spoke of having the knowledge to create anti-gravity! Was this guy actually an extraterrestrial? Did he somehow come upon this futuristic construction miracle technique that appears to have been employed in building his castle? Whatever his secret was, it followed him to the grave.

Is it not abundantly clear that extraterrestrials have visited earth thousands of years ago? Is it not possible that one or more pre-Adamic human civilizations could have existed in prehistory? The non-believers are simply uninformed. The visible physical evidence is beyond denial.

It is hard to imagine that any race of sentient beings, or artificial beings, could not eliminate all life on earth at will, and take over earth whenever they choose. We can only hope that the galaxy has created Federations and Laws that would only permit advanced races to help advance other primitive races, such as us. If not....fade to black.

"Resistance is futile". "Live long and prosper".

P.S. For anyone unfamiliar with "Star Trek", the above two sentences are imbedded in the lore of this enduring sci-fi adventure.

CHAPTER FIFTEEN

RELIGIONS AND THE WRATH OF GOD

"Thou Art GOD." Hindu Sanskrit: "Tat Tvam Tsi". Frequent quote by Valentine Michael Smith, a Martian, from Robert Heinlein's Book: "Stranger In A Strange Land", (1907-1988).

"....and no religion too...." John Lennon, pacifist, musician, (1940-1980). Line from the song "Imagine", sung by The Beatles, 1970, lyrics by Lennon.

"The cause of FREEDOM is the cause of GOD." William Lisle Bowles, English Priest, poet and critic, (1762-1850).

"If you want to get rich start a religion." L. Ron Hubbard, writer, founder of Scientology, (1911-1986).

"We've seen the highest circle of spiraling powers. We have named this circle 'GOD'." Nikosis Kzantzakis, Greek writer and journalist, (1883-1957).

"What has been done is little, scarcely a beginning. Yet it is much in comparison with the total blank of a century past. And our knowledge will, we are easily persuaded, appear in turn the merest ignorance to those who come after us. Yet it is not to be despised, since by it we look up, groping to touch the hem of the Most High." Agnes Mary Clerke, Irish astronomer and writer, (1842-1907).

"Socialism is precisely the religion that must overwhelm Christianity." Antonio Gramsci, (1891-1937), Italian Communist and philosopher.

Before you read this Chapter, please accept my apologies if something written below is found to be inaccurate or offensive to you. Some religious readers will most surely be mortified. I am not a theologian. I have, however, devoted many thousands of hours studying the texts of all "major" religions and some "lesser" ones. Major and lesser are defined here by the number of followers, not by their relative importance.

There are some very interesting, and serious, concepts about our very existence on earth. There are many serious scientists who believe our entire reality is actually a hologram created by a highly advanced civilization many millions of years more advanced than "modern" humans.

Could we be part of an elaborate video game being played by some extraterrestrial teenager? If you are familiar with the four "Matrix" movies (1999, 2003+2003 and 2021) the concept of humans becoming absorbed by Artificial Intelligence machines does not seem all that farfetched. As an existential threat, when the game ends, we are toast!

Does the hologram hypothesis, or the AI machine concept, exclude the possibility of "GOD"? I see no reason why it should.

For hundreds of years there has been a debate as to whether humans do or do not have "free will". Is every single action we take either pre-ordained or guided by the infinitely capable omnipresent hand of GOD? A Stanford University neurobiologist named Robert Sapolsky, after decades of research, has concluded with absolute certainty that free will does not exist!

For all practical purposes I don't see why it matters. "I am what I am." I do what I do, just as everyone else on the planet. If all is pre-ordained, being concerned about it seems silly. As it says in the anonymous beautiful poem "Desiderata": "....no doubt the Universe is unfolding as it should." "Be careful. Strive to be happy." Good advice.

I find what I perceive as good, and sometimes things that are less than good, in every religion studied.

Humans wrote all of the religious texts and humans are imperfect. Many texts supposedly were delivered to a chosen recipient by a heavenly deity and may be pure in words. These may, however, upon reading be subject to very different individual interpretations.

There are three ways in which a religion can be an existential threat: "The Wrath of GOD", the specific directions of a Holy Book and the countless wars fought because "my deity is better than your deity."

I vividly recall back in the 1950s and 1960's in New York City a collection of loose cannons walking around with signs reading: "THE END IS NEAR"! Perhaps others are still there with similar cheery signs.. I presumed they had some advance knowledge from GOD that another Noah incident would descend upon an unsuspecting earth. So far so good.
If you believe that there are any truths in Nostradamus'

1500CE prophecies you can expect a very rough 2024 (or maybe 2025 if his timing is off a bit.) Throughout past five centuries, he made a number of startling predictions that apparently came to pass.

His 2024 predictions are not exactly comforting. King Charles will die. The Pope will poop out. WWIII will start. Climate change will destroy the world. Nothing too serious!

Somehow we survived many predicted existential threats. Anyone older than forty will remember "Y2K". We survived, thanks to Hillary Clinton. Hubby Bill gave her the impossible job of "Y2K Czar" in 1998 in charge of remediation. Does that sound vaguely familiar?

At 12:01 AM Australia time January 1, 2000 most of the world was tuned in to radio and TV to see whether the Aussies, the first possible Y2K victims, were still there! They were. The world breathed collective sigh of relief.

We survived the recent end of the Mayan calendar. We are not yet under water as projected by Al Gore a few decades ago. My life jacket sits unused in my bedroom closet.

Is Climate Change simply GOD's next flood? Probably not. It takes too long!

If the Great Flood was not enough to convince a Believer of the EXISTENTIAL THREAT that is the demonstrated awesome power of GOD's wrath, consider the ten plagues set upon Egypt through GOD's instructions to Noah. One even included infanticide!

These plagues were: Turning the local water into blood; a

massive inundation of frogs; a nasty gnat infestation, followed by a worse fly infestation; livestock disease; horrible painful boils; terrible storms loaded with hail; a horde of locusts; a period of total darkness; and lastly the death of all first-born male children and livestock.

If GOD is in fact capable of all these plagues including infanticide we'd better all try to stay on the good side. I don't believe we are doing a very credible job.

There are four major religions on earth. Christianity with 2.4 billion followers, Islam with 1.91 billion, Hinduism with 1.26 billion and Buddhism with 0.5 billion (500 million).

Christianity has two major factions. Worldwide, Catholics outnumber Protestants 1.4 billion to 1.0 billion. In the United States Protestants outnumber Catholics about two to one, 49% and 23% respectively. Islam, represented by 6.5 million American believers, is 1.8%.

The roughly one-quarter of Americans remaining are atheists or belong to one of the many smaller belief groups.

Incidentally, it is estimated that 35,000 individuals daily become Pentecostals, "Born Again Christians". I highly recommend this practice if it provides personal comfort in this troubled world. Accept Jesus Christ as your Lord and Savior and you have punched your ticket to Paradise.

Many earthly religions do not believe in a "GOD Almighty" at all. Christians refer to "GOD", Islamists to "Allah" which I believe are the equivalent. But Hindus revere "The Brahman". Buddhists revere a long succession of

"Buddhas". Many even believe Jesus was a Buddha! Some other religions with no "GOD" as such include Shintoism, with 100 million followers, and the much smaller Jainism and Confucianism.

Abrahamic Religions, Christianity, Islam, Zoroastrianism and some Judaic sects believe in "Heaven and Hell" or some iteration thereof. I believe in an Almighty, all-knowing, all-controlling entity that guides all of our destinies. "GOD" is a fine designation. The American Indians believe in "The Great Spirit", which also works very well for me.

I find comfort in believing in Heaven and Hell. The Great Spirit will judge all for relative merit and send the evil folk to the eternal hot place. One can only hope they never run out of room. I don't subscribe to the "holding pattern" the Catholics call "purgatory", but you never know. If you ever saw a fully illustrated copy of Dante's "Inferno" and the scary depictions of the "Seven Levels of Hell" you'd never J-walk!

I also strongly believe in reincarnation and "past lives". As a scientist, this makes very little sense. It is in the mainstream teachings of Hinduism, Buddhism, Sikkism, Jainism and Scientology. It is said that only half of the followers of these religions truly believe in reincarnation.

I identify as a non-denominational Protestant Christian. I find much good in Judiasm, Hinduism and Buddhism, and much of Islam. I do not identify as a Buddhist or Hindu, nor am I by any means a pacifist. But in my wallet I carry a number of Buddhist teachings which I find very hard to fault. One is known as the "panca-sila":

To abstain from killing anything that breathes.
To abstain from taking what is not given.
To abstain from illicit sexual indulgence.
To abstain from speaking falsehood.
To abstain from liquor that causes intoxication.

Other Buddhist teachings I carry:

The giving up of all evil.
The cultivation of the good.
The cleansing of ones mind.

By ourselves is evil done.
By ourselves our pain endure.
By ourselves we cease from wrong.
No one saves us but ourselves.

Consider sobriety.
Hear patiently.
Talk courteously.
Decide impartially.

These are all noble ways to conduct one's life, and I try hard to adhere to the principles, not always with 100% success.

In Christian theology we have the story of GOD transmitting a series of Commandments to Moses. The last five of the Ten Commandments reflect some of the above:

Thou shalt not kill.
Thou shalt not commit adultery.
Thou shalt not steal.
Thou shalt not bear false witness against thy neighbor.
Thou shalt not covet.

The first four Commandments refer to GOD and the requirements to be a true believer. I always find the first Commandment to be the most interesting: "Thou shalt have no other gods before me." Does this imply that GOD recognizes the existence of *other* Gods? Can you pray to these other Gods as long as you recognize that there is one primary God?

The Fifth Commandment, "Honor thy father and thy mother" is tough to criticize.

Growing up I always believed that "Do unto others....", the "Golden Rule", was a Christian-derived principle. It was not until I read Indian Vedas and studied Hinduism ("The Eternal Spirit Path") did I learn that this beautiful concept was first articulated five thousand years ago! "Don't do unto others what you don't want done unto you. Wish for others what you wish for yourself."

One bit of non-Christian thought my wife often invokes is "KARMA." Personal example: Leave the toilet seat up, stub your toe an hour later and be certain to hear: "See, BAD KARMA." It doesn't make the toe feel any better. I'm sure you get the idea.

In Hinduism "Karma" is one of the seven principal beliefs. It relates an action or intention to a consequence. You can have both good or bad Karma depending upon your actions.
Not unlike Buddhism, Hinduism has a set of core beliefs:

Action, Intent, and Consequences (Karma);
Ethics and Duty;
Work and Prosperity:

Desires and Passions;
Liberation and Freedom.

There are the five Hindu core principles:

GOD Exists;
All Human Beings are divine;
The Unity of Existence;
Religious Harmony;
Knowledge of the "3 Gs". (These are the **G**anges River for the cleansing of sins; The **G**ita, a sacred Hindu script; and The **G**ayatri, a sacred mantra.

Each of the above, of course, is greatly expanded upon in their Holy Books, and well worth researching. As with Buddhism, there is very little in either faith that I could not adapt in my daily life.

Besides America's three primary religions there are a number of smaller churches.

Mormons (**L**atter **D**ay **S**aints or LDS) number around seven million. Their beliefs are very similar to other Christians. They do not believe, as do most other Christians, that Jesus is one with GOD. Belief in Jesus as The Living GOD allows for salvation through repentance. Mormons see Jesus as a starting point towards salvation, a "conditional" redemption. They do not believe in a triune GOD, the Holy Trinity: The Father, The Son, and The Holy Ghost as do most Christians.

Religious leader David Jeremiah is on TV frequently with a chilling commercial. He speaks of "The Rapture", "The Great Disappearance". All good folk will simultaneously be transported up to Heaven. The rest of us will be doomed to spend our lives here on wretched old Godless Mother Earth. I'm not packing, yet.

Religion is a subject that has been a focus, one of many, of my life-long quest for knowledge. I have found it to be an endless source of fascination and occasional confusion.

Many dedicated scientists are atheists. Religious beliefs are simply so unproven and so "un-provable" that they go against all scientific reason. Multi-blind-proof studies are all that matters. Religion fails those tests, because ideas are impossible to re- create as experiments.

Many in the scientific community believed that if any one person understood GOD's intentions it was Albert Einstein. Here are four of his quotes:

"I believe that whatever we do or live for has its causality. It is good, however, that we do not know what it is." Albert Einstein.

"To have that which is impenetrable to us really existing, manifesting itself as the highest wisdom and most radiant beauty which our dull facilities comprehend if only with the most primitive of forms. This knowledge, this scaling, is at the center of true religiousness. In this sense, and in this sense only, I belong to the ranks of the devoutly religious men". Albert Einstein, from "What I Believe," 1930.
"GOD does not play dice with the cosmos. GOD is subtle, but he is not malicious." Albert Einstein.
I believe in Spinoza's GOD who revealed himself in the Harmony of all Being, not in the GOD who concerns himself with the fate and actions of men." Albert Einstein.

China, one of the world's two largest countries, is officially an Atheist nation. They do, however, recognize, and barely tolerate Taoism, Buddhism, Islam, Catholicism, and Protestantism, Interestingly, they do not recognize Confucianism. They severely suppress a group called the Uyghurs (we know as "wiegers".) An ancient ethnic group of about twelve million, over centuries they have practiced a number of religions. Today most wiegers identify as Sunni Muslims. Considered a threat to Chinese rulers, millions have been rounded up and placed in labor camps.

Another group that is severely persecuted in China is "Shen Yun". As many as one-hundred-million Chinese sympathize with their beliefs. The **C**hinese **C**ommunist **P**arty (CCP) considers this group to be *very* dangerous. Their crime? Efforts to revive and depict the beautiful, truly magnificent, traditional Chinese culture! They show the contrast between pre-communist China and the beauty and glory of centuries past. The contrast is dramatic, and a huge no-no to the CCP.

Shen Yun has an American theater troupe that has performed in over two-hundred theaters nationwide. My wife and I attended a show in Tucson a few years ago. It was beautiful beyond description!

Despite degrees in science and a life-long dedication to the study of diverse scientific disciplines, I am far from being an atheist. Einstein's above quotes are quite in line with my thinking.

Having been raised in a multi-religion family and having been brought up in a very diverse religious neighborhood, my earliest understandings of religion were utterly confused!

My father's family was Italian, and were deeply religious Catholics. As a child I attended mass with my dad. I thought it amusing that no one in the audience could understand the Priest. All services were 100% in Latin! I guess that is one definition of faith.

My father and his older sister (the latter raised me after my mom's early death) said the rosary frequently, while fingering their "Holy Rosary Beads".

"Hail Mary full of grace the Lord is with thee , blessed art thou among women, blessed is the fruit of the womb Jesus. Holy Mary Mother of GOD pray for us sinners now and at the hour of our death. Amen."

As a child I actually recited it every night at bedtime. I had no idea whatsoever what it meant, or even what a womb was! But I was convinced I was damned to Hell if I didn't say the Holy Words.

Both my father and his sister had what they referred to as their "Patron Saint". Theirs was St. Theresa, known as "The Little Flower." In late 1999 her bones were sent from France to New York City to begin an American tour. In honor of my departed Father and Aunt I stood on line for *five hours* to view the stone box that supposedly held her remains. Many wept as they passed the relic. I was not particularly moved. I always hated Disneyland.

My mother and her mom (Granny also helped raise me) were devout Protestants. I was baptized at the Flatbush-Tompkins Congregational Church in Brooklyn, New York.

It is one of the first, and oldest still-surviving churches in America. It happens to be located directly across the street from where I attended High School fifteen years later. Can't say I recall the moment Holy Water was drizzled on me because at age fifteen-days the world is just a happy blur! I try to forget the High School part.

Mom's family was actually quite historic. All were descended from the Tilden (or Tylden) family. Samuel J. Tilden ran for the presidency in 1876, won the popular vote by a majority, but somehow got screwed out of the Presidency by Rutherford V. Hayes. Think we have dirty politics today? Those guys raised it to an art form!

Mom and granny were proud members of the "**D**aughters of the **A**merican **R**evolution", DAR. Hundreds of years before some distant relative allegedly came to America on The Mayflower.

I attended weekly church services with my mom. At least the ministers spoke English, though it might as well have been Latin. Bible quotations had zero meaning to a young child. They are not a whole lot easier to grasp for an adult.

To add to my religious confusion, my neighborhood was one-quarter Orthodox Jewish. My eight closest "brothers" were all "Reformed" Jews. I occasionally attended Schul at Temple Beth Emmeth in Flatbush with my buddies just to fit in. I even learned some Hebrew!

The story of my parents' betrothal is shrouded in mystery. She was actually a well-known model and socialite. This was proven to me by the fact that, under the headline "Beauty To Wed", she was alone on the entire cover of the

Sunday *New York News*, of which I own a yellowing copy!

My father was the unemployed son of Italian immigrants. He was Catholic. She was Protestant. He was 31; she was 17. He was 5' 5", she was 5' 10". He was a WWI Navy vet, star tennis player, and accomplished Ukulele player. She played piano. Oil and water. There must have been a very interesting story there. It was never revealed to me.

Over the years, I learned how much hate religion can cause. It is as much an <u>existential threat</u> to family relationships as it is to countries worldwide.

Everyone in my father's family hated everyone in my mom's family. The near-riots at Easter, Thanksgiving and Christmas would find me as a frightened kid hiding under my bed in tears. All of the people I loved hated each other! I had no idea why.

It didn't help that my maternal grandma married a first-generation German. This was WWII. Niceties such as "dirty Kraut" and "fifthly Wop" were tossed around the table directed at whomever the slur best fit. Each was convinced the other belonged in an American concentration camp along with those "dirty Japs."

Needless to say as an adult I have always found it difficult to enjoy all Holidays to this day. It didn't help that both my parents coincidentally died on Thanksgiving Day, many years apart.

In recognition of the fact that loyal Japanese-Americans were rounded up and put in concentration camps, all of the Italians in my family were in fear that they would suffer a similar fate. Mussolini was not thought of much more highly than Tojo throughout the United States. So the last names "Palmer" and "Anderson" were adopted legally.

Perhaps because of my childhood confusion I set about over the years to read every "Holy Book" I could lay my hands on.

There are actually over four thousand different recognized religions! I never tried to study them all. I did, however, delve deeply into the scriptures of five religious groups: Christianity, Islam, Buddhism, Hinduism and Judaism.

The Old and New Testaments, the religious teachings I am most familiar with, are complex, and subject to the interpretations of the reader. One may take away messages of love, compassion and forgiveness. Another might focus on what they read as violence, hatred and discrimination. Interpretation of various passages are subjective and must be read with an open mind and the willingness to engage in critical thought and debates.

Growing up in a Jewish neighborhood and having a family of mixed Catholics and Protestants, I became quite unconcerned about whatever their diverse beliefs might have been. Having years of intimate contact with this assortment of disparate beliefs I got to know and understand all of them quite well.

I greatly respect the Jewish people. What they endured during WWII was horrible. President Roosevelt was not particularly sympathetic in banning their immigration to escape the Nazis. The fact that there are fewer than fifteen-million Jews worldwide, a minuscule percentage of the overall religion-universe, makes them eternal underdogs.

Personally, I always root for the underdog.

The Old Testament, the Jewish Holy Book, is subject to constant study by scholars. Did you know that there may NOT have been "*Twelve* Tribes of Israel"? How about the growing belief that early Jews were originally Egyptians? Moses is thought to have perhaps been the Pharaoh Akhenaten. Then he became a Jew and, renamed as Moses, led his people out of Egypt. Fascinating stuff.

Ancient Alien theorists believe that Akhenaten was an extraterrestrial. When Moses father first laid eyes on the baby he exclaimed: "This cannot be my child." Apparently the baby Moses did not appear totally human to his dad.

Who, or what is GOD? Is GOD Jesus Father? Is Jesus GOD on earth? Most Christians believe so. Many others such as Mormons do not.

Is the Catholic Pope Francis the manifestation of GOD on earth? Once beyond question as infallible, today many Catholics tend to think not. His "wokeness" and apparent Globalist vision has dismayed many of the Faithful.

The Pope was born in Argentina. The Argentinians refer to "their" Pope Francis as "Poperoni". This is not a clever take on the popular pizza. It refers back to the corrupt "Peronista" rule of Juan & Eva Peron. Their principal was: "To my friends everything. To my enemies, not even justice". This is how they perceive The Pope.

In August 2023 the Pope even criticized American Catholics as having a "reactionary attitude". He may be GOD incarnate, but he is not overwhelmingly popular worldwide. Nostradamus predicts 2024 will be his last as Pope. There is some speculation that he may be ready to retire. As I write this there are reports that he is quite ill.

Personally I believe in a single superior force that can never be understood. Call that force GOD, Allah, Yahweh, The Great Spirit or whatever, all are the same and equal in my mind. Jesus? I do not discount "extraterrestrial", *sent* by GOD.

Does being an atheist and not believing in *any* GOD make GOD as a possible existential threat irrelevant to them?

The only written record for the power of GOD, an all-knowing all-capable force, is the Hebrew Bible, The Old Testament. GOD created everything in a week. Then when he became disillusioned with mankind's evil ways he sent a flood to wipe out every living thing except the pure Noah, his wife. and his arc containing a host of living creatures.

Many other religious texts mention a great flood, so it is not just the invention of a group of religious Jews. Apparently it was a real event.

If GOD got so pissed off at earthlings once, could humans be trying his (or her, or its) patience today? Are we in for another flood or worse? We would only have ourselves to blame.

Surprisingly, there is a great deal of archaeological evidence that a great flood actually happened at the historically correct time. That could well have been accomplished by GOD's wrath. Or by Mother Earth's own retribution? Could GOD *BE* Mother Earth?

There is a mounting volume of evidence from modern archaeological finds that absolutely confirm the facts of various stories from The Old Testament. Many of the ancient temples and cities described as to extent and geographical position have been unearthed exactly as the Bible indicated. Many of these had been considered myths! Dozens of excavations at many different sites continue daily within the Holy Land.

A wonderful magazine, "Biblical Archeology Review" offers details and wonderful photos of dozens of active excavation sites. It really brings the Old Testament to life.

Was Jesus or even Noah not of this earth, extraterrestrials? Many religions hint at this possibility in their own unique creation stories.

The Sumerians, believed to be earth's first "modern-day" civilization, spoke of a people called "The Annunaki". These winged beings came down from the havens to teach civilization to man. Many cultures worldwide have very similar stories.

The Inca believed Viracocha was a visitor from the stars. The Aztecs' Hoitzilopochtli, and the Mayas' Itzamna were believed to have been extraterrestrials. The Australian Aborigines have the same belief about their origin, "sky people". Are these stories all simple myths, or could they be rooted in fact?

I find all religions to be fascinating. Some are quite in contrast with others. As a Christian growing up I learned from Matthew 5:44: "Love your enemies and pray for those who persecute you." I never found doing so particularly easy. My wife says it's due to my Sicilian heritage!

The Judeo/Christian Bible does not teach hatred or inferiority of others.

After the 9/11 attack on the World Trade Center in New York City, I know many Americans who became Islamophobic overnight. They had never previously given Islam a second thought. A friend of mine lost a son, who I knew well, in the collapse of Tower One.

For four years I worked for a company, Century 21 Real Estate, whose Northeast Headquarters occupied part of the top floor of Tower One. My wife did her Securities Broker training with Dean Witter Reynolds in that same building.

Our familiarity with that beautiful structure and its next door twin made 9/11 particularly painful. So did the photos shown on TV of American Muslim families proudly displaying pictures of the tower collapses on the walls of their homes.

The recent inhuman Hamas attack on helpless Israeli women and children didn't go very far to change many negative perceptions.

The killing of our brave soldiers in Afghanistan and the continuing attacks on our ships and bases in the area just add to the general distrust. Iran threatening to obliterate Israel isn't much help either, bolstered sadly by a handful of our own politicians. who openly support Hamas in their conflict with Israel.

Radio and TV personality Glenn Beck wrote a book in 2015

titled: "It IS About Islam". It is the Islamophobe's Handbook. I hope his many premises are wrong, though his sources of information seem valid.

My perception of Islam is that it encompasses more than "just" a religion. It has components that are political, legal, economic and military. That isn't a bad thing. The intolerance aspect is troubling.

The Judeo/Christian Bible is written in direct contrast to the passage in the Qur'an 9:5: "Kill the disbelievers wherever you find them". I wish for neither death nor conversion. Nor do I wish for the death or conversion of any Muslims.

To the best of my knowledge I have never known or even spoken to a member of the Islamic faith. This is unfortunate. I dearly wish I had some Muslim acquaintances. I have a genuine desire to know just how many take the Qur'an passage 9:5 absolutely as their mission in life.

If I understand correctly, the ultimate goal of Islam is a worldwide Caliphate. Adherents are referred to as "Twelvers." Their final goal will happen when the "Twelfth Imam," known as "The Mahdi," comes to earth. This makes **M**utually **A**ssured **D**estruction, M.A.D., total nuclear annhiliation, the MEANS, not the intended deterrent, of life on earth.

Outside of that one scary passage, I see the Qur'an as being very different from all of the other Holy Books I have read. This is not a criticism, just an observation.

I see in Islam a number of qualities that are lacking in

Christianity. One is the fact that the Qur'an has just one version. It is the word of Allah as transmitted to Mohammad, and is immutable. The Bible, quite frankly, is a conflicted confusing mess, as I will discuss below.

Another admirable matter relating to Islam is what appears to me to be a serious and deep profound devotion not shared by many American Christians, or for that matter, Jews. Periodic bowing prostrate in the direction of the Kaaba Holy Shrine in Mecca appears to me to be a sign of a truly deep faith.

Most impressive is the *once-in-a-lifetime* very difficult pilgrimage to Mecca, Saudi Arabia, the Hajj. Its purpose is to visit the Kaaba and view and perhaps even touch the "Holy Black Stone of Mecca". This watermelon-size stone is known as the "Ajar Al-Aswad". It is believed to be a meteorite, a heavenly body, sent to earth by Allah. It was found by, and placed permanently in the wall where it is today, by Muhammad himself.

Most Christians I know make twice *yearly* pilgrimages, but only to their nearest Church and only at Christmas and Easter! There is much to learn from Muslim dedication.
I revered the boxer Muhammad Ali and mourned his death. I had no problem, as some did, when he changed from Cassius Clay to become a devoted follower of Islam.

I have read the Qur'an and many books about the Islamic faith. As opposed to Christians who are split into countless factions worldwide, Muslims seem much less fractured, though certainly not entirely homogeneous.

The two major groups are Sunni, represented by 75% of

Muslims, and Shia the remaining 25%. There are 1.8 billion total Muslims worldwide.

There is also an esoteric, almost mystic faction within Islam called "Sufism". Their predominant views are love, peace and tolerance. They are considered heretics or apostates by most traditional Muslims. Roughly three-hundred-million Muslins, about one in five, identify as Sufi.

I spoke above of the Bible being a mess. Allow me to elaborate:

About two hundred years after the death of Jesus, scribes of varying abilities translated the ancient Aramaic and Greek texts. They were faced with a very serious problem.

Greek text has absolutely no spacing. Aramaic texts have neither spacing nor punctuation, and read from right to left. Consider this: The scribes might see the letters **"E R E H W O N S I D O G."** They reverse the order to left to right **"G O D I S N O W H E R E."**

Now, just how do you suppose that the scribe decides whether the original author intended: **"GOD IS NOWHERE"** or **"GOD IS NOW HERE?"** Same letters, same order, opposite meanings! Flip a coin? Guess? This problem is faced dozens of times in translating any ancient Greek or Aramaic text. The "final" Bible wording was simply the opinion or best guesses of the scribes.

We have two huge archaeological discoveries this century that put the entire modern Bible translations into question. In 1945 a total of fifty ancient manuscripts were discovered. These are known as "The Gnostic Texts." ***All were dated to*** _**the actual time during which Jesus lived!**_

They were written by individuals who actually *knew* Jesus while he was alive. This material was written at least <u>one-thousand years before the scribes made their suspect translations</u> from texts that were derived from oral hearsay hundreds of years AFTER Jesus' death. Which do you suspect is the more accurate?

Did you ever play "telephone" in Grade School? Child one is given a short statement by the teacher. It is passed orally to child two. Child two to child three. This continues until every child has heard it. After each child has passed on the message, the teacher compares the original to the last child's rendition. They are always totally different! This game works at adult parties as well. This is the problem with the oral history that led to the Bible as we know it today.

Much of this new Gnostic material contradicted many passages in the Bible with which we are familiar. There are four previously unknown Books: Thomas, Philip, The Egyptians, and Mary Magdalene.

In Jesus day all Rabbis were married. Jesus was a Rabbi. The book of Mary Magdalene makes it clear that she and Jesus were husband and wife! This is a very different picture from her being a prostitute forgiven and turned follower.

It was also mentioned that Jesus had at least four brothers and two sisters.

Upon learning of these discoveries a prominent Catholic Bishop exclaimed: **"This is an abyss of medieval**

blasphemy against GOD." The Catholic Church is not historically known for open mindedness.

Many theologians believe the scriptures as we now know them contain non-negotiable absolute truths, direct-from-GOD truths. Some "feared" Books contain "Hidden Knowledge" and are locked away for all eternity, many deep in Vatican vaults.

Soon after the discovery in 1945 came an even more important archaeological discovery. In a series of caves in Sherbet Qumran in The British Mandate of Palestine along the Red Sea, a stash of hundreds of scrolls was discovered. These were written *before* Jesus' ministry.

They contain 38 of the 39 Books of the Old Testament. The texts are in fair agreement with the present Old Testament translation. They also contain a wealth of additional material. It is worth your while to seek out the English language translations of The Dead Sea Scrolls.

One must understand that the earliest Christians had absolutely *no idea* who actually wrote the Bible. All of the material was written by scribes <u>anonymously.</u> The religious scholars made a <u>"best guess"</u> at who wrote the various gospels. The assumptions became tradition, and these traditions ultimately became dogma. It is considered by most Bible scholars that it is very unlikely that Matthew, Mark, Luke, John, or Paul, actually wrote **any** of these texts. Some even postulate that the names chosen for the four Books were those of the translating scribes themselves!

The Bible contains so many errors and inconsistencies that there are a number of scholarly books written on the subject. It is also worthy of note that many unpopular "Books" were <u>intentionally</u> left out in the early days because they were considered too controversial.

Most notable is "The book of Enoch". Today it is only included in the 81-book Ethiopian Christian Bible. Enoch's <u>first-person</u> account **deals with his extraterrestrial encounter and his trip into the cosmos in a spacecraft!** The Judeo/Christial Bible only offers a passing reference to Enoch's existence. This Book and volumes of additional material, is classified as "Hidden Knowledge" by theologians.

The first Bible translated into English and approved by the Church of England was "The Great Bible". This was followed by the more easily read "Geneva Bible" published in 1560. Next came the long-used "**K**ing **J**ames **B**ible", or "KJB" version in 1611. Every version either changed or entirely omitted entire verses at the whim of the publishing authority.

My first Bible, THE family Bible was a beautifully illustrated 1800s six-inch thick leather covered beast that weighed at least six pounds! It was a KJB. The language was archaic English and not very easy to read. It was beautifully illustrated. Since then there have been a number of "revisions" to the KJB, unlike the fixed Qur'an. There was the "*New* King James Version" published in 1982, which *omitted* twenty verses from the original KJB. This version was considered easier to read. "The New American Standard Bible" was published in 1995 and also *omitted* some material from the prior iteration.

A book called the "New International Bible" was created in

the 1960s. It was basically started from scratch by hundreds of learned scholars. They did not rely on previous translations. It relied only on the original Aramaic and Greek texts. It was intended to be periodically updated based on new archaeological findings. The latest version was published in 2011.

There continues to be new annotated Bibles advertised in publications such as "Archaeology". My point in all of this is that Christianity, at least through the New Testament Books, is fluid, not fixed. It is based on the whims and interpretations of scholars at various times in history and the questionable accuracy of the original translators. It is further subject to the seemingly endless random omissions of certain chosen "undesired " paragraphs.

Perhaps calling this Bible a "mess" earlier is a poor choice of words that will offend many. I simply cannot think of a better word to describe the long changing history of the most popular book ever written.

The Bible is accepted through a leap of faith to contain the true words as GOD wanted man to read them. All of the "errors" in translation, and the many inconsistencies, are simply GOD's intention. Who am I to argue?

Back in the 1960s I lived with a lovely young talented opera singer. She was a brilliant MENSAN, and a member of The Church of Scientology. She was not exactly a devout follower, but her entire family were deeply involved.
Scientology, a recognized religion, was created *solely for profit* by sci-fi author L. Ron Hubbard. It is considered by many to be a cult. They are said to number 3.5 million members by Scientology officials. Other surveys believe the

number to be closer to 50,000. Some famous Hollywood personalities are members.

Scientologists believe that we are all living with bad unconscious memories that need to be erased. Hubbard named these "engrams". These must be erased permanently. One must also eliminate all "low tone" people from their lives, including those who offer any negative influences. If necessary, this *must* include immediate relatives. Scientology broke up a lot of families.

Only after exorcising engrams and deep-sixing undesirables does one become "CLEAR". Only then is it possible to make all manner of life-decisions in "Real Time". In order to determine an individuals' level of "Clear" a device is used to "audit" members. It was basically a lie detector. Many questions asked, many responses, no needle reaction, "CLEAR"!

Back then a lot of Hubbard's ideas made a lot of sense. Their key precepts were "Reality, Affinity, and Communication". They preached peace. From what I read, today's Scientology, after the 1986 death of its founder, is *very* different and actually could easily be considered a cult.

There exists a large volume of religious texts known as "The Apocrypha". There are fourteen complete "Books". These are texts that are not considered to be "GOD inspired". Certain Christian groups do teach some Apocrypha. Among these are Lutherans and Anglicans.
If you are a true Bible believer, I suggest you read at least some of the Apocrypha. "The Wisdom of Solomon", "The Assumption of Moses" and "The Maccabees" are particularly interesting. The latter work is strongly disliked

within Judaism because it lionizes the Hasmonean Dynasty.

The aforementioned Book of Enoch is often included as Apocrypha.

The Ethiopian Bible contains most of the Books that were excommunicated from the King James Version. It is considered Holy by both the Ethiopian Orthodox Christians and the Ethiopian Jews. I STRONGLY recommend that any Christian or Jew should find and read a copy of this "complete" Bible. Just don't tell your Minister, Priest or Rabbi!

I've done the best I can in a limited space to offer some thoughts I have about the possibilities that over time religion could become an actual existential threat. If there is a GOD controlling my actions, which I do not discount, then I probably have accomplished my goal.

YOU GROK? (An expression from Heinlein's "Stranger In A Strange Land", meaning "Do you fully understand what I am saying?)

END

To My Reader:

Thank you sincerely for reading this book. I hope you found it informative.

I would very much appreciate it if you would send me a letter letting me know your opinion,

good or bad! Also let me know whether I may include your review on a future cover if appropriate.

Thanks again.

JBA

EPILOGUE

Prior to publishing this book I happened to be at my doctor's office for a routine visit. She asked what I was up to lately, and I told her I was just finishing up another book. I explained what it was about, and offered her a copy once it was printed. Her reaction surprised me.

"Oh Heavens no, it sounds much too depressing." This was my first critical review and the book wasn't even printed yet!

I consider myself to be a very happy and upbeat person. I've had a wonderful life, and at eighty-six am blessed with remarkably good health. I love life. I love my country. My dear wife and wonderful dog and I live a very modest life, entirely on Social Security. But I am a realist.

Paraphrasing the Bible, "No one is promised tomorrow." People die every day from unexpected accidents. If you happen to be in the wrong place at the wrong time you'll never hear the sound of the gun that kills you. Children die of cancer before they can begin to enjoy all that life has to offer. Life can seem overwhelmingly unfair.

We live in times today that are *overall* no more dangerous than those in which our ancestors lived. Today, we just have more creative ways to kill each other.

Writing this book was, to me, just another in a long line of books that I hoped would *enlighten, not frighten*. I wrote about Y2K and the Mayan Apocalypse. I wrote about marijuana. I wrote about government programs that I thought were generally misunderstood. I edited a book on personal self-defense. I've been on a life-long quest for knowledge that has led me down many diverse paths, some wonderful, some not so. I do not, however, recall anything I ever read or experienced as being "depressing", just the realities of life. My intention is to share these.

I hope you found this book entertaining. Please do not consider it depressing. My intention is to be a-political, though after reading the book you'll probably brand me a lunatic right-wing terrorist. I'm a good Christian and a registered Libertarian. Those are my excuses.

I hope my readers can apply some critical thinking. Look at every possible side of where the world and America are at today. If you are content, fine, do nothing. If you seek change, VOTE. Elections have consequences. Engage your local and Federal Representatives, on the rash assumption you can identify them. Many cannot.

I have lived through parts of *ten decades*. I'm shooting for twelve! In much of the Orient I would be considered a National Treasure. The elderly are revered, not scorned. In America I'm just a useless grumpy old poop who should keep his opinions to himself and die quietly. Believe it or not one can learn an awful lot about humanity over eighty-six plus years. It is some of this knowledge I try to share, grumpiness aside.

You may or may not be familiar with the verse quoted below. I believe it to be anonymous. It was written hundreds of years ago. The author had greater wisdom and vision that I could ever hope for. I read it often, because the words are profound.

> Go placidly amid the noise and the haste, and remember what peace there may be in silence. As far as possible, without surrender, be on good terms with all persons.
>
> Speak your truth quietly and clearly; and listen to others, even to the dull and the ignorant; they too have their story.
>
> Avoid loud and aggressive persons; they are vexatious to the spirit. If you compare yourself with others, you may become vain or bitter, for always there will be greater and lesser persons than yourself.
>
> Enjoy your achievements as well as your plans. Keep interested in your own career, however humble; it is a real possession in the changing fortunes of time.
>
> Exercise caution in your business affairs, for the world is full of trickery. But let this not blind you to what virtue there is. Many persons strive for high ideals, and everywhere life is full of heroism.
>
> Be yourself. Especially do not feign affection. Neither be cynical about love; for in the face of all aridity and disenchantment, it is as perennial as the grass.

<u>Take kindly the counsel of the years,</u> gracefully surrendering the things of youth.

Nurture strength of spirit to shield you in sudden misfortune. But do not distress yourself with dark imaginings. Many fears are born of fatigue and loneliness.

Beyond a wholesome discipline, be gentle with yourself. You are a child of the universe no less than the trees and the stars; you have a right to be here.

And whether or not it is clear to you, no doubt the universe is unfolding as it should.

Therefore be at peace with God, whatever you conceive Him to be. And whatever your labors and aspirations, in the noisy confusion of life, keep peace in your soul.

With all its sham, drudgery and broken dreams, it is still a beautiful world. Be cheerful. Strive to be happy.

Sean Hannity closes every TV and radio broadcast with the words: "Do not let your heart be troubled." It is a worthy goal.

SUGGESTED READING

The following list of books and literature is suggested reading for anyone who seeks a true understanding of FREEDOM and how FREEDOM can be suppressed or lost entirely. The books are intended to present a wide variety of viewpoints from hyper-conservative to liberal/socialist/communist.

If these works were mandatory reading for students from grade school through college we might produce citizens possessing sufficient information to grasp the ecstasy of FREEDOM and the horrors of suppression of critical thinking. There is a slow, almost unnoticeable loss of freedoms happening today in America.

I do not recommend any one particular book or any one particular viewpoint. They need to be taken as a whole of opposing human viewpoints on freedom. The reader is left to sort out the various ideas and decide for themselves under what philosophy of government they would prefer to live.

Although I consider our Founding Documents and various Holy Books to be critical reading, the following list is offered in absolutely no order of importance. It is a purely random compilation of various viewpoints that came to mind as I wrote this list.

The United States Declaration of Independence.
The United States Constitution and The Bill of Rights.
The Federalist Papers, by Hamilton, Madison and Jay.

The Old and New Testaments, "The Judeo/Christian Holy Bible". (Consider the full 81-book Ethiopian Bible.)
The Qur'an.
The Mormon Bible.
The Hindu Vedas.
The Buddhist Theravadas.

"Atlas Shrugged", by Ayn Rand, 1957.

"The Singularity Is Near", by Ray Kurzwell, 2005.

"Mein Kampf", by Adolf Hitler, 1925.

"Boca's Brain", by Carl Sagan, 1979.

"The Communist Manifesto", by Carl Marx & Friedrich Engels, 1848.

"America's Cultural Revolution – How The Radical Left Conquered Everything", by Christopher F. Rufo, 2023.

"Rules for Radicals", by Saul D. Alinsky, 1971.

"The Radical Mind", by David Horowitz, 2024.

"Don't Bank On It", by Craig Smith and Lowell Ponte, 2014.

"George Soros On Globalization", by George Soros, 2002.

"Imprimis". A free monthly periodical by Hillsdale College, President Larry P. Arnn.

"The Prince", by Niccolo Machiavelli, 1532.

"Cosmos", by Carl Sagan, 1980.

"Chariots of the Gods", by Erich von Daniken, 1968.

"Fugitive Days", by Bill Ayers, 2001.

"The Democrat Party Hates America", by Mark R. Levin, 2023.

"Hot Talk, Cold Science", by S. Fred Singer, 2021.

"The Great Quotations", by George Saldes, 1961.

"The Creature From Jeckyll Island", by G. Edwards Williams, 1994.

"Superintelligence", by Nick Bostrom, 2014.

"1984", by George Orwell, 1949.

"The Wealth of Nations", by Adam Smith, 1776.

"Migration and the 2030 Agenda: A Guide For Practitioners", published by The United Nations' "International Organization for Migration" (IOM), 2017.

"The Green Collar Economy", by Van Jones, 2008.

"The Collected Works of Frederick Douglas", 2020.

"I Have A Dream", writings and speeches by Martin Luther King, Jr., 2003.

"Long Walk To Freedom", by Nelson Mandela, 1994.

"The Story of My Experiments with Truth", by "Mahatma" Ghandi, 1929.

"Open Society – Reforming Global Capitalism", by George Soros, 1998.

"American Marxism", by Mark R. Levin, 2021.

"In Order To Live", by Yeonmi Park, a North Korean defector, 2015.

"The Weight of the Poor: A Strategy To End Poverty", published in "The Nation", 1966, written by Richard Cloward and Francis Fox Piven.

"The Republic", by Plato, 375 BC.

"Climate Change – The Real Story", by Dr. Robert E. Marx, 2022.

"The Art of War", Sun Tzu, 5 BC.

"Nuff Said", by George Murdoch, (Tyrus), 2024.

Do I expect anyone to actually acquire and read all of these works? Hope springs eternal.

I have actually read every word, but of course over many years. Many of these books have been read more than once. My goal is to read at least one book a week, in addition to a number of magazines. I try to read different viewpoints. For example, I subscribe to "Newsmax", as well as "Mother Jones". I view FOX TV, as well as CNN, NBC and CBS.

My wife actually manages to read two books a week. She reads mostly historical fiction and mystery novels, while I'm struggling with archaeological, religious, scientific and financial stuff. I understand that it is impossible to learn everything, but consider it worth trying!

A friend recently asked me where I could possibly find the time to read books and write books. At 86 I also actively day trade stocks, run a small boutique real estate company in Arizona and have two active internet businesses. How is that all possible? I even have time to play daily with my dog!

"TIME" *is* possible for my wife and me because <u>neither of us have succumbed to the single greatest existential threats facing America today</u>....smart phones, tablets, video games, virtual reality devices and especially the many iterations of social media! **These modern time-sucking brain-numbing wonders are destroying our youth and turning much of our society into mindless morons.**

It is said that everything on earth is composed of neutrons, protons and electrons. Add morons. We have a serious imbalance of the latter. Right-brained, left brained, and no brained? Evolution blew it.

There was a cute joke recently, I believe in "The New Yorker." You see a low-flying UFO with two aliens conversing in the cockpit. They are looking down on a crowded city street scene below. One is obviously worried that they could be spotted. The other comforts him: "Don't worry, they never look up!" Smart-phone-insanity.

My wife and I have almost no "social presence" on line, to the astonishment of our family and friends. If we choose to communicate we use our trusty stupid land-line. Fortunately, that ancient invention does not even accept text messages!

The only "clouds" we care about are any that drop precious rain on our Sonoran Desert, usually only about ten days a year. The last and only video "game" we ever played was "PONG" when video games were first conceived as a novelty decades ago! Our friends label us as <u>dinosaurs</u>. We consider it a badge of honor.

If I recall correctly dinosaurs were around a lot longer than humans.

"I am what I am". Popeye

ABOUT THE AUTHOR

James Burton "Burt" Anderson was born in a poor section of Brooklyn, New York, in 1938. He often says that during his eighty-six-plus years he has lived nine very different lives!

Over the years he has visited every state, residing for the longest periods in New York, New Jersey, Pennsylvania, Arizona and Hawaii. Cornwall, England and Queensland, Australia were shorter periods of residence.

His enhanced understanding of other cultures has come from his long visits to thirty-five nations across the globe.

As the child of a poor family, Burt worked by age six delivering pressed suits for a local tailor. He advanced through all manner of menial jobs. He married young, and worked full-time while attending twelve years of night classes and raising a family.

Burt earned degrees in Chemical Engineering at The

Polytechnic Institute of Brooklyn (now NYU POLY), and in Marketing/Finance at CCNY Baruch College of Business. He also holds a Degree of Distinction in Photography.

He is also a Licensed Christian Minister. and today is only one of a handful of original American MENSA members still living. He was elected to the National Management Honor Society.

To say he has had an eclectic mix of vocations would be an understatement! He has often said that four years in one job is two too many!

Over the years he has held licenses as a Private Pilot, SCUBA diver, Journeyman Electrician, Journeyman Plumber, Architect/Builder/Developer, Realtor, Insurance Principal, Loan Originator, Notary Public, Commodities Salesperson, General Securities Principal, Municipal Securities Principal, and Licensed Financial Planner.

After very successful tenures at Dean Witter Reynolds and Smith Barney, and his own small securities firm, Burt joined the Stratton Oakmont organization, headed by the brilliant Jordan Belfort, "The Wolf of Wall Street". He believes that those five years taught him valuable life lessons that should be mandatory curriculum in every college in the country.

He has held upper-management positions in a number of Fortune 500 Divisions, and been on the Boards of Directors of three major firms. He eventually decided to ditch the "rat race" because, as it is said, "Even when you win you're still a rat!"

Burt has been an entrepreneur for almost five decades, primarily as a builder/developer and Wall Street guru. He is credited for inventing a unique water purifier with a fellow ChemE in 1962.

As an accomplished public speaker he has shared the podium with a number of famous educational and inspirational speakers.

He began serious writing in 1970, and has written over twenty non-fiction books, many still in print at Amazon. He was chosen to pen an article for the prestigious "Leaders" Magazine, distributed only to heads of state and corporate CEOs.

Always eager to give back to his community he has served on many local charity and Library Boards. He was the Education Chairman for the Kona-Kohala Hawaii Board of Realtors for five years.

What Burt is most proud of is that he is the only two-time winner of the Burns and Roe Long Island Amateur Golf Open! An avid golfer since his teens, and a scratch for decades, he taught many friends to play excellent golf. He was still able to "shoot his age" well into his 70s.

As a resident of Arizona since the 1990s, he has won over thirty-five medals in the Green Valley and Tucson, Arizona Senior Olympics in sports as diverse as golf, basketball, pistol and rifle, and board-shuffleboard.

An avid athlete all of his life, he began as a track, cross-country and marathon runner in his 20s. Besides golf he was a member of many rifle and pistol clubs, and played basketball for most of his life in various Industrial Leagues.

Around age eighty all of this wear and tear on his body, and a decades long struggle with multiple sclerosis, caught up with him and for the past three years he is confined to a wheelchair unable to stand or walk. He never complains.

Burt, a sci-fi and astronomy buff, spends his days writing books, day-trading, managing an internet business, and spending endless hours with his coin and stamp collections.

He is a Vietnam-era Army veteran and proud member of American Legion Post 66 in Green Valley, Arizona. He has also been a proud NRA member for decades.

Burt has been married to his third wife for almost forty years. He says the brilliant, sexy, yoga-trained and beautiful Melanie, twenty years his junior, is his most proud "trophy".

He has two daughters and two sons by previous marriages, and two grandchildren who live in Germany. Both daughters are schoolteachers, one elementary school, one a college professor and ornithologist.

Both sons are "Sanitary Engineers", members of the Teamsters Union, driving garbage trucks throughout New York City for decades. Whatever you might think of labor unions in general, Burt says the Teamsters have been incredibly generous to his two sons. They are quite well off and happy. Both are past retirement age and plan to keep working. They just can't get enough of those raccoon-size NYC rats!

With a back-log of thirty non-fiction manuscripts Burt plans to live well beyond one- hundred to have time publish them all. We're certain the Library of Congress has room.

ABOUT LIONS PRIDE PUBLISHING

A sole proprietorship since 1970, Lions Pride Publishing produces an eclectic mix of mostly non-fiction books written by a variety of authors. Many are presently in-print and available at Amazon:

1. *Money By Internet, Volumes I & II.* Over 1,000 pages combined! Proven ways to make money from home sitting in your pajamas in front of a computer screen. The author has been an active infopreneur and internet affiliate-marketer for over two decades.

2. *The Black Belt.* Edited. By Master JOHN MAGEE. From the personal notes of this legendary 7th Degree Black Belt karate magazine reporter, this book provides the average person with easy techniques for every-day self-protection.

3. *How To Self-Publish.* Guidance from the author's personal success with his own publishing company for over fifty years.

4. *Reverse Mortgage Dangers.* Valuable information for seniors based upon years of the author's personal experiences as a Loan Officer specializing in Reverse Mortgages.

5. *Reverse Mortgage Risks.* An expanded and updated sequel to 4.

6. *Making Money From Domain Names.* The author has invested in, and profited from, internet domain names and internet commerce since the mid-'90s. He

continues to be involved actively to this day.

7. *Apocalypse 12-21-12 - The Mayan Prophesies.* A scholarly work that is not as outdated as the title might imply.

8. *Marijuana - The Wonder Weed.* Everything you need to know about nature's miracle plant.

AVAILABLE LATER 2024-2025

1. *The Wit and Wisdom of the Tajiks.* Edited. By Evan Bell. Translations and interpretations of Tajik sayings from a Christian missionary who survived life safely for years with his young family, in Muslim Tajikistan!

2. *Digger The Magic Cat.* Edited. By Mike Crolius. An adventure story for young readers, with probing end-of-chapter questions regarding racial and LBTQ+ matters.

3. *The Old Timer.* The biography of an old-time Arizona gold miner and WWII B29B A-Bomb era aviator.

4. *Martial Arts Trailblazer.* The only contracted and authorized biography of Great Grand Master Aaron Banks, the legendary father of mixed martial arts in America, civil rights activist and screen actor. (Check him out on Wikipedia.)

5. *Astrology and Your Pet.* If you believe in human astrology, you'll be fascinated to learn that your pet is similarly influenced!

6. *Modern Reverse Mortgages.* A complete update based on the government's ever-evolving Reverse Mortgage Programs.

7. *CBD, CDG & CBN – The Legal Marijuana Miracles.* The government finally allows hemp growing, leading to a new billion-dollar industry!

8. *How To Sell and Buy Scrap Precious Metals and Jewelry Without Being Screwed.* Self-explanatory title!

And many more in the years to come!